D0772533

Ships and Shipping:
A Comprehensive Guide

SHIPS AND SHIPPING

A COMPREHENSIVE GUIDE

Roy L. Nersesian

PennWell Books
PennWell Publishing Company
Tulsa, Oklahoma

Copyright © 1981 by
PennWell Publishing Company
1421 South Sheridan Road/P.O. Box 1260
Tulsa, Oklahoma 74101

Library of Congress Cataloging in Publication Data

Nersesian, Roy L
   Ships and shipping.

   Includes index.
   1. Shipping. 2. Ships. I. Title.
HE571.N45   387.5   80-25661
ISBN 0-87814-148-0

All rights reserved. No part of this book may be
reproduced, stored in a retrieval system, or
transcribed in any form or by any means, electronic
or mechanical, including photocopy and recording,
without the prior written permission of the publisher.

Printed in the United States of America

1 2 3 4 5   85 84 83 82 81

to Maria

Contents

Introduction

Shipping is not a primary industry in the sense of agriculture or mining, nor a secondary industry in the sense of steel or chemical production. It is a tertiary, or service, industry that responds to the needs of the shipping public. As such, shipping represents the investment of billions of dollars from individual, corporate, commercial, and government lenders.

Ships are only part of the maritime industry. With the aid of shipbuilding and repair yards, marine equipment and propulsion plant manufacturers, vessels are built and kept operational. Ports, navigation aids, berths, terminals, and cargo-handling systems are constructed and maintained to enable ships to enter ports and transfer their cargoes. These investments, employing tens of thousands more shoreside workers than seafarers, satisfy specific objectives. Ore carriers are built in yards throughout the world, and ore-handling terminals are constructed in Brazil and Japan because Japan must import iron ore and Brazil exports iron ore. There is little aesthetic appeal in an oil terminal, yet they are absolutely vital to fuel national economies. Container terminals have been constructed in many ports because containerization is the cheapest and most efficient means of transporting semifinished and finished goods. Low-cost transportation encourages specialization of industrial output. Living standards rise when a country exports products that are manufactured in exchange for products that can be made cheaper elsewhere.

Ships are built to transport goods, raw materials, and commodities. If there are 100 cargoes in the world, then 100 ships are adequate. One other vessel is too many, a waste of capital resources, while 99 vessels cannot meet demand. The signal to owners, builders, and suppliers of capital that 101 vessels are too many and 99 are too few is the level of market rates. Depressed market rates (a weak market) signal excess shipping capacity; high market rates (a strong market) signal a shortage of shipping capacity. A high rate structure induces owners to order more capacity, while a depressed market, at least up until recently, shuts off additional vessels.

Owners do more than respond to the signals of the market. They continually assess the future needs of shippers and charterers investing their resources, in terms of manpower and capital, in new vessel designs, technological improvements, and additional vessel capacity, realizing profits if they are right and losses if they are wrong. In the search for profits, owners maximize the utility value of the capital assets by combining trades wherever possible to reduce the nonrevenue-generating ballast (no cargo) leg in relation to the revenue-generating loaded leg of a voyage by keeping port time to a minimum in order to transport the maximum amount of goods and commodities over a given period of time and by maintaining shoreside overhead expenses and vessel operating costs at a level that maximizes the earning capacity of a vessel or fleet over the course of its life. Doing everything possible to ensure maximum profitability, owners invariably spoil their plans by ordering too many ships.

Strong markets are transient conditions in the world of shipping, lasting 1–3 years per decade. Most of the time, shippers and charterers benefit from low rates. However, sometimes the market turns around from 100 vessels competing for 99 cargoes to 101 cargoes competing for 100 vessels. Rates soar, overhanging debt is liquidated, cash reserves are replenished, and more vessels continue to be ordered until 101 vessels are again competing for 100 cargoes. Periodic boom markets are essential for the long-term commercial viability of shipping.

Some find shipping objectionable. They do not seem to comprehend the benefits of the market system, where profit-seeking entrepreneurs introduce technological advances in industry practices and maximize the use of capital assets. They do not seem to appreciate that enhanced profits and cost savings are eventually passed on to the consumer as lower transportation costs—not out of the kindheartedness and generosity of the entrepreneurs, but by their penchant for overbuilding.

Lowering the cost of transportation since WWII has encouraged the specialization of industrial output by shifts in the comparative price advantage of domestic and foreign-produced goods and has opened remote sources of raw material. World economies have never been as integrated as they are now. Trade is the most powerful binding force in a world filled with incompatible political systems.

The free market impartially profits those who perform well and predict the future and ruins those who cannot compete. It is a disciplinary force par excellence that directs the flow of capital investment and the employment of vessels where they are needed most. From a practical viewpoint of getting the most for one's money, the marketplace, for all its vices and ugliness, produces the best results.

It is impossible to discuss shipping in a vacuum. Certain principles are illustrated by events which occurred between 1972 and 1980. This time frame covers the greatest boom market in shipping history (1973) followed by its greatest depression. In 1973, it was literally impossible not to make money. By 1977, some firms were at the point of exhausting their cash reserves in their attempt to survive the market slump. A few owners had already made their trek to Canossa to implore socialist governments for aid.

Shippers or charterers, lenders, and owners look upon shipping in a parochial way. Shippers and charterers view it as an unavoidable evil whose costs are always too high. Every reduction in the cost of transportation enhances the marketability of their goods in distant lands. Lenders typically view shipping as another source of lending where they buy money at one price and sell it at another. An owner may have some romantic attachment to a vessel or he may consider himself part of a seafaring tradition. Most likely, however, shipping is just a livelihood. If the owner manages to survive and if things work out well, he becomes wealthy.

The feelings toward the industry number about the same as the participants. It would be foolhardy to assume that there is any single approach to this business which is manifestly superior to others, or that any particular approach which has demonstrated its superiority at one time would maintain its preeminence later.

I have tried to represent the feelings and attitudes of users and suppliers, including lenders which support the industry. In addition, I have attempted to suppress my biases by presenting both sides of various issues facing shipping. Some owners, whose lifetimes have been spent in shipping, still consider themselves novices in a business where expectations have not conformed to reality.

Although I would like to express my gratitude to all those who had a part in formulating my thoughts, the list would take pages. However, I would like to express my special thanks to Maria and the children, whose principal sacrifice was to endure my locking myself away for hours on end. In considering the alternative, this may not have been as much of a sacrifice as I thought.

1

The World Fleet

Ships are built for transporting raw materials, commodities, and goods. Tankers transport crude oil from producer regions to terminals in the consuming countries. Ore and bulk carriers are primarily used in transporting raw materials for the steel and aluminum industries. Grain is carried in bulk carriers from nations with surpluses to those with deficits. Finished or semifinished consumer goods and manufactured items are carried as break-bulk cargo on a general cargo vessel or are stuffed in containers for shipment by container vessel.

A vessel's gross registered tonnage is its internal volume, figured on a basis of 100 cubic feet (cf) per ton. In 1979, the world merchant fleet employed in the oceanborne movement of goods and commodities numbered over 71,000 vessels totaling 413 million gross registered tons (grt). The remaining 4% of the world fleet covers a wide spectrum of vessel types—chemical, livestock, and automobile carriers, tugs, dredges, cable ships, and ice breakers.

Table 1.1 does not accurately reflect the diversity of the world fleet. For instance, *general cargo vessel* has a broad meaning. Of the 22,000 vessels listed in Table 1.1, 1,000 (over 5 million grt) are refrigerated ships which exclusively carry fresh and frozen produce and meat. Other general cargo vessels specialize in a particular segment of the forest product trades, while some (multipurpose vessels) serve a variety of general, containerized, and bulk cargo trades. The listing of 7,000 tank-

TABLE 1.1
1979 WORLD MERCHANT FLEET

Vessel	Types of cargoes	Number of vessels	Percentage of total grt of world fleet
Tankers	Crude oil and refined oil products	6,950	42
General cargo vessels	Finished and semifinished goods	22,000	19
Ore and bulk carriers	Iron ore, coal, grain, bauxite, alumina, phosphate rock	4,200	20
Combination carriers	Crude oil, iron ore, coal, grain	430	6
Fishing vessels including fish carriers and fish factories		20,000	3
Container vessels	Containers stuffed with finished and semifinished goods	600	2
Passenger liners, vessels, and ferries		3,150	2
Liquefied gas carriers	Petroleum gases cooled to a liquefied state	580	2

*Data taken from the 1979 Statistical Tables of Lloyd's Register for vessels of 100 grt and over, compiled by the Institute of Shipping Economics, Bremen, Germany.

ers does not adequately explain the international trade of crude oil and refined products. On major international crude trades, one seldom finds tankers of less than 20,000 deadweight tons (dwt), a measure of cargo-carrying capacity. Only 2,700 of the 7,000 tankers are over 20,000 dwt.* The remaining 4,300 tankers of less than 20,000 dwt account for 10% of the carrying capacity of the world tanker fleet and are usually used on coastal and intraregional trades. Even among the vessels over 20,000 dwt, the large tankers dominate; 60% of the carrying capacity of the world tanker fleet is concentrated in the 940 tankers above 125,000 dwt. The table also does not show trends within the shipping industry. The fleet of liquefied gas carriers, while making up only 2% of the world fleet, is rapidly expanding to the cost of billions of dollars.

Gross registered tonnage is only one measure of the world fleet. Since a vessel's gross registered tonnage is its entire internal volume converted to tons at a rate of 100 cf per ton, it is a handy gauge for

*Drewry Shipping Statistics and Economics, H. P. Drewry (Shipping Consultants) Ltd., London (1979).

shipbuilders who use it to describe their past accomplishments or the state of their order books for new vessel construction (newbuildings). From a shipper's viewpoint, the volume of a vessel dedicated for machinery and propulsion is of academic value because no cargo can be carried in these spaces. A vessel's net registered tonnage is the internal volume of its cargo-carrying spaces, measured at 100 cf per ton. This appears to be a more practical measure of the world fleet.

A vessel carries cargoes, and the revenue it receives for performing this service determines its commercial value. Deadweight tonnage is the maximum weight in long tons (2,240 lb) of a vessel's cargo, including the weight of its stores, water, and fuel (bunkers). For bulk cargoes of crude oil, ores, coal, and heavy grains, the cargo-carrying capacity of a tanker or bulk carrier is about 90–95% of its deadweight tonnage. Hence, the commercial value of tankers and bulk carriers is best determined by their deadweight tonnage and not by their gross or net registered tonnage. Gross and net registered tonnage, along with Panama and Suez net tonnage, are derived values listed on a vessel's registration papers. They are used mainly for calculating insurance premiums, registration fees, port charges, and canal tolls.

Deadweight tonnage is not an appropriate measure of the usefulness of a vessel in carrying other types of cargoes. It is the number of containers which can be carried onboard a container vessel, the cubic feet of refrigerated space in a refrigerated vessel, the number of accommodations or cabins on a passenger vessel, the number of automobiles which can be transported on a car carrier. For light-density cargoes, the critical factor for determining the commercial value of a vessel is the volume of its cargo-carrying spaces (holds). For a cargo of locomotives, the commercial value of a vessel is determined by the configuration of the holds, the size of the hatches, and the lifting capacity of the vessel's gear.

All vessels are registered in a nation and are owned by an individual or a company incorporated in the nation of registry. The stock of a ship-owning company may be owned by an individual, by another corporate entity, or by any combination thereof. By definition, all vessels are under the jurisdiction of the maritime authority of the nation of registry and are bound to abide by its laws and regulations. Since the degree of control exercised by sovereign nations varies greatly, there is a distinction made between a vessel registered under a national flag or under a flag of convenience/necessity. National flag vessels are usually under greater control by government maritime agencies than vessels under flags of convenience/necessity.

Vessels registered in most maritime nations are considered to be national flag vessels. Varying rules apply to national flag vessels, mandated by each nation's maritime laws. For example, a U.S. flag vessel must be owned by a U.S. citizen or a corporation where the majority of the shares of stock is in the hands of U.S. citizens or interests. Owners of U.S. flag vessels are subject to all the rights, privileges, rules, and regulations affecting any U.S. citizen or corporation, including access to the U.S. judicial system and the obligation to pay taxes on profits. To trade between U.S. ports or be a recipient of maritime subsidies, U.S. law requires that a vessel be built in a U.S. shipyard according to the rules and regulations of the American Bureau of Shipping and the U.S. Coast Guard, be manned by duly-licensed U.S. merchant officers and seamen, and be registered in the United States. To fly the Scandinavian flag, owners must have Scandinavian crews, but the vessels are not required to be built in Scandinavia. A vessel flying the British flag does not have to be built in Britain, and only the principal officers are required to be British citizens. Similarly, a vessel registered in Greece does not have to be built in Greece, and only the principal officers have to be Greek citizens. Owners of Greek-registered tonnage pay a fixed fee to the government of Greece based on the size and age of their vessels, whereas Scandinavian and British owners are subject to an onerous tax on profits.

The two most important flag-of-convenience/necessity nations in the world are Liberia and Panama. Ownership of a one-ship holding company registered in flag-of-convenience/necessity nations is open to all, regardless of their citizenship or place of residence. The actual ownership of the stock may not be known by the local authorities if the stock is issued in bearer form (he who possesses the stock owns the company which owns the ship). The maximum loss (limitation of liability) an owner of a one-ship holding company must face is the loss of the vessel. An owner of a flag-of-convenience/necessity vessel is not required to file financial statements or pay taxes on profits to the nation of registry. He may build the vessel anywhere in the world as long as the vessel is under the purview of an authorized classification society which inspects it during construction and periodically throughout its life for seaworthiness and compliance with international conventions on safety of life at sea. He may man his vessel with any nationality or combination of nationalities, as long as the principal members are duly licensed to serve on a recognized national flag vessel. For instance, a British officer serving on a Liberian registered vessel as chief engineer is granted a Liberian license if the officer already has a valid license issued by British maritime authorities to serve as chief engineer on a British flag ship.

During the early stages of World War II, U.S. government officials encouraged registering ships under Liberian, Panamanian, and Honduran flags to aid the cause of the Allies without direct involvement by U.S. flag vessels. The program survived the war, and today about 25–30% of the Liberian flag fleet is considered American-controlled shipping, i.e., the ownership of the Liberian-registered one-ship holding companies is held by foreign shipping subsidiaries of U.S. corporations or by U.S. citizens. In time of war or national emergency, the owners agreed to place these vessels under the jurisdiction of U.S. authorities. In return, the American owning interests were exempt from taxation on profits made by the foreign shipping subsidiaries and received, for a very small premium, war risk marine insurance for damage or loss from hostile acts of foreign governments.

Since flag-of-convenience/necessity vessels serve a large portion of the shipping needs of the United States, U.S. maritime interests have opposed flag-of-convenience/necessity shipping because of the loss of job opportunities in shipbuilding and ship operation. The phrase *flag of convenience* aptly describes their position that the whole setup is convenient for owners: limited liability, no taxes, and freedom to change the nationality of crews at will. The critics of convenience flag vessels, who in recent years have spread beyond U.S. shores, argue that the inspection of a vessel with regard to manning with the proper number of duly-licensed, competent personnel and with regard to the vessel's seaworthiness and compliance with international conventions on safety by officials of the country of registry is either insufficient or non-existent. This, in conjunction with a possible language barrier between officers and crew, results in the poor safety record for flag-of-convenience ships.

The flag-of-necessity proponents retort that all this grumbling stems from spokesmen of high-cost shipyards and high-cost maritime labor unions who are fighting for their survival by trying to legislate away competition. They argue that eliminating flag-of-necessity vessels would increase the cost of transportation, which might depress international trade among the developed nations and thwart the industrialization of the developing nations. Thus, the interests of exporters, importers, consumers, and producers are sacrificed for the benefit of a relatively small number of members of shipbuilding and merchant seamen unions who have managed to price themselves out of the world market. The supporters of flags of necessity maintain that, in addition to the efforts of classification societies inspecting the seaworthiness of a vessel and its adherence to international safety conventions, it is in the owner's selfish interest to safeguard his investment by ensuring that his vessel is seaworthy and properly manned. The charges of a poor safety record are challenged using the same sources of data on safety as the critics of flags of convenience. The resulting battle of statistics is similar to the one on the safest mode of travel, where airline casualty rates are much more impressive if expressed in deaths or injuries per mile rather than per hour of travel. Even conceding the poor safety record of Cyprus, Singapore, and Somali flag vessels, proponents of flag of necessity point out that these small fleets should not condemn the Liberian flag-of-necessity fleet whose safety record is comparable to most national flag fleets.

The unrelenting pressure on flag-of-convenience/necessity vessels has been growing recently. In the United States, foreign shipping subsidiaries of U.S. corporations lost their tax-exempt status in the Tax Reduction Act of 1975. That year, war risk insurance for American-controlled shipping was terminated but was quietly reinstated in 1976. In the early 1970s, British, Scandinavian, and Australian dockside and harbor unions affiliated with the International Transport Workers' Federation (ITF) boycotted flag-of-convenience/necessity vessels which had not been issued a Blue Certificate or Blue Ticket certifying that the owners were paying crew wages above minimum ITF standards. Spokesmen for flag-of-necessity vessels called this discriminatory since the ITF took no action against national flag vessels whose pay scales were far less than the ITF standards, e.g., the Soviet fleet. The situation worsened in 1975 when the Scandinavian branch proposed boycotting all flag-of-convenience vessels throughout Norway, Sweden, Denmark, and Finland on principle alone, regardless of the pay scale of the crew. The proposed boycott, which did not materialize, provoked the criticism of Indian and Pakistani maritime authorities, who pointed out that this job substitution—not job creation—ploy would wipe out the means of livelihood for their merchant seafarers whose compensation, while small compared with North American, European and Japanese standards, is much more than what they can earn in their own countries.

In 1976 in another move against flag-of-convenience vessels, the International Labor Office (ILO) adopted a convention which, if ratified and approved by maritime nations, would give port authorities the right to force vessels, regardless of flag, to comply with ILO standards. Opposition was expressed by spokesmen for flag-of-necessity shipping interests and by representatives of national flag fleets of developing nations who did not like having to adopt Western standards on their vessels. In 1979, the United Nations Conference on Trade and Development (UNCTAD) proposed that flag-of-convenience vessels be forced to register under national flags by 1991.

TABLE 1.2
MOST IMPORTANT NATIONS OF REGISTRY FOR OVER 300 GRT (1976)*

Flag	Number of ships	Percentage of world fleet in grt or dwt	Average dwt per ship
Liberia**	2,457	22	53,600
Japan	4,166	12	15,500
Great Britian	1,872	9	27,100
Norway	1,134	8	40,900
Greece	2,389	8	17,600
Soviet Union	2,750	4	7,200
Panama**	1,973	4	12,200
United States	1,067	4	18,800
France	499	3	36,100
Italy	986	3	17,200
West Germany	1,165	2	12,000
Sweden	435	2	29,400
Spain	697	2	14,900
Netherlands	774	2	11,300
Singapore**	546	2	15,800
India	351	1	21,800
Denmark	708	1	10,900
Mainland China	456	1	11,300
Brazil	349	1	13,800
Cyprus**	722	1	5,900
Poland	325	1	13,000

*Data taken from the Institute of Shipping Economics, Bremen, for vessels of 300 grt or greater. The world fleet of vessels of 300 grt or greater totaled 334 million gross registered tons (grt) or 566 million deadweight tons (dwt) in 1976.
**Countries of registry considered to be flag-of-convenience/necessity nations.
Includes 31,200 ships

The top ten maritime nations account for three-quarters of the world fleet in terms of gross registered or deadweight tonnage. The larger average size of Liberian flag vessels reflect, in part, the tankers, bulk and ore carriers, and other vessel types owned by Liberian shipping subsidiaries of U.S. oil, steel, and aluminum companies, grain trading houses, shipping companies, and citizens, who may also own U.S. flag vessels in addition to their Liberian and other foreign flag vessels. The remaining 70–75% of the Liberian flag fleet is owned by citizens and shipping companies of other nationalities and nations.

TABLE 1.3
RELATIVE STANDINGS AMONG NATIONS OF REGISTRY

Flag	Ranking, 1976	Ranking, 1979	Percentage of world fleet in grt or dwt*	
			1976	1979
Liberia	1	1	22	20
Japan	2	2	12	10
Great Britain	3	4	9	7
Norway	4	5	8	6
Greece	5	3	8	9
Soviet Union	6	7	4	4
Panama	7	6	4	5
United States	8	8	4	4
France	9	9	3	3
Italy	10	10	3	3
West Germany	11	11	2	2
Sweden	12	17	2	1
Spain	13	12	2	2
Netherlands	14	18	2	1
Singapore	15	13	2	2
India	16	15	1	1
Denmark	17	16	1	1
Mainland China	18	14	1	2
Brazil	19	19	1	1
Cyprus	20	**	1	—
Poland	21	21	1	1

*Institute of Shipping Economics, Bremen. The world fleet in 1979 totaled 377 million grt or 647 million dwt.
**Cyprus dropped to 25th place and South Korea rose to 20th place between 1976 and 1979.

An investigation's findings into the sinking of a Liberian flag vessel in 1977 criticized the standards of inspection by Liberian maritime authorities. Toughening these standards made some owners switch to other flags of convenience/necessity, seen by Liberia's small drop between 1976 and 1979 and by gains by Panama and Singapore (Table 1.3). Another contributing factor was the success of Greek maritime authorities in persuading Greek owners to shift from flags of convenience/necessity to the national flag of Greece by promising to preserve most of the traditional freedom of action associated with flags of convenience/necessity. Moreover, a vessel flying the Greek flag would not be boycotted by the ITF. The same vessel with the same crew receiving the same remuneration flying a flag of convenience/necessity could be boycotted if it called on British, Scandinavian, or Australian ports.

Losses in the percentage of the world fleet registered in Japan, Sweden, Norway, and the Netherlands were caused primarily by owners forced to liquidate a portion of their fleet holdings because of low market rates and high operating costs. The buyers of these vessels were mostly Greek and Hong Kong owners who could take advantage of their low operating costs to expand their fleets in a depressed market. Mainland China boosted its standing by purchasing about 200 bulk and general cargo carriers in 1977–78. These vessels were shrewdly purchased at the very bottom of the market; the investment had more than doubled in 1979.

Cross traders are vessel owners whose fleets serve the needs of other nations. The British were the major cross traders at the turn of the century, owning and operating half the world fleet. They are still considered cross traders because the size of their fleet far exceeds the shipping requirements of Britain. The other major cross traders are the Norwegians, Greeks, and Hong Kong Chinese. Norwegian shipowners operate under the national flag of Norway, the Greeks under both the national flag of Greece and under flags of convenience/necessity, and the Hong Kong Chinese under flags of convenience/necessity. U.S. and Japanese owners are not considered cross traders because their fleets are primarily dedicated to serving a portion of their respective nation's shipping needs. The French and Italian fleets are sized to the level of imports and exports of their respective nations. Recently, the Soviet Union has emerged as a major cross trader as its expanded fleet of general cargo and container vessels nudges into the trade between non-Soviet bloc nations.

With the exception of the Soviet bloc and Mainland China, the world fleet is largely privately owned. Owners may be individuals or shipping companies serving the needs of end users of transportation capacity or the shipping subsidiaries of the end users themselves. Tankers are the one major segment of the world fleet where the end users, the major oil companies, own a significant portion of the tanker fleet. Even here, ownership is dominated by individuals and shipping companies who serve the needs of all oil companies.

Other end users owning sizeable fleets are the major steel, aluminum, and grain-trading companies. The remainder of the world fleet is owned by individuals and shipping companies who serve the transportation needs of shippers and charterers.

TABLE 1.4
PERCENTAGE OF WORLD TANKER FLEET FOR VESSELS
OF 10,000 DWT OR GREATER

Ownership	%
Private	
Individuals and shipping companies	64
Shipping subsidiaries of oil companies	35
Public	
Government agencies	1

Data taken from *World Tanker Fleet Review* published by John I. Jacobs, London (1976).

2

Tankers

Integrated oil companies explore for oil and develop finds. They realize profits on these activities by refining the crude and marketing the products. Transporting crude oil from the fields to the refineries and oil products from the refineries to the consumer is a cost of business, not a source of profits. The major oil companies feel it is more profitable to allocate most of their capital for exploring and developing oil fields and refining and marketing oil products than to build tankers. At the same time, it is absolutely vital to their operation that there is a smooth, uninterrupted flow of crude oil. To guarantee this, the Seven Sisters (Exxon, British Petroleum, Texaco, Royal Dutch Shell, Mobil, Gulf, and Standard Oil of California) own or control through captive fleets much of their tanker needs.

Captive tanker fleets are chartered to oil companies for most or all of their useful lives on a cost-of-service basis. Under cost-of-service contracts, owners bear little or no financing or operating risks. These risks are borne by the oil companies. Owners with these contracts sell their ability to manage and operate vessels. Through these arrangements, the oil companies have access to the ship management talents of competent ship operators for a relatively modest fee. In addition, oil companies can, to a certain degree, resort to off-balance sheet financing through captive fleet owners. The actual percentage of owned and controlled fleets to total tanker needs varies considerably among the major oil companies, depending on their experience with ownership, their relationship with independent tanker owners and tanker-owning shipping companies, the business philosophy of the chartering managers, their perception of future tanker needs, and the availability of corporate funds for acquiring tankers.

11

The basic relationship between a charterer and an owner is that a charterer is a buyer and an owner is a seller of a service. Chartering managers of major oil companies with in-depth staff support attempt to minimize their transportation costs; tanker owners in the same economic environment with little or no staff support try to maximize their profits.

When there is no excess tonnage available to satisfy an incremental demand for tanker capacity, oil companies must select other means to satisfy their need. They may order tankers for their own account, enter into a life-of-asset transportation agreement with a captive fleet owner, or arrange a charter (contract) with an independent tanker owner or tanker-owning shipping company on a long-, medium-, or short-term basis. Charter parties (written contracts) are concluded after considering the owner's past performance and reputation as a ship operator and his proposed rates and terms.* A charter is fixed if the rates and terms are satisfactory to both the charterer and the owner; that is, when the business objectives of both parties are satisfied. They are negotiated in an extremely competitive environment with numerous owners attempting to garner contracts from a few major charterers who rank among the world's largest corporations.

Economy of Scale of Large Tankers

In the late 1940s and early 1950s, there was a plentiful supply of war-built tankers of about 16,000 dwt. These later became known as handies for their versatility in serving every oil terminal in the world. Many of the 20 or so individuals who dominate today's world tanker business started—or restarted, for those who lost their fleets during the war—by purchasing handies for a few hundred thousand dollars each. By the mid-1950s, world economic activity had sopped up all the excess war-built tonnage. In response to a growing demand for tanker capacity, certain shipyard managers, oil company chartering managers, and owners developed, ordered, and built larger-sized tankers of 20,000, 25,000, 30,000, and 35,000 dwt. From 1950–1974, owners who pursued this development made the correct business decision, witnessed by their wealth. Those who lingered with the handies were left in the backwaters of the shipping business because the larger-sized tanker satisfied charterers with low-cost transportation and owners with high profits.

*An owner may be either an individual or a shipowning company.

In the 1950s, the 50,000-dwt supertanker made its debut. The vessel required the same size crew as a handy or a smaller crew as automation took over some of the more mechanical functions of running a ship. Since the supertanker carried three times the cargo of a handy-sized tanker, the crew cost component of the total cost to transport one ton of crude for one mile (cents per ton-mile) was reduced by at least two-thirds. Maintenance, repair costs, and fuel consumption were not three times larger than a handy, so their respective components in the total cost of transportation (cents per ton-mile) were less for a supertanker than for a handy. Nor did the physical weight of steel increase proportionately with tanker size.* Less steel per ton of carrying capacity meant less capital cost per ton of carrying capacity. Measured in terms of carrying capacity, insurance premiums were also lower because premiums are based principally on capital costs. The combination of lower operating costs and capital servicing charges to transport a ton of crude for one mile is known as the economy of scale of large crude carriers.

In summary, since WWII, increased economic activity has resulted in a greater crude oil consumption. The growing oceanborne movement of crude oil caused a demand for more tanker capacity. Larger-sized tankers gave the owners an opportunity to offer transportation services at rates that enhanced their profits and lowered the cost of transportation to the oil companies. The degree of economic sharing was determined both by the state of the market, which sets the tone of the negotiations between a charterer and an owner, and the respective negotiating skill of the chartering manager and the tanker owner.

The development of the supertanker was a sharp break with the past and was not easy to accomplish. There were numerous obstacles to overcome, such as constructing larger building berths by shipyards and larger dry docks by repair yards, building new terminal berths and oil storage facilities by oil companies, dredging channels for the deeper draft tankers, and other harbor improvements by port authorities. Yet the rise in the worldwide consumption of crude oil and the dramatic savings in transportation costs from the economy of scale of large crude carriers fully justified these enormous investments.

Japanese shipyards were the first to recognize the market potential of large crude carriers. Large crude carriers were big ticket earners of foreign exchange for a trading nation such as Japan which imported

---

*This can be seen by considering the doubling of a spherical shell. While the amount of steel necessary to construct the shell is increased fourfold, its internal volume, or capacity to carry cargo, increases eightfold.

most of its energy and raw materials. Construction of large crude carriers employed thousands of Japanese shipyard workers and consumed as much as 15% of the output of the Japanese steel industry. At the same time, large crude carriers reduced the cost of transporting Japanese crude oil imports.

Japanese shipyards pioneered mass production techniques in the building of ships, similar to Henry Ford's achievement in mass-producing automobiles. Instead of building a ship stick by stick, huge subassemblies of ship structure weighing 300–900 tons were lifted into graving docks by the world's largest cranes and welded into place to form the main structure of the ship.* The entire flow of material—from steel mills and marine machinery manufacturers to the yard storage areas, from the storage areas to the subassembly and assembly areas, and from there to the graving docks—was monitored and controlled with the aid of computers. Once the vessel's hull and main structures were completed and the main propulsion plant installed, the graving dock was flooded, its gates were opened, and the vessel was towed to a pierside location for final fitting-out before sea trials. After the vessel was towed and the gates were closed, the graving dock was pumped dry to begin assembling the next vessel. Sometimes several graving docks were building different segments of a vessel: one for the bow section, another for the stern section with the propulsion plant, and others for tank sections. As each section was completed, it was floated out of the flooded graving dock and welded underwater to the other sections.

Shipyards began to specialize in constructing one or a very few off-the-shelf vessels of standard design. Shipyard productivity, measured in man-hours per ton of erected steel, was greatly enhanced as the shipyard eliminated design problems and production bottlenecks associated with constructing the first of a series of vessels. Construction time for large crude carrier was cut from two to three years to nine months.** The Japanese yards' early entry into building large crude carriers, their pioneering efforts in advancing shipbuilding techniques, their access to low-cost steel produced by efficient mills and to a low-cost, highly dependable and industrious work force, their encouragement by government agencies, and the availability of government shipyard credit facilities to prospective owners helped Japan capture half of the world order book for new vessel construction (newbuildings).

*The Kockum Shipyard's goliath crane in Sweden can lift up the 1,500 tons of ship structure.
**The world record is 2 weeks between keel laying and launching for the much smaller WWII Liberty vessels built in U.S. yards.

As each quantum jump in tanker size occurred, commentators announced that the world had finally seen the ultimate in vessel size. This was particularly true for the 50,000–60,000-dwt supertanker, the largest tanker that could transit the Suez Canal fully loaded (the Sumax tanker). It did not seem practical to build above Sumax size, for it could trade only in a partially loaded condition on the most important crude oil route in the world—the Persian Gulf to Europe via the Suez Canal. Even at that time, some owners were predicting the day when large crude carriers on the 4,500-mile longer trade route around the Cape of Good Hope (South Africa) would be fully competitive with Sumax tankers.

Shortly thereafter, they ordered the next generation of tankers larger than the Sumax, ignoring everything the pundits said. This new generation of tankers of 70,000–80,000 dwt were used on trade routes such as the Persian Gulf to Japan where there were no physical impediments on vessel size. The transportation cost savings offered by the economy of scale of larger-sized tankers were much too impressive to be stopped by something as limiting as the depth of the Suez Canal. However, this new generation of supertankers began the age of tanker specialization to trade routes, ending the era of trading flexibility epitomized by the handy-sized tanker. This loss of trading flexibility increases with vessel size; the world's largest tankers in the mid-1970s were restricted to the major terminals on the most important long-haul crude trades.

In 1966 and 1967, the first tankers of over 200,000 dwt, Very Large Crude Carriers (VLCCs), were delivered. The projected world fleet at that time was 20 VLCCs by the end of 1968. The market for tankers was depressed because the supply of vessels exceeded the number of available cargoes. Even without an apparent economic incentive, certain oil companies, owners, and shipyards continued to push the development of large crude carriers. The principal builders of this fleet were the Japanese shipyards of Mitsubishi Heavy Industries (MHI) and Ishikawajima Harima Heavy Industries (IHI). Half of this fleet was owned by the Shell Group and a third by three independent tanker owners: D. K. Ludwig, an American who took delivery in 1968 of the world's first Ultra Large Crude Carrier (ULCC) of over 300,000 dwt built by MHI; Sig. Bergesen, a Norwegian shipowner; and A. P. Møller, a Danish shipowner. The remaining vessels were delivered to tanker owning shipping companies, principally the Japanese shipping firm Idemitsu Tanker (*The Tanker Register*, H. Clarkson and Company, London.)

By 1970, the world VLCC/ULCC fleet numbered 130 vessels. Exxon, Texaco, and Shell owned about a third; Greek owners Aristotle Onassis,

B. P. Goulandris, Stavros Niarchos and C. Y. Tung of Hong Kong were added to the roster of owners, who collectively owned another third of the fleet. The remaining third was owned by Idemitsu Tanker, Japan Line, and the British shipping company, Peninsular and Orient Steam Navigation (P & O). In addition to MHI and IHI, other Japanese shipyards building this fleet were Mitsui Zosen, Kawasaki, Hitachi Zosen, and Sasebo. Traditional European shipbuilding yards Odense Staalskibsvaerft (Denmark), Chantiers de l'Atlantique (France), Howaldtswerke Deutsche Werft and A. G. Weser (West Germany), Italcantieri (Italy), Akers (Norway), Nederlandsche Dok (Netherlands), Gotaverken and Kockums (Sweden), Swan Hunter and Harland & Wolff (Britain) began building VLCC/ULCCs.

The Suez Crisis

In 1967, a few oil companies, owners, and shipping companies had access to the existing VLCC/ULCC building berths of a shipbuilding industry just gearing up for this new market. At that time, a study replete with lengthy computer printouts so persuasively projected an oversupply of tanker capacity in the future that one shipowning firm sold its entire fleet. The bleak market conditions taxed the patience of financial institutions who had lent funds for building large crude carriers, for which there was no apparent demand. The prospects for tankers were bleak right up to the day the Suez Canal closed in 1967.

The closing was an unforeseen event which lengthened the world's largest crude oil movement from 6,500 to 11,000 miles. This prompt, quantum jump in demand for tankers turned a surplus of tanker capacity into a shortage. Rates for chartering tankers on a single voyage or spot basis soared. Oil companies rushed out to order more tonnage; if tanker owners beat them to the punch, they had to deal on the owners' terms.

Owners of uncommitted tonnage on hand or under construction were in the driver's seat for a change, and they enjoyed every minute of it. Each reacted according to his best business judgment. Some remained in the single voyage or spot market, reaping the windfall profits. Others took advantage of the situation and arranged long-term, full-payout charters where the length of the charter (the charter period) extended as long as the underlying debt that financed the acquisition of the vessel. After completing a full-payout charter, the vessel would be free of all debt; its entire residual value at that time belonged to the owner. Full-payout charters sacrificed near-term profits for long-term security, although the ravages of inflation in the first half of the 1970s destroyed the economic basis of these fixed rate contracts. Other owners fixed vessels on a variety of less than full-payout short- and medium-term charters. They were influenced in their chartering decisions by the attitudes of the financing institutions supplying the bulk of the funds necessary to acquire the tonnage.

Other independent tanker owners acquiring large fleets of VLCC/ULCCs after 1970 were Norwegian shipowners Hilmar Reksten and Hagbart Waage; Swedish shipowner Sven Salen; Greek shipowners G. S. Livanos and C. M. Lemos; and Hong Kong shipowner Y. K. Pao. Also included were the Japanese shipping companies K Line, Mitsui OSK, NYK Line, YS Line and Sanko; foreign flag shipping companies of U.S. corporations: Gotaas Larsen,* Marine Transport Lines;** the New York independent shipping company Overseas Shipholding Group; the Norwegian independent shipping firm Fearnley & Eger, the Israeli independent shipping firms Zim Israel and Maritime Fruit Carriers; and, of course, all the major oil companies. More VLCC/ULCC shipyards were constructed in Japan, in the traditional shipbuilding nations in Europe, in the U.S., and in newcomers such as Spain, Greece, Portugal, Korea, Yugoslavia, and Taiwan. By 1973, the largest crude carriers on order were 550,000 dwt, and mammoth crude carriers of 750,000, 1,000,000, and 1,500,000 dwt were being proposed.

On top of the closing of the Suez Canal, crude oil consumption was growing at a fast pace as the economies of the industrial nations climbed toward their cyclical peaks. Per capita living standards were advancing, the world population was growing, and crude oil was playing a more dominant role in satisfying global energy needs in relation to coal and natural gas. To make things even better for tanker owners, the United States, historically self-sufficient in oil, became a major crude oil importer. Although an annual growth rate of 5% in U.S. crude oil consumption coupled with a 3% annual decline in U.S. domestic production did not seem to be spectacular, the effect on U.S. crude oil imports over a relatively short period of time was dramatic.

Suppose crude oil is consumed at 14 million barrels per day (MMbpd) growing at 5% per year and domestic production is 11 MMbpd declining at 3% per year, leaving a difference of 3 MMbpd

---

*Gotaas Larsen was a Norwegian-based shipping company acquired by the U.S. firm of IU International. In 1979, IU International spun off the Gotaas Larsen division.
**Maritime Transport Lines is a division of GATX, a U.S.-based corporation.

imported. The growth in imports over a five-year period would be as in Table 2.1.

TABLE 2.1
GROWTH OF IMPORTS

Year	Consumption of crude oil (MMbpd)	Domestic production of crude oil (MMbpd)	Import level to meet the difference between consumption & production (MMbpd)	Annual growth of imports from preceding years
1	14.0	11.0	3.0	
2	14.7	10.7	4.0	33%
3	15.4	10.4	5.0	25%
4	16.2	10.0	6.2	24%
5	17.0	9.7	7.3	18%

Over this period, imports would increase by 250% in the face of only a 20% growth in consumption. The demand for tankers is keyed not to the growth of domestic consumption of crude oil but to the growth of crude oil imports. The increasing U.S. reliance on foreign crude oil stimulated tanker orders.

Marine Insurance

Lacking any record of losses and claims, marine insurance underwriters are reluctant to be the first to insure a new vessel class. Underwriters tend to mark up their rates to compensate for a greater perceived risk until a loss record is established. The larger size of supertankers in relation to handies did not result in any extraordinary losses, and the initially higher premium rates quickly fell back to former levels. At times, competitive pressures among marine underwriters resulted in little or no change in the structure of hull insurance rates when a new class of tanker appeared on the scene. Suddenly, in 1969 and 1970, underwriters had to bear the risk of a new class of vessel when several large crude carriers were lost at sea during tank-cleaning operations.

At that time, it was the customary practice to let fresh air displace the cargo of crude as it was pumped ashore. The cargo tanks were then cleaned during the ballast voyage from the discharging port to the loading port. A high-velocity sea-water spray from a rotating nozzle apparatus suspended in each cargo tank washed away the oily residue. This had never presented a problem in smaller-sized tankers; however, the cavernous spaces of the VLCC cargo tanks mimicked a thunderstorm environment. Lightning from static electricity, created by the impact of the high-velocity water striking the sides of the tanks, ignited the fume-laden atmosphere. This triggered an explosion, ripping open the ship. Once the cause was diagnosed, an engineering change was made to substitute the oxygen-depleted exhaust from the main engines for fresh air in displacing the crude oil in the cargo tanks as it was pumped ashore. The tanks were purged again and kept under slight pressure to prevent the entry of fresh air prior to and during tank cleaning, ensuring insufficient oxygen to support an explosion. As long as this inert gas system was properly operated, casualties of this sort ceased. Insurance rates, which had risen because of these problems, subsequently fell back to their former levels.

Oil Pollution

A tanker on a ballast voyage back to a loading port is about one-third loaded with sea water for proper stability. Since water sloshing in a partially full cargo tank can capsize a vessel under certain weather conditions, some of the cargo tanks are completely full of sea water ballast while others are empty. Prior to taking on sea water ballast, the cargo tanks are cleaned to reduce oil pollution when the ballast water is pumped overboard at the next loading port. Tank cleaning ensures the tanks are gas-free for inspection by ship's personnel and shoreside inspectors. Tank cleaning also removes the crude oil residue in the tanks, which, if not removed, would simply build up voyage after voyage, reducing the vessel's cargo-carrying capacity. The cry for segregated ballast tanks used exclusively for sea water ballast does not eliminate the need for cleaning the cargo tanks and the problem of disposing oily residues.

Pollution by tankers is caused primarily by overboard discharges of the washings from tank cleaning and of oily bilge water from the engine room. Everyone clearly recognizes the environmental issue of polluting the seas with oily residues, but there is also an economic issue at stake for not polluting the ocean's waters, made even more poignant by the large crude carrier.

If the residue in the cargo tanks after discharging a 200,000-dwt VLCC were 0.5% of the cargo, this would amount to 1,000 tons of crude oil. If all this were dumped overboard as a result of tank-cleaning operations, the financial loss would be $17,500 at pre-1973 oil prices (1,000 tons × 7 bbl/ton × $2.50/bbl) per voyage. Figuring seven voyages a year, the annual loss would be $122,500. As post-1973 prices of $11 per barrel, the loss is marked up to $539,000 per year. At 1980 prices of $30 per barrel, the loss of $1,470,000 per year provides a clear economic incentive to keep the crude residue onboard a tanker, regardless of environmental considerations.

Since the 1960s, tankers have been built with slop tanks that settle out the oily residue in tank washings and bilge water prior to pumping the water overboard. Although the oily residue is retained onboard the tanker as part of the next cargo, the water from slop tanks is still contaminated with oily substances. Large crude carriers have oil separators installed onboard, and some have adopted load on top procedures for discharging crude oil to reduce the amount of contaminated water pumped overboard. Slop tanks, separators, and proper procedures can keep oily discharges to less than 1/30,000 of the cargo carried as required by a United Nations' international convention.

In 1975, there was a surplus of tanker capacity in relation to demand. One partial solution to the surplus tanker problem was the proposal to use tankers as floating slop tank reception facilities. The tanker would thoroughly treat the slop tank water prior to discharging it into the harbor. This did not occur, for about this time a new tank-washing technique using crude oil rather than seawater as the cleaning agent was developed independently by British Petroleum and Exxon. Crude oil washing systems are now being installed on existing vessels and on newbuildings.

Today, the amount of pollution per ton-mile of oil carried on the high seas has dropped significantly. Shoreside or floating slop retention facilities, crude oil washing systems, and segregated ballast tanks will further reduce pollution of the ocean waters. The main offenders are old tankers that have not been modified to reduce oil discharges, but their numbers rapidly dwindled in the mid-1970s in the wake of massive scrapping brought on by a surplus of tanker capacity.

Chartering

Historically, 90–95% of the transportation needs of the major oil companies is filled by ownership, control of captive fleets, and an assortment of long-, medium-, and short-term chartered-in tonnage. The remainder is satisfied by open market chartering of tanker capacity on a single-voyage basis called the spot market. If the chartering manager of an oil company must transport crude oil between two ports on a specified loading date and there are no suitably sized tankers in the company's owned, controlled, or chartered-in fleet which can meet the date, the chartering manager will attempt to charter-in a vessel from the spot market. Usually he contacts brokers who, for a commission, seek out tanker owners of uncommitted, suitably sized, advantageously positioned tonnage. The search extends not just to owners but also to other oil companies.

The practice of oil companies chartering out owned or chartered-in tonnage to competitors is called reletting. An oil company relets a tanker to another oil company with a specific objective in mind, not as a general service to the industry. Perhaps there may have been a shift in its sources of crude oil supplies, leaving its tanker fleet poorly positioned to meet its immediate needs. By judicious reletting, an oil company can distribute its tanker fleet, earning incremental revenue to compensate for the expense of relocation. Or if an oil company's tanker, owned or chartered-in, is desirably positioned but no cargo is available for immediate lifting, the oil company may relet the vessel and earn incremental revenue rather than have a vessel sit idly by. Another common problem is bunching owned and chartered-in tankers at a loading or discharging port. Reletting restores a smoother schedule of arrivals and departures for an oil company's tanker fleet as it increases utilization and optimizes distribution.

A tanker on the spot market is under charter only for the duration of the loaded leg of a single voyage, which may last from a few days to a month. Once the cargo is discharged, the vessel is free to compete for another cargo wherever it happens to originate to wherever the destination, as long as the vessel is suitably sized for the intended cargo, is physically sized to come alongside the loading and discharging berths and to pass through intervening canals and restricted waterways, and can meet the desired loading date. The spot market is an extremely sensitive indicator of the marginal demand and supply of tanker capacity, a key signal to oil companies and owners on whether or not to expand the world stock of tanker capacity, and a means to allocate the worldwide fleet of tankers among the many crude oil trade routes.

Worldscale

Rates of freight in the spot or single-voyage market are expressed in Worldscale or Worldscale Points to facilitate the decision-making process for fixing tankers. Worldscale equates the daily revenue-earning rate of a tanker independent of any specified trade route. For example, if an owner has a tanker in the Persian Gulf and receives two offers—one to transport a cargo of crude from the Persian Gulf to Europe via the Cape of Good Hope and the other to Japan both at Worldscale 100 (W100)—in theory, he would be indifferent because both offers would generate the same daily revenue. From a practical viewpoint, he is not indifferent. He may select the Persian Gulf to Japan (PG/Japan) to have his vessel in the Far East to take advantage of a low-cost repair yard for planned maintenance. Or he may select the longer-distance PG/Europe voyage because he feels spot market rates may be falling and wants to maintain the current daily earning rate longer. If he thinks rates are going up, he may select the PG/Japan voyage because its shorter duration would increase the vessel's earnings in a rising spot market more than selecting the longer PG/Europe voyage.

The pre-October 1973 Worldscale 100 rate per ton of cargo on the PG/Europe voyage was $10 and $5.70 on the PG/Japan voyage. The round-trip time at a speed of 15 knots to complete the PG/Europe via the Cape of Good Hope voyage is about 64 days, 40 days for the PG/Japan voyage. If an owner fixes his vessel at W100 on either voyage, the gross receipts of tons of cargo carried multiplied by the W100 rates less bunker (fuel) costs, port charges, and canal tolls divided by the round-trip voyage time would yield essentially the same daily earnings rate for both voyages. Out of the daily earnings rate, the owner must pay all operating costs (crew, maintenance, insurance, and stores) and any financing charges. The underlying basis for computing Worldscale rates by the International Tanker Nominal Freight Scale Association for over 50,000 voyages is the preservation of the earning power of a standard tanker at the base rate of W100 regardless of the voyage.

TABLE 2.2
FREIGHT RATE PER TON OF CARGO CARRIED

	PG/Europe	PG/Japan
W100 (1973)	$10.00	$ 5.70
W200	20.00	11.40
W50	5.00	2.85

Worldscale 100 (W100) means 100% of the published or base rates. W200 is 200% and W50 is 50% of the published rates.

Worldscale 100 rates were adjusted annually to compensate for changes in port and canal charges and bunker costs. These changes were minor up to October 1973, but the next revision after 1973 listed W100 on the PG/Europe trade at $14.50. This was an unprecedented 45% hike from the previous $10 rate per ton of cargo as a result of the sharp rise in the cost of bunkers and the rapid escalation of port charges. By 1980, the W100 rate had risen to $20.00.

Spot market rates for a given size class of vessel are usually listed as a single value as if rates were the same all over the world. However, rates fluctuate regionally, signifying mismatches between supply and demand in place and time. For instance, suppose that Worldscale rates average W150 for vessels of 40,000 dwt. If the movement of crude oil between the Caribbean and the United States picks up in volume simultaneously with a fall-off in the movement of crude oil between Indonesia and Japan, a tanker owner with a vessel in Indonesia may receive W135 for a shipment of crude oil to Japan while his competitors with vessels situated in the Caribbean are obtaining W165. There is now an economic incentive for the tanker owner to move his tanker from the Far East to the Caribbean. To reduce his repositioning expenses, the owner will attempt to secure a cargo from Indonesia to the United States. Since the purpose of this cargo is to position the vessel in a more profitable trade, the owner may come under the market to guarantee the securing of a cargo, e.g., W130 to a U.S. West Coast port. He might even bid W120 for a U.S. East Coast destination to bring his vessel closer to the desired location and have the charterer, through the Worldscale rate structure, pay for the Panama Canal tolls. Whatever the owner does, he is motivated to maximize his earnings. Perhaps an owner's greed knows no bounds, but the world is at least assured that his capital assets are always optimally utilized.

Chartering vs. Ownership

The cost of acquiring and operating a fleet by an oil company establishes the internal cost of transportation. The internal cost of an owned vessel reflects the actual costs of operating a vessel, including a pro rata share of the cost of the shore-based support organization and the cost of capital tied up in acquiring the vessel. If a major oil company expects to earn a certain return on its investments in exploring, producing, refining, and marketing, then that same rate of return should apply to its investments in ships and be part of the derivation of the internal costs of transportation.

Independent tanker owners and tanker-owning shipping subsidiaries may be able to offer rates on a medium- or long-term basis which are less than an oil company's internal costs. Perhaps this is a result of a lower profit objective, an ability to man and operate a vessel at less cost, a smaller shoreside staff, a lower acquisition cost, or any combination. Oil companies do not own all their tanker needs because owners can perform a vital service at less than internal costs and because a portfolio of short-, medium-, and long-term charters with staggered expiration dates allows an oil company to shed excess capacity at no cost. An oil company's need for tanker capacity may diminish because of declining economic activity, mild winter weather which reduces heating oil consumption, or a greater reliance on sources of crude oil supplies closer to refinery locations. If the oil company owned all its tonnage requirements, it would have to lay up vessels (assuming there are no profitable reletting opportunities). This involves a cost of funds tied up in an unused capital asset, whereas letting charters expire without entering into new transportation arrangements sheds tanker capacity at no cost to the oil company. The brunt of a tanker surplus, but by no means all of it, is borne by owners.

One may argue that the spot market, filling only a small portion of an oil company's needs, is of little economic value. Even when spot market rates are high and owners are profiting, a major oil company's average cost of transportation hardly budges because 90% or so of the cost of their tanker requirements is fixed by virtue of ownership and term charters. Yet nothing could be further from the truth.

The spot market, the proverbial tip of the iceberg, is an extremely sensitive barometer to changes in the marginal demand for tankers. It plays a major economic role in the decision-making process by oil companies and owners to build, buy, sell, charter, and scrap vessels. It plays an enormous psychological role in the negotiations between charterers and owners. In a strong spot market when rates are high, an owner negotiates from a position of strength because failure to conclude a medium- or long-term charter means that the oil company will pay a higher rate of transportation on the spot market and the owner will earn more (at least in the short run) by remaining in the spot market. The tables are turned completely when the spot market is depressed. The charterer has the upper hand since a depressed spot market means a surplus of tanker capacity in relation to demand. If an owner fails to conclude a medium- or long-term charter, he may be forced to lay up his vessel. This is not a terrible alternative if there are no debt servicing charges because the operating costs for a vessel in layup can be cut to the bone. It is not the lack of employment that bankrupts owners, but the existence of debt on unemployable assets.

In a strong spot market, an oil company may be forced to introduce a layer of chartered-in tonnage whose costs are far higher than its internal costs. When the spot market is depressed, the oil company can meet its future needs with a layer of chartered-in tonnage whose costs are far below its internal costs. With the passage of time, the spot market serves just desserts to all.

The most important point to note for a tanker on the spot market is that the market rates depend on the supply and demand for tanker capacity; costs, in the form of operating and financing charges, are independent of the level of the spot market. Any change in spot market rates is immediately felt as a change to profitability. The success of a tanker owner depends on his feel for the market, his timing in concluding charters during favorable market conditions, and his quickness in making decisions. In a strong market, negotiations among charterers, brokers, and owners reach a fever pitch. It is no place for a person who takes his time making decisions nor for an organization where decision making is spread over several layers of management. Independent tanker owners are one-man shows, and tanker-owning shipping companies are also largely run in a highly centralized, autocratic manner.

Although the period 1968–1973 was marked by very high growth rates in the oceanborne movement of crude oil, it was not one continuous boom for tanker owners. The spot market rates for tankers of 50,000–100,000 dwt were W20 before the closing of the Suez Canal in 1967 and peaked a few months later in 1968 at W140, a 700% jump in the revenue-generating capacity of charter-free tonnage.* An owner of a tanker on a term charter did not enjoy this bonanza because the revenue stream of the tanker is fixed by the charter party. It is possible for the charterer to relet the vessel at the higher rates and pocket the difference for himself.

After peaking at W140, the spot market fell back to and fluctuated around W60 throughout 1968 and 1969, rising again to a peak of W170 late in 1970 in response to an increase in the marginal demand for tanker capacity. Eight months later in mid-1971, the spot market fell back nearly 75% to W40 levels and fluctuated around W40 to mid-1972. Then the market took off on its highest flight in history, averaging W240 (some individual fixtures were much higher) in October 1973.

At W40, a 100,000-dwt crude carrier on a two-month, round-trip voyage PG/Europe via the Cape of Good Hope grossed $380,000 (95% cargo tons per dwt × 100,000 dwt × $10 per ton of cargo at W100 × 40%). Netting out $20,000 in port charges, $130,000 in bunker costs

---

*All tanker rates in this chapter are taken from Drewry's Shipping Statistics and Economics, H. P. Drewry (Shipping Consultants) Ltd., London.

(110 tons per day × 60 days × $20 per ton) and $120,000 for two months' operating costs (crew, maintenance, insurance, and stores), the cash surplus as a return on investment or to support debt servicing obligations (if any) was $100,000. If by chance the owner had fixed the vessel at W240 on this same voyage in October 1973, the gross revenue was $2,280,000 (95% cargo tons per dwt × 100,000 dwt × $10 per ton of cargo at W100 × 240%). The gross revenue net of the same $270,000 in port charges, bunker costs, and two months of operating costs was $2,010,000. This voyage alone generated a cash surplus equal to 18 voyages, or three years of employment, at W40 rates.

Spot market rates reached historic highs just before the oil crisis because of a simultaneous peaking of the North American, European, and Japanese economies, the emergence of the United States as a major importer of crude oil, and perhaps some inventory stockpiling in anticipation of a sharp markup in the price of crude. The stratospheric spot market levels once again gave tanker owners the opportunity to expand their fleets on the basis of favorable charters arranged with oil companies, to fix their existing vessels on favorable charters, or just to sit back and accumulate huge cash reserves by operating in the spot market. Oil company chartering managers who had failed to take advantage of the previous depressed state of the spot market to fix low-cost transportation paid extraordinarily high rates for tanker capacity. Lingering memories of the 1967, 1970, and 1973 tanker markets induce oil companies to keep their exposure to the spot market within manageable limits. It is not comfortable for a chartering manager to negotiate with owners in a strong spot market.

Coping with a Tanker Surplus

The problems plaguing the tanker industry in the 1970s were a direct result of the 1973 tanker market boom. With all the benefit of hindsight, the tanker boom of 1973 was radically different from its predecessors by the lack of natural constraints. In previous booms, most orders for newbuildings came from traditional tanker owners who began their careers in shipping prior to or just after WWII. This time, the orders came from firms with little experience in tankers. They were blinded by the high spot market rates and mesmerized by the thought of tripling the size of a fleet simply by ordering one VLCC/ULCC. For example, an owner who spent his life building up a fleet of ten 15,000-dwt general cargo vessels could triple his fleet capacity with one 300,000-dwt ULCC.

Second, the previous booms were marked by limited shipyard berth facilities to build ships. By 1973, the expansion of shipyards had markedly increased the world capacity to build large crude carriers. In 1966, 10 million dwt of tankers were delivered by the world's shipyards; in 1973, 29 million dwt; and by 1975, when shipyard expansion programs were for the most part complete, 45 million dwt were delivered (Fearnley and Egers Chartering Inc., Oslo). This was over four times the 1966 level of newbuilding deliveries. The rapid growth in shipyard capacity was partly market oriented and partly sponsored by governments fostering industrialization and reducing unemployment.

Third, the previous booms were supported by public and private sources of debt insisting on an owner fixing the vessel on an acceptable charter prior to the drawdown of funds. This traditional approach to ship financing recognized the volatility of the spot market where an owner might well own a capital asset whose earnings potential was far below that required to meet debt servicing obligations. However, in 1973 a floodgate of available credit opened to support speculative orders for large crude carriers. Syndicates of financial institutions were formed to finance newbuilding orders where many of the members had no previous experience in ship financing. The high market rates for spot fixtures lured owners to place orders for tankers, and neither the capacity of shipyards to build large crude carriers nor the caution of lenders in supplying funds could restrain them. As a consequence, orders were placed for 130 million dwt of tankers in the last quarter of 1972 and throughout 1973 on top of an existing fleet of 200 million dwt. Many of these orders were speculative; the owners had no charters from oil companies to support the associated debt obligations. Adding the orders already placed on the books prior to the last quarter of 1972, the projected world fleet, if all the vessels were built, would have been 480 million dwt by 1980.

The few voices of caution in 1972 and 1973 about a possible oversupply of tankers were silenced by the fact that the capital investment in a large crude carrier could be completely amortized in a few round-trip PG/Europe voyages. Just as the unforeseeable closing of the Suez Canal made hash of the computer projections based on the premise that the future is merely an extrapolation of the past, so too did the unforeseeable quadrupling of the price of crude utterly destroy everyone's perceptions of a continuing boom in the tanker market.

The initial impact on the tanker market was not the quadrupling of the price of crude oil but the embargoes of oil shipments to the U.S. and Rotterdam, the world's largest crude oil importing port. This shifted the marginal demand for tanker capacity from a shortage to a surplus. Rates for the 50,000–100,000-dwt class of tanker collapsed from W240 to W80, a 67% fall. By the time the embargoes were lifted, crude oil consumption was declining as nations began to respond to a new era of high-cost energy. Tanker owners and oil companies now had to cope with a surplus of tanker capacity which lasted for years.

Shedding excess tonnage through the normal expiration of charters was too slow for the oil companies. Since there were few reletting opportunities, the oil companies trimmed their cargo-carrying capacity by ordering their fleets to slow steam. A 25% reduction in the average speed of a fleet should reduce bunker costs by nearly 60% because fuel consumption theoretically varies with the cube of speed. In practice, the fuel savings are not quite this impressive. Some oil companies differentiated on the slow steaming speed between the loaded and ballast legs of a voyage to reflect inventory carrying charges of a cargo of high priced crude oil. A 400,000-dwt ULCC with 390,000 long tons of crude oil, or 2.73 million barrels (114,660,000 gallons), has a cargo value of $30 million at $11 per barrel. At $30 per barrel, the value is close to $82 million. The loaded leg had a higher speed than the ballast leg and the higher bunker costs of the loaded leg were compensated by the lower inventory carrying costs over the shorter voyage time.

By 1975, spot rates had fallen so low that large crude carrier owners on the spot market were earning only enough to pay for bunker costs and port charges; all other operating and financing charges had to come out of cash reserves or other cash-generating assets. Under these circumstances, the major oil companies laid up some of their more inefficient tonnage and chartered-in shortfalls from the spot market. Shipowners considered the use of their assets at such depressed rates a form of subsidy to the oil companies. This was no subsidy; the low market rates merely reflected the magnitude of the surplus of vessel capacity.

Scrapping is another way of reducing excess tonnage. In the life of any vessel, the thickness of the steel in the hull and the condition of the propulsion plant require a substantial investment to keep it operational. In a robust market environment, the investment is justified by the continued earning capacity of the ship; in a depressed market, the same vessel is sold for scrap—usually to ship-breaking companies in Taiwan and Spain.

The scrapping of tankers in 1975 and 1976 was unique in that the type of propulsion plant was important in the decision on whether or not to scrap. Propulsion plants are either steam turbine or diesel engine.

In steam propulsion, the lowest grade of refined oil products (Bunker C) is burned in boilers to heat water which produces the steam to drive the turbines which, through reduction gears, turn the propeller shaft. A diesel engine uses a slightly better grade of refined product and may turn the propeller shaft without any intermediary gearing arrangement. A steam turbine plant is less efficient thermally and requires more fuel than an equivalent shaft horsepower rated diesel engine. A diesel engine is more costly to install and expensive to maintain. The total cost of operation, including capital charges, for both types of propulsion plants was about the same at pre-October 1973 crude prices. The choice of propulsion plant was essentially a matter of personal preference on the part of the owner.

A 50,000-dwt tanker burns about 85 tons per day of Bunker C with a steam propulsion plant and about 55 tons per day of low-grade diesel fuel with a diesel plant. The pre-October 1973 costs of operation were about the same for both types of propulsion plants. Any rise in the price of crude oil above $2.50 per barrel placed the steam propulsion plant at an economic disadvantage. The price of crude increased by about $9 per barrel after the 1973 oil crisis, or $63 per ton, or $1,890 per steaming day ($63 per ton × 30 tons per day differential between the two types of propulsion plants). Assuming 250 steaming days a year, the extra cost of a steam turbine plant over a diesel plant was $472,000 per year. This provided the economic justification for preferring to scrap steam-propelled rather than diesel-propelled tankers. By the end of 1979, the economic disadvantage of a steam turbine plant had increased to nearly $1,500,000 per year.

Another way for an oil company to reduce fleet capacity is by selling vessels. This would have involved taking substantial book losses because of the depressed state of the second-hand or sales and purchase (S&P) market. The major oil companies accomplished vessel disposals in two unique ways to avoid excessive book losses. One was to form joint ventures with the OPEC nations desiring tanker fleets that were managed and operated by OPEC personnel. Through joint venture arrangements, the OPEC nations acquired the vessels and the proper personnel indoctrination and training while the oil companies disposed of a portion of their excess fleet capacity.* The other way was to extend the charter period for charters expiring in the latter part of 1970s or early 1980s at a reasonably profitable rate for the owner. The price the owner had to pay to ensure continuity of profitable employment for

*The one notable example of this was a joint venture between British Petroleum and the National Iranian Oil Company.

his assets in the future was to buy a large crude carrier from the oil company at a premium above the S&P market. In the eyes of an oil company chartering manager, the benefits of disposing of excess capacity, usually an older large crude carrier at better-than-market prices, exceeded the cost of committing the company to a charter which commenced three to five years in the future. In the eyes of an owner, the benefits of securing employment for his assets in the future exceeded the cost of purchasing a large crude carrier at a premium over its market value.

In the post-1973 environment, order cancellations for large crude carriers were fairly common. Although the oil companies succeeded to some degree in postponing delivery by having the yard eliminate overtime and, in a few cases, renegotiating the contracts for other types of tonnage, few orders were actually cancelled. To be fair, it was not the oil companies who were primarily responsible for the massive ordering of tanker capacity. Moreover, a shipyard will be much more insistent on the contractual obligations being fulfilled on an order from a major oil company than from an owner who placed his order through a Liberian one-ship holding company capitalized at $500.

Unlike owners who receive spot market rates for their unchartered vessels, oil companies charge AFRA (Average Freight Rate Assessments) for their transportation services to their affiliates. AFRA rates reflect the overall cost of transportation for oil companies. They are set by a panel of London brokers partly based on past charter fixtures for various periods of time and partly on the internal cost of ownership by an oil company. Since AFRA rates remained higher than spot-market rates after the 1973 oil crisis (they were lower than the spot market preceding the crisis), the oil companies earned a return on their tanker investments while the owners with tonnage on the spot market suffered significant cash shortfalls.

Major oil companies could not entirely avoid the consequences of overcapacity by hiding behind AFRA rates. If one major oil company transported a shipment of crude from the Persian Gulf to Europe on its own vessel and charged the average 1975 AFRA rate of W55, which was $8.53 per ton (55% × $15.50, the W100 base rate in 1975), the proceeds were largely dedicated to servicing the vessel's operating and capital costs. If a competing oil company chartered-in a large crude carrier at the average 1975 spot market rate of W25 and charged W55 for its transportation services, then the difference of 30 Worldscale points, or $4.65 per ton, was pocketed as incremental profits. Thus, the overall profitability of competing oil companies was influenced by the size of their commitment to tankers relative to their transportation needs.

Perhaps if the major oil companies were the only force in the world oil business, the AFRA rate structure might protect their $10 billion in tanker investments (100 million dwt × estimated book valuation of $100 per dwt). Unfortunately for the majors, a significant share of the world's oil business is conducted by smaller integrated oil companies and by independent refiners and oil trading companies who collectively own little of their transportation needs. They can, and did, price their product on the basis of actual spot rates for tanker capacity. The major oil companies were not immune to the competitive inroads of these firms, nor could they escape the unpleasant reality that they have suffered a loss in the capital stock of their tanker fleets in recent years.

A tanker owner must face the consequences of an oversupply of capacity more squarely than an oil company executive. The independent tanker owner, largely responsible for the speculative binge in ordering large crude carriers, was forced to cancel, renegotiate, or walk away from newbuilding contracts. More than one yard had the unpleasant experience of an owner not showing up to take delivery of a large crude carrier. Whereas in 1973 the projected 1980 tanker fleet was 480 million dwt, by 1977 this figure was trimmed to about 350 million dwt. Cancellation did not come cheaply because penalty charges, or loss of paid-in capital, were often part of the final arrangement with the shipyard. Many owners converted their large crude carrier contracts to other types of vessels to avoid large losses in paid-in capital.

In a free market environment, the only way to restore an equilibrium capacity when the supply of vessels exceeds the demand for vessels is for rates to sink so low that owners are forced to lay up vessels, thus removing capacity from the marketplace. Some owners installed dehumidifiers, placed protective coverings on critical electrical equipment and machinery, and took other actions to prevent deterioration of a vessel in lay up. Others took no precautionary actions at all. Laying up also entails mooring or anchoring the vessel in a safe berth or anchorage that is approved by the insurance underwriters. Once laid up, operating costs can be cut by disbanding the crew except for a security watch, eliminating further maintenance, and reducing insurance premiums. At first, owners had difficulty finding suitable lay-up berths or anchorages. Large crude carriers had never been laid up before, and underwriters were reluctant to cut the insurance premiums until they were first satisfied with the proposed lay-up berths or anchorages and the precautionary safeguard measures.

Although a small- or medium-sized tanker can be laid up for only a few thousand dollars a month, the lay-up costs of a large crude carrier turned out to be $500,000–$1,000,000 per year plus the cost of preparing the vessel for lay up and the cost of reactivating the vessel prior to returning it to service. One reason why rates sank so low during the mid-1970s was that owners preferred to operate a vessel at less than breakeven rates as long as the losses did not exceed the lay-up cost.

An improperly laid-up vessel will suffer from steel corrosion in the hull and electrical equipment/machinery deterioration. Some vessels were plagued with metal-eating microbes, thriving in the phosphate and nitrate compounds found in lube oil additives. Heating the lube oil by an engine killed the microbes, and the normal maintenance programs of a crew restored the condition of electrical equipment and machinery. A vessel laid up for an extended period of time without proper prior preparation and some sort of an ongoing maintenance program will physically deteriorate. Many tankers in lay up during the 1970s deteriorated beyond the point of ever returning to service and were subsequently scrapped. However, most vessels laid up in 1975 were reactivated in 1976 in response to higher market rates and to preserve the vessels from further deterioration.

Although the oceanborne movement of crude oil was about the same in 1976 as it was in 1973, the fleet had grown by 50% in the interim (300 million dwt in 1976 compared with 200 million dwt in 1973). The excess capacity of 100 million dwt was concentrated in the VLCC/ULCC-size categories and was by no means shared equally by other classes and types of tankers. The excess capacity of tankers of 70,000 dwt and less was about 10% in 1976—enough to wreck the spot market rate structure but not a situation which couldn't be remedied by a modest growth in the world movement of crude oil. Small- and medium-sized tankers have not been built in large numbers since 1965 when most owners turned their attention to larger-sized tankers. Since small- and medium-sized tankers dominated the older segment of the world tanker fleet, they have made up most of the 45 million dwt of tankers broken up between 1974 and 1979. During 1979, newbuilding orders were placed for nearly 100 tankers of about 80,000 dwt, primarily as replacements for vessels already scrapped and anticipated to be scrapped during the 1980s.

Another type of tanker with brighter prospects than large crude carriers is the products carrier. Crude carriers transport crude oil to refineries, while products carriers transport refined oil products (gasoline, jet fuel, and home heating and industrial heating oils) from refineries to the consuming areas. The many types and grades of oil products require maintaining product integrity. Each product must have its own independent tank and cargo-handling system known as segregated tanks. Moreover, the higher grades of oil products require special coatings (commonly an epoxy) on the inner surfaces of the cargo tanks to prevent contaminating the cargo with rust. Typically, a products carrier has six, eight, or more segregated and coated tank systems for versatility in the clean products trade. Products carriers are more sophisticated and costly to build than an equivalent-sized crude carrier because the latter has a simpler tank arrangement for carrying two grades of crude in its uncoated tanks and a one-cargo handling system.

The lower grades of refined oil products such as heating oils do not require coated tanks nor the total sophistication of a typical products carrier. Some products carriers have only two or three segregated and uncoated tanks and participate either in the heating oil segment of the products trades or in the crude oil trades as dictated by the market. In the products trades, there is a difference in shipping demand between clean or white products such as gasoline and dirty or black products such as heating oils.

Asphalt is the waste of the refining process and is transported in asphalt carriers. Since asphalt, along with Bunker C and certain heavy and waxy grades of crude oil, is too viscous for the cargo pumps at ambient temperatures, heating coils are built into the tanker to keep the cargo at the proper viscosity. For waxy crudes, the required temperature may be 120°F while asphalt must be kept at a temperature of 350°F. The heating coils use steam or heated water from the residual heat of steam turbine plants or from auxiliary or donkey boilers installed for this specific purpose. Asphalt carriers have strengthened hull support members to transport the heavy 350°F cargo of asphalt safely. No insulation is needed around this hot cargo because a thin layer of asphalt cooled on contact with the ship's hull insulates the rest of the cargo.

Since most refineries are located close to or in major population centers, the world product carrier fleet is much smaller in size and number than the crude carrier fleet. Before offshore refineries were constructed in Singapore to serve the Japanese market and in northeastern Canada and the Caribbean Islands to serve the U.S. market, the typical products carrier was 15,000–25,000 dwt. Newer product carriers built to serve these offshore refineries are 25,000–35,000 dwt. As the proposed Middle Eastern refineries come on stream, there will be another jump in the demand for products carriers and a shift in the mix of tanker types serving these nations. In anticipation of this new market, oil companies and owners have a number of 50,000-dwt product carriers on order that will be able to transit the Suez Canal fully loaded. The largest products carrier in existence is 110,000 dwt.*

In summary, the independent tanker owner and tanker-owning shipping companies satisfy a portion of the core and all the marginal tanker needs of the major oil companies, and much of the total tanker needs of the small integrated oil companies, the independent refiners, and oil trading companies. The reasons for this are an unwillingness on the part of the oil industry to commit all the capital necessary to be self-sufficient in tanker capacity, the desire to shed excess tanker capacity at no cost to itself, and the ability of owners to satisfy transportation needs at less than internal costs through lower profit objectives and greater operating efficiency. A charter market provides oil companies the opportunity to charter in low-cost transportation capacity during depressed market conditions or to pass on to the owners' accounts the ravages of inflation on operating costs through fixed-rate charters that were arranged in more stable times. Yet the successful tanker owner has flourished in this environment. Increased worldwide consumption of crude oil is the cause of the growing demand for his services with charters from some of the world's largest corporations providing the means to acquire the necessary capital.

*Prior to WWII, most tankers were product carriers because refineries were built at the oil fields. At that time, the U.S. was the world's major exporter of refined oil products. The crude carrier is actually a post-war development in the tanker business.

3

Forecasting Tanker Demand

In a competitive, market-oriented environment, corporate managers conduct their business and formulate their plans looking toward the future. Their perception is strongly affected by recent developments and current trends in their respective industries. This peering into the future is a consequence of today's business decisions being judged by tomorrow's unfolding of events. The future need for tanker capacity is as much on the minds of those responsible for oceanborne transportation of crude oil in large and small integrated oil companies and in independent refinery, oil-marketing, and trading companies as it is on the minds of managers of tanker-owning shipping companies and independent tanker owners. Large corporate planning staffs of major oil companies assess the probable course of events in the many vital areas of interest in the oil business, one of these being tankers. Most projections are extrapolations of the current situation with existing trends remaining essentially intact. Vast input is required to collect and sort the raw data to establish the status of the current situation and to identify the trends.

Of all the vessel types and trades, projecting tanker demand for the crude oil trades should be the easiest because of its simple structure. Of the world oceanborne movement of crude, 40% is transported to Europe, 20% to North America, and 15% to Japan (*1975 British Petroleum Statistical Review*, British Petroleum, London). These three areas account for 75% of crude oil imports. Two-thirds of oceanborne crude exports emanate from the Middle East with most of the remainder being Caribbean, North and West African exports to North America and Europe, and Indonesian crude exports to Japan and the United States. Oil consumption in the crude-importing nations has historically followed their economic growth patterns fairly closely. Knowing the present volume on world crude trades, forecasting economic activity, and determining the sources of the incremental crude necessary to satisfy energy demand, one can project tanker demand.

The supply of tanker capacity is easily projected by taking the existing fleet and laying out the schedule of tanker deliveries from the world's shipyards less an allowance for scrapping and losses at sea. A forecast of a tanker shortage or surplus can be made by comparing the projected demand for tanker capacity with the projected supply of tanker capacity. If it is correct, a forecast of tanker supply/demand will help oil company chartering managers minimize transportation costs.*

Chartering managers are more interested in projected shortages of tanker capacity than in projected surpluses. In a surplus market, low rates let a chartering manager introduce a layer of transportation capacity whose cost is below the internal costs of his fleet. If a shortage of vessel capacity is projected, the only way for a chartering manager to minimize transportation costs is to complete his transportation arrangements before the actual shortage occurs. The funds dedicated to forecasting the relationship between tanker supply and demand are well spent if the results help the chartering manager perform his task. The success or failure of such efforts has a direct impact on the prospects for tanker owners.

The Mechanics of a Forecast

Projections are like peeling off the layers of an onion where the scope of the problem is narrowed by removing each successive layer until the end result, lying at the very core, is exposed. The first layer of a tanker demand projection is a projection of total energy demand for the major crude oil-importing regions of the world independent of the actual source of energy. Since overall energy consumption closely parallels economic activity, the initial step in the analysis is a forecast of economic activity for each major oil-importing region. This includes

*Anyone who charters a vessel, including an owner, is a charterer. Chartering manager in this chapter refers to a manager of a marine department of an oil company who is responsible for the oceanborne transportation of crude oil.

the entire industrialized world (North America, Western Europe, and Japan) plus crude oil-importing nations in South America (Argentina, Brazil, and Chile), South Africa, and Asia (India, Pakistan, the Philippines, Korea, Taiwan, Singapore, and Hong Kong). Energy consumption is also influenced by noneconomic factors such as the severity of weather (the consumption of heating oils and natural gas in winter and the usage of air conditioning in summer) and political considerations in energy pricing. For instance, during the 1970s Americans believed they could consume high amounts of energy because the government kept the price of the bulk of U.S. domestic production of crude oil and natural gas far below the international levels.

Having projected total energy demand, the second layer of analysis is to determine the future role of crude oil, coal, natural gas, nuclear, hydro, and other sources of energy in satisfying total energy demand for each of the major categories and subcategories of energy usage (electric generation, residential and commercial users, industry, and transportation). The approach to this problem in the past was to net out the contribution of coal, natural gas, nuclear, and hydro sources from total energy demand to establish the role of crude oil. Crude oil is no longer merely a filler in satisfying the gap between total energy demand and the contribution of other energy sources. Some nations have imposed a limit on the quantity of imported crude oil to conserve their foreign exchange reserves. Other oil exporters have limited production to conserve their reserves. Nevertheless, North America, western Europe, and Japan account for 55% of the world's appetite for energy, 80% if the Soviet bloc and Mainland China are excluded (Table 3.1).

TABLE 3.1
BREAKDOWN OF ENERGY SOURCES (1975)

	Crude oil	Natural gas	Coal	Hydro	Nuclear
North America	43%	29%	18%	7%	3%
Western Europe	56%	13%	21%	8%	2%
Japan	70%	2%	20%	6%	2%

The relative contribution of each source in satisfying total energy demand changes with time. King Coal supplied half of U.S. energy needs in the 1940s and was eventually displaced by crude oil and natural gas. In the late 1960s and early 1970s the growth in natural gas consumption leveled off and began to decline as a consequence of government pricing policies which discouraged exploration and development of new gas fields.

In projecting the role of natural gas in satisfying future U.S. energy needs, one must predict (1) the future pricing policies of FERC,* (2) the effect of these policies on exploration budgets of oil and gas companies, (3) the success of finding new gas fields for any given level of exploration activity, and (4) the nature of FERC rulings on liquefied natural gas (LNG) imports into the United States. The future role of coal involves predictions on the effects of legislation on strip mining, mine safety, and pollution standards on the production of coal and the availability of capital and labor to develop and operate new mines. While nuclear energy was once expected to satisfy 10–15% of total U.S. energy needs in the mid-1980s, construction and licensing delays in completing nuclear plants, the old question of uranium supplies for refueling reactors, and public attitudes toward nuclear power plants cast some degree of doubt on its future role. This vision of the future contribution of each energy source must be repeated for each crude-importing region, and each region has its unique characteristics. During the 1970s while natural gas production was declining in the United States, European supply rose from the development of the Groningen gas fields in the Netherlands, Soviet/Iranian natural gas pipeline imports, LNG imports from North Africa, and associated gas from North Sea crude oil and gas field production. A trans-Mediterranean natural gas pipeline between Libya and Italy is under construction. When completed, this will enhance the role of natural gas as a source of energy in Europe.

After projecting the role of crude oil in meeting total energy needs, the third layer of analysis is to project domestic crude production and crude oil pipeline imports to establish the future level of oceanborne crude oil imports. This is easy for Japan, which has no domestic crude production and pipeline imports and must import all its crude needs by tanker. For many years western Europe was in a similar position, having only modest domestic production of crude plus some Soviet crude oil pipeline imports. However, North Sea oil fields are expected to supply a third or more of western European needs by the mid-1980s. The eventual production level and the rate at which it is achieved depend on the size of future oil discoveries and the timetable of laying underwater pipelines and setting up production platforms. These, in turn, are

---

*The pricing of natural gas came under the jurisdiction of the Federal Power Commission (FPC) in the 1950s. After a government reorganization in 1977, the functions of the FPC were taken over by the Federal Energy Regulatory Commission (FERC) of the U.S. Department of Energy.

influenced by the Norwegian government's decisions on restricting oil production within its sector of the North Sea for conservation purposes and the British government's decisions on taxes and royalties and the respective role of government and private capital in developing its sector of the North Sea.

Domestic oil production in the United States is influenced by the pricing policies of the Economic Regulatory Administration (ERA) of the U.S. Department of Energy which, in 1979, held the price of old oil at about $6 per barrel while OPEC oil sold for $30. Offshore exploration activity is constrained by the timing of lease sales conducted by the Department of the Interior and by the public's opposition to drilling off beaches. While the Trans-Alaska Pipeline reduced U.S. reliance on crude oil imports, the decision of Canadian Authorities to curtail crude oil pipeline exports to refineries in the northwestern United States increased U.S. reliance on oceanborne imports. Canadian exports, which were as high as 1,000,000 bpd in 1973, were cut to 600,000 bpd in 1975, 300,000 bpd in 1978, and are expected to be phased out in the 1980s.

Canada once exported its crude oil production, which is concentrated in its western provinces, by pipeline to refineries in the northwestern United States and imported crude oil from Venezuela and the Middle East to feed its refineries in the eastern provinces. As a result of its policy to cut back exports to the United States, a new tanker route emerged from Vancouver to eastern Canadian refineries via the Panama Canal. These refineries either had terminals on the St. Lawrence River, which were inaccessible during the ice season, or were linked by pipeline to an ice-free oil terminal in Portland, Maine. This tanker trade disappeared in 1976 when pipeline extensions connecting the eastern Canadian refineries with western Canadian oil fields were completed.

Tanker demand is not just a function of tons per year of crude oil imports. It depends on ton-miles per year of imports, which takes into consideration the distances between exporting and importing nations. The fourth layer of analysis is a country-by-country assessment of who supplies how much crude to whom over the projected period. About one-third of world crude import needs are accounted for by estimating the future production levels of Libya, Algeria, Nigeria, Indonesia, Venezuela, the Soviet Union, Mexico, and Mainland China. Their production, net of domestic consumption, determines the available crude for export that is then assigned to various crude oil importers. In the past, the remaining bulk of crude import needs was assumed to flow from the Middle East (Saudi Arabia, Iran, Kuwait, Iraq, Abu Dhabi, Dubai, Qatar, and Oman). The assumption that the Middle East can satisfy any level of demand for crude is no longer valid because leaders of these nations are aware that their large crude reserves are finite and that oil in the ground may be more valuable than money in the bank.

The fifth layer of analysis is an assessment of the sharing of tanker traffic for alternative voyage routes. Once the flow of crude oil from all sources to all destinations has been projected, tanker demand can be calculated. This is done by a straightforward arithmetic relationship that exists between barrels per day of crude oil throughput and dead-weight of tanker capacity required for any given voyage. Unfortunately, even this calculation is complicated by the presence of alternative voyage routes between two ports.

Genoa is a major crude oil-importing port and Kirkuk is a major oil field in eastern Iraq. The Kirkuk oil field is linked to the port of Basrah (Iraq) in the Persian Gulf and to the Mediterranean ports of Dortyol (Turkey), Banias (Syria), and Tripoli (Lebanon) by pipelines (Table 3.2).

TABLE 3.2
VOYAGE DISTANCE FOR ALTERNATIVE ROUTES

Voyage distance*	Voyage
11,000	Basrah/Genoa via Cape of Good Hope
4,800	Basrah/Genoa via the Suez Canal or the use of the Sumed pipeline in Egypt or the Trans-Israel pipeline that connects oil terminals in the Red Sea with terminals in the Mediterranean
1,500	Dortyol/Genoa
1,500	Banias/Genoa
1,500	Tripoli/Genoa

*Data taken from the British Petroleum Distance Tables published by British Petroleum, London.

Obviously, the tanker capacity required for a given throughput volume of crude from the Kirkuk oil fields to Genoa depends on sharing the trade among five routes whose distances vary between 1,500 and 11,000 miles.

Although tanker demand is influenced by the extent of the usage of the Suez Canal, its parallel pipelines, and the Middle East pipelines terminating in eastern Mediterranean ports, their throughput volume is in turn affected by the level of spot market tanker rates. For example, depressed tanker rates in 1975 caused a sharp cutback in the through-put volume of the Trans-Arabian Pipeline which connects the eastern Saudi Arabian oil fields with the port of Sidon, Lebanon. The cost of Saudi Arabian crude at Sidon is marked up in comparison to the price of crude at ports in the Persian Gulf by the pipeline tolls, which cover the cost of operating the pipeline, its capital servicing charges, plus the transit fees paid to Jordan, Syria, and Lebanon. The low tanker rates in 1975 made it less expensive for a North European importer to purchase Saudi Arabian crude for delivery at a port on the east coast of Saudi Arabia than the much nearer port of Sidon in the Mediteranean. Simi-larly, low tanker rates made the opening of the Suez Canal in 1975 the nonevent of the year in the tanker business. The cost of transporting crude oil on a large crude carrier between the Persian Gulf and Northern Europe via the Cape of Good Hope was less than the Suez Canal tolls alone on a per ton of cargo basis. Spot market tanker rates play an important role in establishing the level of tolls for the Suez Canal and the Middle East pipelines.

Therefore, the assessment of the throughput volume of the Suez Canal and the Middle East pipelines requires an assessment of future spot market rates, which, as a manifestation of a surplus/shortage situ-ation in tanker capacity, is the object of the projection. This problem may be sidestepped by assuming a fairly high utilization rate for these facilities. This would be appropriate during tanker shortages (high spot market rates), bearing in mind that chartering managers are more in-terested in projected shortages than in projected surpluses of tanker capacity.

The utilization of these facilities is not, however, strictly a matter of economics. Political, not economic, factors shut down the Iraq Petro-leum Company (IPC) pipeline branch serving Haifa, Israel, in 1948, closed the Suez in 1967, and reopened it in 1975. The Lebanese Civil War shut down the IPC pipeline branch in Lebanon. The Trans-Arabian Pipeline was shut down over a dispute on the price of crude taken from the pipeline by Jordan and Lebanon and over the amount of pipeline transit fees to be paid to Jordan, Lebanon, and Syria. Tanker demand will be affected by the outcome of any decision made by Singapore maritime authorities on the minimum allowable clearance below the keel of tankers transiting the Malacca Strait. If large crude carriers are forced to divert from the Malacca to the Lombok Strait, the loaded leg of the voyage between the Persian Gulf and Japan would be increased by 1,000 miles.

If the projection compares overall tanker demand with overall tanker supply, then assessing the sharing of alternative tanker routes completes the demand side of the task. However, chartering managers do not make decisions on tankers as though all tankers were identical. Decisions are made on tankers of a particular deadweight size. In order for a tanker demand projection to be useful for decisionmakers, the sixth layer of analysis—breaking down the crude oil trades based on various tanker size categories, taking into consideration port and terminal limitations and development projects—is necessary.

Suppose, for example, there is a projected movement of crude oil from the Persian Gulf to a refinery on the Delaware River near Philadelphia. The refinery terminal berth has sufficient water depth for a fully laden 60,000-dwt tanker and sufficient length for a partially loaded 100,000-dwt tanker to moor alongside. There are five choices of size classes of tankers to handle this movement, considering alternative voyage routes and possible port development projects.

A. The 60,000-dwt Sumax tankers employed from the Persian Gulf direct to the refinery berth via the Suez Canal on a round-trip voyage basis.

B. The 100,000-dwt tankers employed from the Persian Gulf via the Cape of Good Hope on the loaded leg with the option of transiting the Suez Canal on the ballast leg of the voyage. The tankers are lightened of some of their cargoes in the sheltered waters of the Delaware Bay to awaiting barges before proceeding to the refinery berth to complete the offloading. When the Suez Canal is deepened from its present depth of 38 feet to 55 feet in 1981, tankers of about 150,000 dwt (the new Sumax vessels) will be able to make round-trip voyages through the Canal.

C. VLCCs may be used from the Persian Gulf to the southern terminus of the Sumed Pipeline in the Red Sea with 60,000 and 100,000-dwt tankers completing the movement from the northern terminus of the pipeline in the Mediterranean to the Philadelphia refinery.

D. A single point mooring (SPM) system is a shoreside tank farm linked by an underwater pipeline to a floating buoy situated in deep waters. A large crude carrier anchored nearby pumps its cargo through a floating hose to the buoy and then to the storage tanks via an underwater pipeline. The movement of crude from the storage tanks to the refinery is completed by pipeline or by barges and small coastal tankers. If an SPM were located in ocean waters off Delaware Bay (depth of 75 feet), 250,000-dwt VLCCs could be employed via the Cape of Good Hope on the loaded leg of the voyage with the option of transiting the Suez Canal on the ballast leg. If the SPM were situated further out in deeper waters of 100 feet, then ULCCs of 350,000 dwt or larger could be employed.

E. VLCCs or ULCCs can off-load their cargoes in any of several Caribbean transshipment ports with 60,000-dwt shuttle tankers completing the movement to the refinery. A growing practice in the Caribbean is ship-to-ship transfer of crude from VLCC/ULCCs to the shuttle tankers in sheltered or open waters. The Louisiana Offshore Oil Port (LOOP) project, a grouping of SPMs under construction off the mouth of the Mississippi River, or the Seadock project, a proposed fixed dock in deep waters off Texas, are other possible alternatives for off-loading VLCC/ULCCs. The completion of the crude oil movement to the Philadelphia refinery can be accomplished if suitable connections were made to existing pipelines or by U.S. flag tankers. U.S. flag tankers are required by the provisions of the Jones Act, which establishes a protected trade for U.S. flag vessels for all goods and commodities shipped between U.S. ports.

The U.S. Gulf to U.S. East Coast crude oil and oil products trade is the prime source of employment for the U.S. flag handy-sized (15,000–35,000-dwt) tanker fleet. This fleet holds the longevity record among the world's oceangoing fleets, with some active units 35 years old compared to the nominal 20-year life for most tankers. Their longevity is linked to the amount of steel originally built into the hulls and hull structures and to their remarkably reliable steam propulsion plants. Furthermore, the declining movement of crude from the U.S. Gulf to U.S. northeastern ports encouraged extending the useful life of the fleet rather than scrapping and building anew. The other major protected trade for U.S. flag tankers is the transport of North Slope crude from the terminus of the Trans-Alaska Pipeline in Valdez, Alaska, to refinery terminals on both coasts of the United States. A fleet of 80,000–160,000-dwt tankers was built to handle this movement.

One of the distinguishing features of the tanker market in the 1970s was the effect of port development projects on tanker demand. The large crude carrier was intended for the long haul trades from the Persian Gulf to Europe, the United States, and Japan. However, the low-cost transportation provided by VLCC/ULCCs and the low cost of installing an SPM in areas where deep waters are relatively close to shore brought about the increasing use of VLCC/ULCCs on short- and medium-haul trades. SPMs installed off West Africa allowed large crude carriers to be employed transporting West African crude to refineries in Europe and in the Caribbean. West African crude oil was transported to refineries in the United States by VLCCs utilizing the Caribbean transshipment terminals. Upon completion of the LOOP project, about 25% of U.S. crude imports will be transported in large crude carriers directly into the United States without requiring the Caribbean transshipment terminals and shuttle or lightening vessels. Large crude carriers have transported North African crude from an SPM offshore Libya on short voyages to Italy. VLCCs are, or will be, able to participate in Persian Gulf exports to nearby India and to South Africa, Taiwan, and Hong Kong because of existing or proposed SPMs. This penetration of VLCCs into medium- and short-haul trades, something never envisioned when the first vessels were constructed in the late 1960s, has lessened demand for small- and medium-sized tonnage on these trade routes. The need for a newbuilding program for medium-sized crude carriers, which became apparent in 1979, was caused not so much by a growth in demand for these tankers as by a shrinkage of supply of vessel capacity from scrapping.

There are other considerations to be made besides port and terminal development projects. One example involves refinery characteristics. Refineries are built for particular feedstocks, or grades of crude. Many European refineries are designed for sour crudes from the Middle East, while U.S. refineries are designed to refine mainly domestic sweet crudes. Since North Sea crude is sweet, it may make sense to export some North Sea crude to the United States for refining while continuing to import Middle East sour crudes to European refineries rather than adapt European refineries for a different feedstock.

By tallying up the demand for tanker capacity by deadweight classes on all trades over a period of time, one obtains a projection of demand by size category. The projection of supply of tanker capacity by size categories is obtained by taking the existing fleet plus newbuilding delivery schedules adjusted for new orders, cancellation of existing orders, and slippage in shipyard delivery schedules. Further adjustments must be made for losses at sea and scrapping. Scrapping depends on the age distribution of vessels in each size category and the state of the spot market, which again presumes a foreknowledge of the results of the forecast. A forecast of the relationship between the supply and demand for tanker capacity for each size class of tanker under consideration is finally obtained by comparing the supply and demand projections.

Interpreting Forecast Results

A good forecast provides valuable insights for chartering managers instituting policies and plans that may lower the cost of transportation. The forecast does not in any way relieve management of the necessity of exercising their business judgment because the forecast is not infallible. The data base in the supply and demand projections may not be accurate or cover all aspects of the crude oil business because competing oil companies are not eager to exchange privileged information.

Projecting total energy demand requires an economic forecast to project total energy consumption. Recent forecasts have been as reliable as the practice of reading the future in the entrails of chickens. While economists rivet their attention on macroindices of economic activity such as the Gross National Product, millions of consumers and businessmen are making microeconomic personal decisions which, time and again, have made a shambles of official economic predictions. Projecting the role of all energy sources squeezes the projection of crude oil demand between a margin of error, or variance, of economic activity on one hand and four variances on the respective roles of coal, natural gas, nuclear, and hydro sources on the other. Therefore, the future role of crude oil is not a series of definite numbers, but a range of likely values which widens as one projects further. This blurring worsens as one descends through the successive layers of analysis.

In the real world, a mismatch of only a few percentage points from a balance between the supply and demand for tanker capacity can cause spot market rates to rise or fall to the point where oil companies are either forced to absorb a layer of high-cost transportation or have an opportunity to introduce a low-cost layer of transportation in satisfying their shipping needs. This kind of accuracy in a tanker supply/demand forecast is far beyond the realm of human effort. Even if a corporate planning staff is convinced of the accuracy of the results of its forecast, line managers of a chartering department would rightfully resent having their decisions dictated to them by a staff study.

The upshot of all this is that a chartering manager, buried under sheafs of computer printouts, may not be in any better position to make a business decision than a tanker owner who conducts his business over a morning cup of coffee. The inability to predict the relationship between the supply and demand for tanker capacity accurately means that the decisions made to minimize the cost of transportation essentially rest on the business judgment of the chartering manager. The corollary to this is that a tanker owner does not merely respond to the immediate needs of the oil companies. He may be just as good in assessing the future transportation needs of the oil companies as the chartering managers themselves. In fact, a common business practice in shipping is for owners to assess the future shipping needs of charterers and order a vessel before its demand becomes apparent to all.

Tanker owners are independent businessmen fulfilling an entrepreneurial role. Some tanker owners have broadened their business horizons to associated shipping activities such as ship repairing or shipbuilding or to energy-related projects with the idea of locking up the transportation requirements for their own accounts. They may be involved in nonshipping-related businesses such as real estate, manufacturing facilities, and mineral resource development projects.

Chartering managers and tanker owners are intelligent people who keep one eye on today's transportation needs and one eye on the future. Chartering managers, however, are salaried executives who exercise their best business judgment to minimize the cost of transportation. They can also leave their mistakes behind as they advance in their careers. Owners, on the other hand, are entrepreneurs who exercise their best business judgment to maximize their future worth. They live with their mistakes until the mistakes are liquidated by the course of events. Owners invest their capital resources in a business environment which enriches those who correctly judge the market and ruthlessly cuts down those who don't. The risk in a shipping venture is being wrong; the reward is being right.

4

Bulk Carriers

Bulk carriers carry iron ore, coal, grain, and a host of other dry-bulk cargoes. These cargoes are loaded directly into the holds of the vessel by shoreside material-handling facilities. Cargo is transferred from the terminal storage areas into the open holds of the vessel until the total weight of cargo, bunkers (fuel), stores, and water is equal to the deadweight of the vessel or until the holds are completely full of cargo. Hatch covers are secured over the holds prior to sailing.

A vessel loaded to its full deadweight capacity is loaded to its marks. Viewed from dockside, the waterline of the vessel is at the Plimsoll marks on the hull, which show whether the ship is loaded to its full summer, winter, or tropical deadweight capacity in salt water or to its full summer and tropical deadweight in fresh water. A 70,000 summer dwt tanker taking on crude oil in Alaska or a 70,000 summer dwt bulk carrier taking on iron ore in Sweden during the winter is loaded to its winter marks (about 68,200 tons). The same vessels loading crude oil in the Persian Gulf or iron ore in Brazil during the summer are loaded to their tropical marks (about 71,800 tons). Load line zones, which delineate the geographic areas and set the times of the year when winter, summer, and tropical deadweight apply, are established by the Load Line Convention administered by the United Nations Intergovernment Maritime Consultative Organization (IMCO).

Aside from revenue considerations, an ideal cargo completely fills the holds of a vessel and loads it to its full deadweight capacity. This rarely occurs in practice. A bulk carrier's holds may be only one-third filled with an iron ore cargo when loaded to its full deadweight capacity. A cargo of light grain will cube out, i.e., completely fill the holds

47

before the vessel is loaded to its marks. Cubing out is not the only reason for being unable to load a vessel to its marks. Water depth restrictions at berths or channels at either the loading or discharging ports or at intermediate points on a voyage may limit the draft of a vessel. A vessel loading in a tropical load line zone for discharge in a winter zone can take on cargo only to the extent that it can enter the intervening summer zone at its summer marks and the subsequent winter zone at its winter marks.

A geared bulk carrier has cargo-handling cranes and derricks installed on its main deck to load and unload a cargo, while a gearless bulk carrier depends entirely on shoreside handling facilities for loading and unloading. A better use of capital resources is to have one shoreside material-handling facility serving the needs of all vessels on important trade routes rather than each vessel having its own infrequently used cargo-handling system. Regardless if a vessel is geared or gearless, cargo handling is a critical function. If improperly handled by shipboard personnel, a vessel may be subject to damaging stresses or strains in port or be in an unstable condition for sailing at sea.

TABLE 4.1
COMMODITY MOVEMENT, 1975–1979

	Trillion ton-miles	Percentage distribution
Crude oil and refined oil products	9.7	71
Major dry-bulk commodities	3.1	23
Minor dry-bulk commodities	0.9	6
Total	13.7	

Gearless bulk carriers are primarily used in the major dry-bulk commodity trades. Geared bulk carriers are usually employed in the minor dry-bulk commodity trades: forest products; agricultural products other than grains (rice and sugar); ore concentrates and minerals (manganese, chrome, lead, zinc, copper, nickel, titanium, gypsum, asbestos, and pyrites); fertilizers (potash, urea, and phosphates); pig iron, scrap, structural steel and steel products in the form of billets, sheets, plates, bars, coils, rods, pipe and automobiles; cement; limestone; sand; gravel; sulphur; soda; ash; salt; and petroleum coke. Although the volume of each individual minor bulk trade is miniscule compared to the iron ore, coal, and grain trades, the aggregate employment on the minor bulk

TABLE 4.2
MAJOR DRY-BULK COMMODITY TRADES

	Percentage distribution
Iron ore	45
Grain	25
Coal	20
Phosphate rock	5
Bauxite and alumina	5

trades is nearly half the combined movement of the major bulk cargoes in terms of tons of cargo and about a third of their shipping demand in terms of ton-miles. This reflects the relatively short voyages in some of the minor bulk commodity trades. The minor bulk trades offer ample opportunity for owners of small- and medium-sized geared bulk carriers to earn their livelihood by concentrating their efforts and resources on a particular market segment.

Iron Ore

The single largest dry-bulk commodity in oceanborne trade is iron ore (about 300 million tons). Bulk carriers built exclusively for the ore trade are called ore carriers. Ore carriers have a smaller cubic capacity, or internal volume, than bulk carriers of the same deadweight designed to carry less-dense cargoes of coal and grain in addition to ores.

The trading patterns of iron ore and other commodities are not solely established to minimize shipping distances. Although most Swedish iron ore exports are to Northern Europe, 20% of Australian ore exports are shipped to Europe and one-third of Brazilian ore exports are shipped to Japan. Diversity of supply improves the bargaining position of steel companies in dealing with iron ore exporters. Higher transportation charges are compensated by potentially lower ore costs at the mine and greater supply security.

The same incentive for growth in vessel size exists for bulk carriers in the iron ore trade as for tankers. The transportation cost savings fully

The sources of all data in this chapter are Fearnley & Egers Chartering, Oslo, and H.P. Drewry Shipping Consultants, London. The data typifies the pattern of trade in the latter part of the 1970s.

justify the investments in harbor improvements and in berths, terminals, and ore-handling facilities to accommodate ore carriers of 175,000 dwt and ore/oil carriers, capable of trading in ore or crude oil, of 300,000 dwt. Terminals located in waters too shallow for large ore carriers or without available storage areas for individual shipments of 200,000 or 300,000 tons would not appear to be able to enjoy the transportation cost savings of large ore carriers. Multiporting, calling on two or more terminals at either end of a voyage, prevents these capital investments from becoming obsolete. A large ore carrier calls on the shallow water loading terminal first for a part cargo of iron ore, topping off at a deepwater terminal. Similarly, the ore carrier first calls on a deepwater receiving terminal, lightening the vessel so that it can then call on the shallow water receiving terminal. If three steel mill receiving terminals can take only 50,000-ton shipments of ore at a time because of limited storage areas, they can still take advantage of the transportation cost savings of a 160,000-dwt ore carrier by having the vessel call on each terminal with a 50,000-ton shipment.

TABLE 4.3
IRON ORE TRADE

Sources		Destinations	
South America (1)	30%	Europe	46%
Australia	25%	Japan	43%
West Africa (2)	13%	United States	10%
Sweden	11%	Other	1%
Canada (3)	7%		
India	7%		
South Africa	2%		
Other	5%		

(1) Brazil, Venezuela, Chile, and Peru. Brazil, along with South Africa and India, is developing large-scale iron ore exporting projects.
(2) Liberia and Mauritania
(3) Canadian oceanborne iron ore exports only. The data does not include shipments to the United States handled by the Great Lakes fleet.

The fallout to owners of introducing larger-sized bulk and ore carriers was an increased demand for their services because low-cost transportation encouraged steel companies to diversify their sources of supply. Now, security of supply, political aspects of contractual arrangements between iron ore exporting and importing nations, and the grade, quality and cost of the ore have greater impact on decisions

than the length of the voyage between mine and mill. Large ore carriers
have limited trading flexibility and serve between a few modern deepwater loading terminals in Brazil, eastern Canada, Australia, West
Africa, and South Africa and a few modern deepwater receiving terminals in Japan and Europe.

Iron ore is a dense cargo well-suited for rapid material-handling
techniques. A 100,000-dwt ore carrier requires 2.5 days of total port
turnaround time (both ends), and a 240,000-dwt ore carrier requires six
days at a modern loading or receiving terminal that can handle 80,000
tons per day. Unlike bulk carriers, tankers have their cargo discharge
pumps sized to the power output of the propulsion plant. Tankers can
discharge their cargoes in 24 hours regardless of their deadweight. The
port turnaround times indicated for ore carriers and tankers do not
include time to come alongside a berth and make the vessel ready for
cargo handling. These times also assume no port or berth congestion,
no shoreside or harbor labor disputes, sufficient availability of cargo
(stems) at the loading terminal, and sufficient storage capacity at the
receiving terminal.

Iron ore and coal can be mixed with water to form a slurry. Handling
dry-bulk commodities or raw materials as a slurry speeds up cargo
transfer rates, which reduces port turnaround time. Marcona Corporation pioneered adapting slurry techniques to the iron ore trades. A mixture of crushed ore and water is pumped aboard a specially adapted ore
carrier. The water is decanted and the ore is transported in a solid state.
At the receiving terminal, the ore cargo is reslurried by a shipboard-
installed water agitation system and pumped ashore.

It is usually less expensive to bring a liquid cargo to a ship moored
in deep waters by pipeline than to bring a ship to a shoreside cargo by
dredging a deeper channel. Marcona's approach to shipping was not to
transport a cargo between two ports but, by means of slurry techniques,
to offer transportation services from the inland location of the mine to
the site of the steel mill. By offering a lower-cost method of accomplishing this broader task and having the technique to fulfill its promises,
Marcona secured long-term employment for its uniquely designed ore
carriers for transporting iron ore from New Zealand and Peru to steel
mills in Japan and the U.S. West Coast. Following this same approach, a
number of coal slurry projects are under consideration, such as the one
to pipeline coal from mines in Appalachia to bulk carriers on the East
Coast or to pipeline coal from Utah to the West Coast.

U.S. oceanborne iron ore imports of about 33 million tons in the
1970s were from Venezuela, Brazil, Peru, and eastern Canada for steel

mills located on the East and West Coasts. Midwestern steel mills imported another 14 million tons from Canada which were transported by the Great Lakes fresh water fleet of bulk and ore carriers. Bulk carriers transporting ore from terminals on the St. Lawrence River to midwestern steel mills are restricted in size to 35,000 dwt by the dimensions of the Welland Canal locks between Lakes Ontario and Erie. Ore carriers of 60,000 dwt work the interlake ore trade from Lake Superior to Lake Erie.

The Great Lakes Fleet

Trade between Great Lakes ports is reserved by law for U.S. and Canadian flag vessels. This fleet has been built specifically for the Great Lakes and not for open ocean trading. It would not be competitive in international trade even if constructed for open ocean trading because of the ships' relatively small cargo-carrying capacity and high manning costs. During the four-month ice season, part of the fleet serves as a floating grain storage facility. All maintenance is completed during the ice season in anticipation of the hectic eight-month trading period of carrying ore from the St. Lawrence and western lakes iron ore terminals to the U.S. midwestern steel mills, grain from the western lakes to export elevators on the St. Lawrence River, plus handling a large interlake traffic in coal, cement, sand and other commodities.

Since the Great Lakes fleet has a forced four-month idle period for upkeep and maintenance and is not exposed to the corrosive action of salt water nor to the abuse of open ocean weather (although some vessels have been lost riding out storms on the Great Lakes), a few Great Lakes vessels have been in active service for 70 years. Whereas U.S. flag handy-sized tankers have had steel replaced in their hulls or have been jumboized with new forebodies of greater cargo-carrying capacity to prolong their useful lives, the older vessels of the Great Lakes bulk carrier fleet have run through a succession of propulsion plants starting with coal-fired steam turbines.

Most of the Great Lakes bulk carrier fleet depends on conventional shoreside cargo-handling facilities for loading and unloading the ore, grain, and coal cargoes. The distances between many Great Lakes ports and between eastern Canadian and U.S. ports are relatively short, and much of the voyage time is spent in port. For example, a voyage may take two days to load, two days in transit (round-trip basis), and six days to discharge for a total voyage time of ten days. A self-unloader, consisting of a hopper-fed conveyor belt built into the bottom of the ship to transfer the cargo to shore, may be able to reduce the discharging time from six days to two days. With voyage time cut from ten to six days, the utility value of the vessel to transport cargoes is increased by 67%. Self-unloaders are quite costly, and the decision to install a self-unloading system or build a self-unloading vessel is based on the availability of cargoes (stems), the level of freight rates, and the possibility of term employment.*

Coal

Transporting coal is the second most important source of employment for large gearless bulk carriers, yet it is only one-third the size of the iron ore trade. The two distinct markets in the coal trade are metallurgical coal and steam coal. Metallurgical or coking coal is heated to form coke which is consumed in the production of steel. The grade of metallurgical coal plays a major role in determining the efficiency and performance of blast furnace operations. The coal performs both a chemical function in reducing iron oxides to pure iron and a mechanical function in supporting the internal contents (iron ore, coal and limestone) of a blast furnace. The best grades of metallurgical coal in the world are in the United States. These are often blended with inferior grades of coking coal from other nations to produce an acceptable grade of coking coal for steel production. Steam coal, on the other hand, is mostly burned in coal-fired electric generating plants and is valued for its heat, ash, and sulphur content, the latter of prime importance in meeting environmental emission standards. The distinct nature of the two types of coal can be demonstrated by a bulk carrier transporting Polish steam coal to a U.S. East Coast electric utility and returning with a cargo of metallurgical coal for a steel mill in Germany.

Most Polish and Soviet oceanborne coal exports are to nearby western European nations in small bulk carriers (coasters) and barges. A small amount of Polish coal is exported to Japan and 15% of Australian coal exports are shipped to Europe. This again illustrates there is more to world trading patterns than minimizing shipping distances. The three most important long-haul coal trades are U.S. East Coast/Japan, Australia/Japan, and U.S. East Coast/Europe. The Australia/Japan trade has modern deepwater terminals that can accommodate up to 150,000-

*Tanker owner D. K. Ludwig spearheaded the development of Mexican salt reserves and lined up Japanese purchasers who were attracted by the low delivered price of the salt, made possible in part by a uniquely designed 150,000-dwt self-unloading bulk salt carrier.

dwt bulk carriers. 100,000-dwt bulk carriers have carried coal from western Canada (Roberts Bank near Vancouver) to Japan. Although both these trades can accommodate large bulk carriers, much of the coal is actually shipped in medium-sized bulkers of 50,000–70,000 dwt.

TABLE 4.4
COAL TRANSPORTED, 1975–1979*

Sources		Destinations	
United States and Canada	43%	Japan	52%
Australia	23%	Europe	46%
Poland	19%	Other	2%
Soviet Union	7%		
Other	8%		

*Represents 125 million tons of coal.

A Panamax vessel of about 80,000 dwt serving the U.S. East Coast/ Japan coal trade has the largest beam (width) which can pass through the 110-foot wide locks in the Panama Canal: 106 feet. The locks transfer the vessel on its southeasterly transit from the Atlantic to the Pacific, or on its northwesterly transit from the Pacific to the Atlantic. The depth of the water in the canal depends on the amount of rainfall replenishing the highland lakes feeding the locks. This results in a two to three-foot variation in the depth of the water between the dry summer and the wet winter seasons. At the summer lows, an 80,000-dwt Panamax bulk carrier or tanker may only be able to carry 50,000 tons of cargo compared with 60,000 tons during the winter season. A natural Panamax vessel of about 60,000 dwt is designed to transit the Panama Canal nearer to its fully laden draft.

Another restriction on vessels hauling coal between the U.S. East Coast and Japan is the 45-foot draft limit on vessels calling on U.S. coal exporting ports (Hampton Roads, Norfolk, and Baltimore). Most shipments from these ports are 50,000–70,000 tons. Since the channels in these ports rest on bedrock, dredging is prohibitively expensive. However, multiporting by large bulk carriers can bypass the necessity of massive port improvement projects. A 150,000-dwt bulk carrier can take on a part cargo of coal at Hampton Roads, proceed to iron ore terminals in Brazil, eastern Canada, west Africa, or south Africa, top off with an ore cargo (in different holds than the coal cargo), and proceed to Japan via the Cape of Good Hope. A large bulk carrier, with its economy of scale, can successfully compete for cargoes from relatively shallow water ports on a 5,000-mile longer voyage against toll-paying medium-sized bulk carriers transiting the Panama Canal. Closing the canal would have no lasting disruption on this trade.

The future oceanborne movement of coal depends on the level of Japanese and European steel production and developments in steel-making technology which lessen the quantity and quality of coking coal per ton of steel produced. While a greater reliance on the electric furnace reduces the demand for metallurgical or coking coals, the role of steam coal in satisfying world energy needs has expanded in the wake of high crude oil prices. A potential loss of shipping demand for one type of coal may be compensated by the growth in demand for the other.

Although Europe and Japan import roughly the same quantities of iron ore and coal, about 25% of European iron ore imports are from Sweden and nearly half of its waterborne coal shipments originate in Poland and the Soviet Union. Since the Pacific Ocean is twice as wide as the Atlantic and the nearest source of iron ore and coal for Japan is 3,500 miles away in Australia, the most important factor shaping the market for large gearless bulk carriers is the level of Japanese steel production. While Japan and Europe receive about the same in the volume of iron ore and coal imports, Japan has a far greater impact on shipping demand.

TABLE 4.5
EUROPEAN/JAPANESE IRON ORE AND COAL IMPORTS

	World share of imports, tons*	World share of imports, ton-miles*
Iron ore		
Japan	43%	55%
Europe	46%	38%
Coal		
Japan	52%	72%
Europe	46%	24%

*Figures apply for mid-1970s.

Another factor influencing large bulk carrier demand is inventory adjustments of raw material stockpiles. Steel companies, as a group, maintain a few months' supply of raw materials on hand, based on current production rates. If steel production increases by an incremental amount, the demand for iron ore and coal increases by an even greater amount as inventory levels are expanded to restore the desired number of months of raw material supplies at the higher level of steel production. Similarly, a reduction in steel production cuts back on shipping demand as inventories are liquidated to adjust the size of the stockpiles. This phenomenon is prevalent in all bulk trades.

Phosphate Rock

Phosphate rock (phosrock) is a raw material for the production of fertilizers and industrial phosphate chemicals. The two most important phosrock exporters are Morocco, with a 34% share of the world market in 1974, and the United States (Florida) with a 23% share. Other exporters are the Soviet Union, Togo, Senegal, Tunisia, Jordan, Israel, and the Pacific islands of Naura, Ocean, and Christmas. Phosrock was the fastest-growing major dry-bulk commodity until 1974 when Morocco quadrupled the price of phosrock. Farmers cut back on the use of higher-priced fertilizers and the ton-mile demand for shipping capacity in the phosrock trade fell by 25% in 1975. By 1978, world trade in phosrock was back to 1974 levels.

The phosrock movement between Morocco and southern Europe is handled by small geared bulk carriers. These vessels are best suited for short voyages to ports without shoreside cargo-handling facilities. A large 50,000-dwt bulk carrier is not appropriate for a 100,000-ton annual movement where loading and discharging rates may be only 2,000 tons per day. The economy of scale of this vessel is meaningless if it sits in port for 25 days to load and another 25 days to off-load a cargo after a two-day sea voyage; the entire annual movement of phosrock is completed in two voyages. A 5,000-dwt bulk carrier making 20 voyages spread out over the year with a port turnaround time of five days is more appropriate but still may not be the best-sized vessel for this trade. The optimal vessel size would minimize the cost of transportation, taking into consideration the desired size of the shipments, the hire rates for various-sized vessels, port and berth restrictions, port congestion, cargo handling rates, and terminal storage capacity. The process of selecting the optimum-sized vessel is never-ending, because the party paying for the transportation charges evaluates every available vessel and bargains in a competitive market environment for the one that minimizes his costs. The free market automatically selects the best-suited vessel without any outside assistance.

U.S. phosrock exports are in shipments of 40,000 tons or less because of water depth restrictions in Tampa and Jacksonville. Pacific island terminals can handle 50,000-dwt bulk carriers for phosrock shipments to Japan, and 50,000-dwt bulk carriers also carry North and West African phosrock exports to destinations east of Suez. However, much of the phosrock trade is in bulkers of less than 30,000 dwt because of restrictions at the receiving terminals.

Expanded phosrock production beyond domestic needs does not necessarily mean more phosrock exports. In the United States, the expected increased production of phosrock in the Carolinas will be exported in the form of phosphate fertilizers, a processed form of phosrock. Morocco exports a portion of its phosrock production as phosphoric acid. On the surface, creating industrial processing plants in the raw material exporting nations should reduce shipping demand. Actually, shipping demand merely changes form. For instance, Moroccan phosphoric acid production has opened up a whole new market for phosphoric acid carriers. The production of phosphoric acid consumes sulphuric acid. The incremental loss of business for unsophisticated phosrock-carrying bulkers is compensated by a new market for highly sophisticated and costly phosphoric acid and, possibly, sulphuric acid carriers. The OPEC refinery and petrochemical plant projects will generate shipping demand for more costly ($/dwt) products and chemical carriers at the expense of less-sophisticated crude carriers. The desire of raw material exporting nations to process a portion of their exports generally increases the degree of sophistication of their shipping requirements.

Bauxite and Alumina

Aluminum is made from the electrolytic reduction of alumina, a concentrate of bauxite. Half the world movement of about 43 million tons of bauxite and alimina in the latter part of the 1970s was shipped to North America. Aluminum plants on or near the U.S. Gulf receive most of their imports from the Caribbean and South America (Jamaica, Surinam, Dominican Republic, Haiti, and Guyana) plus some shipments from Guinea and Sierra Leone. Aluminum plants in the U.S. Pacific Northwest import their raw materials from the Caribbean, South America, and Australia. The Gulf plants utilize 20,000–40,000-dwt bulk carriers, and the Pacific Northwest plants employ larger bulk carriers of 35,000–50,000 dwt. Europe imports 30% of the world's oceanborne trade from West Africa, the Caribbean, South America, Greece, Yugoslavia, and Australia. Japan accounts for another 15% of the market, receiving most of its supplies from Australia, Indonesia, and Malaysia. Bulk carriers of 70,000–80,000 dwt are employed on the Australian bauxite trades to Europe and Japan.

Two pounds of bauxite are required to produce a pound of alumina; two pounds of alumina are consumed to produce one pound of aluminum. For a given level of bauxite production, shipping requirements fall 50% for each increment of alumina production facilities built in bauxite exporting nations. One would expect declining bulk carrier demand in this trade because alumina made up only 10% of all bauxite and alumina shipments in 1965, grew to nearly 25% in 1974, and is expected to increase to 30% in the early 1980s. On the contrary, demand for bulk carriers in the alumina and bauxite trades has been increasing yearly. The reasons for this are the increasing consumption of aluminum products, the lengthening of the average voyage distance caused by the inability of nearby sources of alumina and bauxite to satisfy U.S. and European demand, the emergence of Australia as a major alumina and bauxite exporter, and the diversification of raw material supplies by the aluminum companies. While bulk carrier demand would have grown more rapidly had all exports been in the form of bauxite, ship owners were compensated for this loss of business by the necessity of the bauxite exporters to import large quantities of caustic soda, a heavy corrosive liquid consumed in the production of alumina.

Grain

The most important influence on the movement of bulk commodities and raw materials, other than grain, is the level of economic activity. Even the severity of winter weather on crude movements is secondary. Regional grain surpluses and shortages, caused by shifting weather patterns, may or may not be balanced out as cargoes for bulk carriers. Grain provides more demand for shipping capacity than coal, but there is a limit to its buffering ability to absorb excess tonnage during economic contractions because it accounts for 25–30% of all trading opportunities. Besides, no law states that grain shipments must rise when economic activity declines.

Grain shipments are mainly wheat. They may also include corn (maize), barley, oats, rye, soybeans, oilseeds, and sorghum. Excluding intra-European waterborne grain movements where France is a net grain exporter, the principal sources of oceanborne grain exports are the United States and Canada (65%), Australia (10%), and Argentina (7%).

Although the respective shares of the market shift from year to year, these four nations account for over 80% of the world grain trade. Other grain exporting nations besides France are South Africa, Thailand, and Brazil.

Grain importing nations have considerable variations in their annual needs, depending on the weather. India, usually a major grain importer, produced a surplus in 1976; part of this had to be sold overseas because of insufficient storage capacity. The record for variability of grain import demand is held by the Soviet Union.

TABLE 4.6
SOVIET GRAIN IMPORTS

	Soviet grain imports, millions tons	Percentage of world oceanborne grain trade
1970	3	4
1971	4	5
1972	15	17
1973	24	17
1974	7	5
1975	22	16

Taking 1974 as a representative year, nearly 30% of all oceanborne grain shipments were to Europe, 15% to Japan, 15% to other Far Eastern nations, 10% to the Indian subcontinent, 10% to South America, and 10% to Africa. Grain trades are more diffuse than other bulk commodities. The irregularity of grain imports to many nations means that many grain-receiving terminals have limited storage capacity and inefficient transportation connections to the populated hinterlands. The lengthy port times and limited storage capacity of receiving terminals discourage the use of large bulk carriers except on certain important trades connecting North America with Europe and Japan. The grain trades, along with large segments of the bauxite, alumina, phosrock, and the minor bulk trades, provide the major sources of employment for handy-sized bulk carriers of 15,000–35,000 dwt.

The problem of discharging grain cargoes in many areas of the world can be appreciated by considering the time involved loading 30,000 tons of grain on a 35,000-dwt bulk carrier at a U.S. Gulf grain elevator operating under SHEX WWD 2,000 TPD terms. Unlike crude oil, iron ore, and coal trades where cargo handling is a 24 hours a day, seven days a week operation, grain loading in the United States is generally limited to an eight-hour day by longshoremen contracts. SHEX means that Sundays and holidays are excluded as working days. The flow of grain from elevator chutes into the open holds of a bulk carrier cannot take place during inclement weather. As long as it is not a Sunday or a holiday and as long as weather working day (WWD) permits eight hours of loading, 2,000 tons of grain a day can be transferred from the elevator to the ship.

TABLE 4.7
PORT SCHEDULE FOR 35,000-DWT CARRIER

Day	Date	Weather during 8-hour day	Tons of cargo loaded	Tons on board vessel
Wednesday	December 22	Good	2,000	2,000
Thursday	December 23	Good	2,000	4,000
Friday	December 24	Good	2,000	6,000
Saturday	December 25	Holiday	0	6,000
Sunday	December 26	Sunday	0	6,000
Monday	December 27	Rain	0	6,000
Tuesday	December 28	Rain	0	6,000
Wednesday	December 29	Rain for 4 hours	1,000	7,000
Thursday	December 30	Good	2,000	9,000
Friday	December 31	Good	2,000	11,000
Saturday	January 1	Holiday	0	11,000
Sunday	January 2	Sunday	0	11,000
Monday	January 3	Good	2,000	13,000
Tuesday	January 4	Good	2,000	15,000
Wednesday	January 5	Good	2,000	17,000
Thursday	January 6	Good	2,000	19,000
Friday	January 7	Good	2,000	21,000
Saturday	January 8	Good	2,000	23,000
Sunday	January 9	Sunday	0	23,000
Monday	January 10	Good	2,000	25,000
Tuesday	January 11	Rain	0	25,000
Wednesday	January 12	Good	2,000	27,000
Thursday	January 13	Rain for 6 hours	500	27,500
Friday	January 14	Rain for 6 hours	500	28,000
Saturday	January 15	Rain for 4 hours	1,000	29,000
Sunday	January 16	Sunday	0	29,000
Monday	January 17	Good	1,000	30,000

On December 18, a 35,000-dwt bulk carrier arrived at the grain terminal where another vessel was being loaded. After four days, the bulk carrier moored alongside the loading berth, hatch covers open, ready to take on cargo by the start of the working day. Total port time at the loading port was 31 days: 4 days waiting for the berth to become available and 27 days to load. If the vessel were taking the grain to a Third World nation that has not suffered a crop failure, the vessel could come alongside a receiving terminal possibly within a week or two of arrival. The discharging rate might be only 1,000 tons per day using vacuvators, air pumps similar to vacuum cleaners that dump the grain on the pier. At some ports, the cargo could be bagged onboard and carried off the vessel by dockside workers. If there were no rain and if the vessel could be worked Sundays and holidays included (SHINC terms), the vessel would be off-loaded in thirty days.

If the nation suffered a crop failure, the situation would be quite different. First of all, it would take two or three months just to get alongside a berth. The terminal would be clogged with grain and the means of transport from the terminal bogged down with grain shipments. If it were the monsoon season, weather working days would be few and far between. The grain couldn't be off-loaded because of the weather. When it could be dumped on the pier, there would be no room in the terminal to store it. The grain already stored in the terminal couldn't be shipped to the hinterlands because of congested transport systems. Under these circumstances, it would not be unusual for half the cargo to be eaten by rats or ruined by rain.

Large bulk carriers are useless in trades where port time is measured in months and receiving terminals have limited storage capacity. Storage capacity has been temporarily expanded at some grain-importing nations by chartering-in large crude carriers to serve as floating storage facilities. Certain grain terminals on the St. Lawrence River, the U.S. Gulf, and the Pacific Northwest can accommodate bulk carriers of 100,000 dwt. A few modern deepwater grain terminals in Europe and Japan routinely receive 60,000–80,000-ton shipments in bulk carriers that are unloaded in excess of 20,000 tons per day by shoreside air flow-type grain handling systems. Although these terminals are small in number, they handle a large percentage of European and Japanese grain imports from North America.

5

Combination Carriers

A vessel earns revenue carrying a cargo on the loaded leg of a voyage while the ballast leg of a voyage merely positions it to secure another revenue-generating cargo. A tanker carrying crude oil between two ports is only 50% utilized. The earnings from the loaded leg of the voyage must bear the expense of the ballast leg. Always seeking to maximize the earnings capacity of their assets, shipowners seize any possibility to reduce nonearning ballast voyages.

The U.S./Soviet grain deals during the 1970s provided employment for many handy-sized bulk carriers and tankers hauling grain from U.S. East and Gulf Coast ports to Black Sea ports. Most of the vessels returned in ballast because backhaul cargoes were not generally available, but a few tankers were able to secure backhaul cargoes of Soviet heating oil exports. The Soviet managers were just as keen for the tanker owners to combine the eastbound grain and westbound heating oil cargoes on the same vessel as the tanker owners were eager to secure these cargoes.

Concluding massive purchases of U.S. grains, the managers of the Soviet grain importing agency, acting through selected brokers, had to acquire shipping capacity to transport the grain to the Soviet Union. Suppose that an owner of a 35,000-dwt tanker is willing to commit his tanker to the U.S./Soviet grain trade if he can obtain $18/ton for several consecutive voyages. The tanker owner expects to earn $8,140 per day in this trade.

Voyage Time

Round trip distance in nautical miles (1)	11,200
Total days at sea (15 knots) (2)	31.1
Days in U.S. port awaiting berth	2.0
Days to load (5,000 tpd SHINC) (3)	6.4
Days in Black Sea port awaiting berth	3.0
Days to discharge (3,000 tpd SHINC)	10.7
Voyage time	53.2

(1) A nautical mile is one minute of arc of a great circle of the earth equal to 6,080 feet.

(2) One knot is one nautical mile per hour. A 15 knot vessel sails 360 nautical miles a day. Usually a 4% or so allowance is added for loss of headway in rough seas and loss of speed from fouling of the ship's hull by marine growths. This allowance has already been included in the 15-knot assessment on vessel speed.

(3) 5,000 tons per day loading rate working seven days a week. For simplicity, the demurrage terms of the contract is assumed to compensate the owner for any port delay beyond that indicated in the calculations.

Voyage Expenses (Bunker and Port Charges)
   Vessel fuel consumption per day
     At sea: 45 tons per day (tpd)
     In port: 2 tpd
   Fuel consumption

At sea (45 tpd × 31.1 days)	1,400 tons
In port (2 tpd × 22.1 days)	44 tons
Bunkers consumed	1,444 tons
Bunker costs at $90/ton	$130,000
Port charges	
United States	$ 8,000
Black Sea	5,000
Voyage Expenses	$143,000

Daily Vessel Earnings Rate

Gross revenue ($18/ton × 32,000 tons) (1)	$576,000
Voyage expenses	143,000
Net vessel earnings	$433,000
Daily vessel earnings or hire rate	
during 53.2 day voyage	$ 8,140

(1) Brokerage commissions are neglected in all the calculations. The 32,000
     net cargo tons is a side calculation taking into consideration the weight of
     bunkers, stores and water, load line zones, the density of the cargo and the
     cubic capacity of the vessel.

The owner's bid of $18/ton is somewhat above the rates being
quoted by others in recognition of the magnitude of Soviet shipping
needs, which could easily result in a short-term shortage of shipping
capacity. The owner could earn $7,800/day trading his vessel in crude.
However, he wants some incentive to trade in grain to compensate for
the risk of excess port delays, which are usually not fully covered by
demurrage, and for the greater demands which will be placed on his
operating organization when the vessel is trading in grain. The Soviet
grain importing agency negotiates with the owner on rate and terms
through its brokers. The owner remains firm on his offer. The Soviet
grain importing agency, motivated by the urgency to move the grain,
accepts his offer of $18/ton for several consecutive voyages.

Meanwhile, the Soviet oil exporting agency has just sold a quantity
of home heating oil to a distributor in Boston and is in the market for
tanker capacity. The transportation cost of chartering in a 35,000-dwt
tanker at $7,800 per day is $11.72 per ton:

Round trip distance:	10,300 miles
Days at sea (15 knots)	28.6
Days to load and discharge	3.0
Voyage time	31.6
Hire paid to owner (7,800/day × 31.6 days)	$246,500
Bunker costs	
At sea (45 tpd × 28.6 days × $90/ton)	$115,800
In port (40 tons × $90/ton) (1)	3,600
Port charges for both ports	9,000
Voyage expenses	$128,400
Hire paid to owner plus voyage expenses	$374,900
$/ton for 32,000 tons of cargo	$11.72

(1) Most of the fuel consumed in port is to operate the cargo pumps at the
     receiving terminal.

There are few secrets in shipping. The owner knows, through brokers' enquiries, of the heating oil shipments. Realizing that the cost of
transportation for the Soviet oil exporting agency is $11 to $12 per ton,

the owner calculates that he can bid as low as $2/ton and still maintain his daily earnings rate of $8,140 per day:

Voyage Distance

Fronthaul cargo of grain from Baltimore to Black Sea	5,600 miles
Ballast voyage between Black Sea grain receiving and oil loading terminals	300
Backhaul cargo of heating oil from Black Sea to Boston	5,150
Ballast voyage from Boston to Baltimore	700
Voyage distance	11,750 miles

Voyage Time

Days at sea (15 knots)	32.6 days
Days to load and discharge grain cargo	22.1
Days to load and discharge heating oil cargo	3.0
Voyage time	57.7 days

Voyage Expenses

Tons fuel at sea	1,467 tons
Tons fuel in port	84
Total:	1,551 tons

Bunker costs (1,551 tons × $90/ton)	$140,000
Total port charges	22,000
Tank cleaning costs in preparation of grain cargo (1)	7,000
Voyage expenses	$169,000

(1)   All ships carrying grain and other foodstuffs must pass government inspection prior to loading and prior to discharging. A vessel cannot tender notice of readiness to load or discharge a cargo of grain until it has passed this inspection. The calculations assume that there is sufficient time to clean the tanks in preparation for the grain cargo on the ballast voyage between Boston and Baltimore and during the time awaiting a berth in Baltimore (about four days). As a practical matter, 5–7 days may be required to clean the tanks.

Freight Rate Calculation

Total hire desired by owner	
($8,140/day × 57.7 days)	$470,000
Voyage expenses	169,000
Total revenue required from both cargoes	$639,000
Less revenue from grain cargo	576,000
Minimum revenue required from heating oil cargo	$ 63,000
Minimum $/ton on 32,000 ton cargo of heating oil	$1.97
Maximum discount from market rate of $11.72/ton for transporting the heating oil	83%

Any amount above $2/ton is lucrative for the owner. The managers of the Soviet oil exporting agency fully realize the magnitude of the discount inherent in combining trades. They are also aware that they are in the driver's seat in the negotiating process because there are more inbound grain-carrying tankers entering the Black Sea than there are available outbound cargoes of heating oil. Motivated by the same desire of any charterer, the Soviet oil exporting agency, through its brokers, plays one owner off another to obtain the lowest possible rate on the most favorable terms. Owners are not offended by this behavior, for this is what they contend with in all their business dealings. While negotiating with the brokers representing the Soviet oil exporting agency, the owners are contacting brokers representing Mediterranean oil exporters in their search for backhaul cargoes. If an owner can confirm a fixture for a backhaul cargo of crude from Libya to the United States within one hour's time, he may well make a final offer to the brokers representing the Soviet oil exporting agency, at a rate that is more profitable for the owner than the Libyan transaction, good for one half hour. Failing to respond to this offer, the owner will fix his vessel for the Libyan cargo and the Soviet oil exporting agency has one less owner to churn in the pot.

A shipowner is often in a position to satisfy the transportation needs of two different clients for substantially less cost than each charterer taking care of his own needs. Suppose a European aluminum company imports some of its bauxite from Australia and a Japanese steel company imports some of its iron ore from Brazil. Both companies are thinking of acquiring a 125,000-dwt bulk carrier at a cost of $35 million. Assuming each company has identical operating costs and capital charges, the cost of transportation for their respective movements is:

Cost of 125,000-dwt bulk carrier	$35,000,000
Cost of capital	15%
Annual capital charges (15% × $35,000,000)	$ 5,250,000
Annual operating costs	1,250,000
Total annual costs	$ 6,500,000
Allowing 15 days off-hire per year for maintenance and dry-docking, the daily hire rate for both companies ($6,500,000 divided by 350 days) is:	$18,570

TABLE 5.1
MOVEMENT STATISTICS

	European aluminum company bauxite movement Australia/Europe via Cape of Good Hope	Japanese steel company ore movement Brazil/Japan via Cape of Good Hope
Round trip distance	30,000 miles	23,000 miles
Loading rate (tpd SHINC)	25,000	40,000
Discharging rate (tpd SHINC)	15,000	20,000
Days at sea (15 knots)	83.3	63.9
Days in port		
Awaiting berths	2.0	2.0
Loading	4.7	3.0
Discharging	7.9	6.0
Total days	97.9	74.9
Bunkers		
At sea (90 tpd × days at sea)	7,497	5,751
In port (2 tpd × days in port)	29	22
Total tons	7,526	5,773
Cost of bunkers ($90/ton)	$677,000	$520,000
Total port charges	30,000	35,000
Voyage costs	$707,000	$555,000
Hire per voyage		
($18,570/day × voyage time)	$1,818,000	$1,391,000
Total cost of transportation	$2,525,000	$1,946,000
Net cargo tons	118,000	118,000
$/ton	$21.40	$16.49
Vessel utilization rate	50%	50%

A ship-owning company or a shipowner, with the same operating costs and capital charges, desires to bid for both cargoes. The owner first calculates the total freight rate of both cargoes that meets his profit objectives:

Distance iron ore Brazil to Japan	11,500 miles
Distance ballast Japan to Australia	3,000
Distance bauxite Australia to Europe	15,000
Distance ballast Europe to Brazil	5,000
Total distance	34,500 miles
Utilization rate $\dfrac{\text{(length of loaded legs of voyage)}}{\text{(length of loaded and ballast legs)}}$	77%
Days at sea (15 knots)	95.8
Days in port iron ore trade	11.0
Days in port bauxite trade	14.6
Total days	121.4
Hire desired by owner ($18,570/day × 121.4 days)	$2,254,000
Fuel	
At sea: 90 tpd × 95.8 days	8,622 tons
In port: 2 tpd × 25.6 days	51 tons
Total	8,673 tons
Cost of fuel at $90/ton	$ 781,000
Total port charges	65,000
Total cost of transportation	$3,100,000
Net cargo tons of each bauxite and iron ore cargo	118,000
Combined freight rate of both cargoes	$26.27
Cost of transportation ($/ton) for the Japanese steel company to haul iron ore from Brazil to Japan on a ballast back basis	$16.49
Cost of transportation ($/ton) for the European aluminum company to haul bauxite from Australia to Europe on a ballast back basis	$21.40

Total transportation cost ($/ton) of both commodities on a ballast back basis	$37.89
Total cost of transportation ($/ton) of a shipowner or a shipping company hauling both commodities on a combined basis	$26.27
Total potential cost savings for the steel company and the aluminum company of contracting for their cargoes rather than owning their own vessels	$11.62
Potential savings as a percentage of the total transportation charge of $37.89	30%

The shipowner can provide a transportation cost savings of 30% to both companies if they contract for their tonnage requirements on a combined basis rather than transporting the ore in their own vessels on a ballast back basis. On a ballast back basis, the utilization of the vessel, defined as the ratio of the distance of the loaded leg of the voyage to the round trip voyage distance, is 50% while the shipowner achieves a utilization rate of 77% by combining both trades. For this reason, the owner earns the same rate of return as the steel or the aluminum company on his investment for any combination of freight rates for the bauxite and iron ore cargoes as long as the total freight rate for both cargoes is $26.27 per ton.

The shipowner is constrained in his rate offers by the ballast back transportation rate of each commodity. The shipowner would not offer a rate to the steel company exceeding $16.49, or $21.40 to the aluminum company, for then each company would be better off owning the vessel. If the owner offered a rate of $16.49 to the steel company, then the minimum rate he could offer the aluminum company which preserves a total rate of $26.27 is $9.78. Conversely, if the owner offered a rate of $21.40 to the aluminum company, then the corresponding minimum rate he could offer the steel company is $4.87.

Maximum offer to the steel company	$16.49
Minimum offer to the aluminum company to preserve a total rate of $26.27	9.78
Maximum offer to the aluminum company	$21.40
Minimum offer to the steel company to preserve a total rate of $26.27	$ 4.87

The $26.27 combined rate for both cargoes is a theoretical calculation based on actual operating costs and real capital charges containing an implicit profit margin. Whether or not an owner can negotiate a combined rate of $26.27 depends on the state of the market, which reflects the current state of and the anticipated changes to the relationship between the supply and demand for vessel capacity. There is no connection between what a shipowner desires and what the market offers. There is an economic principle that states, over the long run, market rates must average at a level which covers an owner's operating costs and provides some sort of a return on his capital investment in order for shipping to remain a viable business. This principle, however, has no impact at all on the day-to-day business between charterers and owners. An owner cannot negotiate this transaction in a depressed market where rates for hauling these cargoes are far below a total of $26.27. Conversely, in a strong market, he may negotiate a combined rate which is above his minimum hurdle rate.

Another factor entering the negotiations is the size of the backhaul commodity movement relative to the fronthaul movement. Since iron ore, coal, and grain movements from the Atlantic basin to the Far East far outweigh Australian dry bulk exports to the Western Hemisphere, the competitive pressure of many bulk carriers seeking relatively few backhaul cargoes in the Far East tends to drive down the rates for the bauxite cargoes. In other words, the economic benefit of combining the two cargoes would be unequally apportioned. The European aluminum company is in a position to garner the lion's share.

To illustrate the impact of large bulk carriers, modern terminals, and combining commodity movements on world trade, suppose the European aluminum company could negotiate a rate of $11/ton for its Australian bauxite imports. The company also imports bauxite from West Africa where the loading terminal can accommodate vessels up to 40,000 dwt and can transfer bauxite to bulk carriers at 12,000 tpd. This is less than half the rate for the more modern cargo handling facilities in Australia. In addition, there are no backhaul cargoes available on the Europe/West Africa trade. The ballast back cost of transportation for this trade is:

Cost of 40,000-dwt bulk carrier	$14,000,000
Cost of capital	15%
Annual capital charges	$ 2,100,000
Annual operating costs	750,000
Total costs	$ 2,850,000

Daily hire (350 days per year)	$8,140
Round trip distance from West Africa to Europe	6,200 miles
Days at sea (15 knots)	17.2
Days at load port awaiting berth	1.0
Days to load (12,000 tpd SHINC)	3.2
Days awaiting berth at discharge port	1.0
Days to discharge (15,000 tpd SHINC)	2.5
Total days	24.9
Total hire ($8,140/day for 24.9 days)	$ 203,000
Fuel	
At sea: 47 tpd × 17.2 days	808 tons
In port: 2 tpd × 7.7 days	15 tons
Total	823 tons
Cost of fuel at $90/ton	$ 74,000
Total port charges	12,000
Total cost of transportation	$ 289,000
Net cargo tons	38,000
$/ton	$7.60

From the point of view of the economic cost of transportation, which incorporates actual operating costs and capital charges with an adequate margin for a return on capital, the cost of transporting bauxite from West Africa to Europe is 70% of the transportation charge from Australia even though the distance to Australia is five times greater than the distance to West Africa. The development of large bulk carriers by owners attempting to improve their competitive position, the decisions by Australian port authorities and raw material exporters to build modern, deepwater loading terminals, and the search by owners for any opportunity to combine east and west-bound cargoes to enhance the earning capacity of their vessels have opened up the whole world as a potential market for Australian raw material exports. Owners, who had initiated low-cost transportation in dry-bulk commodities, were rewarded by more business opportunities as world trade in bulk commodities expanded and the average voyage distance increased, caused in part by low-cost transportation.

The actual opportunities for tankers to combine the oil and grain trades are few since most grain shipments are in bulk carriers. The U.S./ Soviet grain deal was an exception because one-third of the shipping requirements were reserved for the U.S. flag fleet where tankers far out-number bulk carriers. The ability of bulk carriers to combine trades is limited in scope because the preponderance of bulk commodity move-ments are in one direction. North and South American exports of iron ore, grain, and other dry-bulk commodities to Europe are not counter-balanced with opposite moving bulk commodities; and Western Hemi-sphere dry-bulk commodities to the Far East dwarf Australian exports to the Atlantic. Crude trades provide the potential of successfully com-bining trades. If a vessel transporting coal U.S./Japan via the Panama Canal (9,800 miles) made a ballast voyage to the Persian Gulf (6,400 miles) for a cargo of crude oil back to the U.S. via the Cape of Good Hope (11,900 miles), the utilization rate would be 77%—an obvious improve-ment over the 50% utilization rate of a tanker in the crude trade or a bulk carrier in the coal trade. However, a tanker cannot carry coal and a bulk carrier cannot carry crude.

In response to this situation, Erling Naess, an independent ship-owner, developed the concept of the combination carrier. He took deliv-ery in 1965 of the 71,000-dwt *Naess Norseman*, the first ship able to participate in both the crude oil and dry bulk trades. The principal types of combination carriers are ore-oil (O/O) carriers and ore-bulk-oil (OBO) carriers. O/O carriers combine the ore and oil trades but do not participate in the coal, grain, and other less dense bulk trades. OBOs are more versatile, designed to participate in the crude oil and all the dry bulk commodity trades. In 1978, the world's first PROBO was delivered (refined oil-ore-bulk-oil).

Combination carriers cost about 15% more than tankers and bulk carriers of the same deadweight capacity because they must have a pip-ing system and cargo pumps of a tanker and the large movable hatch covers and smooth inner cargo hold surfaces of a bulk carrier. Com-bination carriers must be seaworthy regardless of the cargo type. As a consequence, there is some loss of cubic capacity and earning capacity for cargoes of lighter grades of crude oil and less-dense grades of coal and grain compared to tankers and straight bulk carriers of the same deadweight.

O/O carriers between 200,000 and 300,000 dwt are well suited in size and achieve close to 80% utilization on their most common trade of iron ore Brazil/Japan combined with crude oil Persian Gulf/Brazil. OBO carriers range in size to 170,000 dwt. A common trade for large combi-nation carriers is hauling a part cargo of U.S. coal with a part cargo of iron ore from eastern Canada, West Africa, South Africa, or Brazil for a full shipment of coal and ore to Japan via the Cape of Good Hope. They return with a cargo of Persian Gulf or Indonesian crude or a cargo of Australian ore, coal or bauxite. Large OBOs in the grain trade frequently take only part cargoes of 60,000—80,000 tons because of terminal restrictions. An 80,000-dwt Panamax OBO is better sized for the grain trade. An ideal trade for Panamax OBOs is to participate in the U.S./ Japan coal movement combined with backhaul cargoes of Indonesian crude or Australian bauxite. These vessels can also combine the U.S./ Europe coal and grain trades or the eastern Canada or South America/ Europe iron ore and grain trades with backhaul cargoes of crude oil from North or West Africa.

Combination carriers have opened up the possibility of exporting iron ore, coal, and bauxite to the Middle East for conversion into steel and aluminum products. These energy-intensive processes could use the vast quantity of natural gas associated with crude production that is being flared off in the Middle East. Combination carriers could achieve close to 100% utilization returning with crude oil to the United States for another coal cargo, to eastern Canada or South America for another iron ore cargo, or to Australia for another bauxite cargo.

Combination carrier owners enter into contracts of affreightment (COFA) to service a number of charterers with the same vessel. A COFA is an agreement to transport a stipulated number of tons per year of a commodity between two ports, or a range of ports, for a number of years at a certain rate ($/ton) with a designated number of liftings per year of a desired quantity of cargo. For example, a contract of affreightment for 600,000 tons of coal between Hampton Roads and a range of ports in Japan for five years may call for 12 liftings a year (once a month) of 50,000 tons each. A combination carrier owner can conveniently service the needs of several charterers with a portfolio of contracts of affreightment.

Since a contract of affreightment does not mention the name of a particular vessel, an owner is free to nominate for the charterer's approval his own or a chartered-in vessel. This allows the owner to practice arbitrage. Suppose an owner enters into a COFA for coal U.S./ Japan where his combination carrier earns $3,000 per day when servicing the contract. One year later, the market rate for bulk carriers turns out to be $4,000 per day and tankers are obtaining $7,000 per day. The owner charters out the combination carrier in the crude trade for $7,000 per day and charters in a bulk carrier at $4,000 per day to fulfill his obligation under the contract of affreightment. The incremental loss of

$1,000 per day of the bulk carrier servicing the COFA cargoes is compensated by the $4,000 per day in incremental income of having the combination carrier trade in crude oil. This arbitrage, which adds $3,000 per day to the owner's income, is made possible by the dual role of combination carriers to trade either in crude oil or dry bulk commodities and the freedom of action permitted by contracts of affreightment. Arbitrage is not possible nor can an owner service the transportation needs of several charterers with the same vessel if the combination carrier is under a bareboat charter or time charter because the charterer then has exclusive control over the vessel's employment.

In 1973, about 85% of the world fleet of combination carriers of 40 million dwt was trading exclusively in crude oil because of high spot market rates for tankers and the preference of financing institutions to support the acquisition of a combination carrier on the basis of a major oil company charter rather than a portfolio of contracts of affreightment. When the spot market collapsed, tankers in the spot market lost their source of employment while combination carriers in the spot market shifted their employment into the profitable iron ore and coal trades. By late 1974, 50% of the combination carrier fleet was trading in crude oil. This meant that 14 million dwt (35% of 40 million dwt) had abandoned the crude oil trades from the year earlier. This did little to reduce the tanker surplus because almost 40 million dwt of new tanker capacity was delivered from the world's shipyards in the interim.

Looking at the other side of the coin, the iron ore and coal trades in late 1973 were served by 15% of the combination carrier fleet, or 6 million dwt, plus 32 million dwt of large bulk and ore carriers with 50,000 dwt or more. The total fleet of large bulk ore and combination carriers in the iron ore and coal trades was 38 million dwt. The shift of 14 million dwt of combination carriers into the iron ore and coal trades was equivalent to adding over 35% in fleet carrying capacity in less than a year. This was more than sufficient to wreck the rate structure for large bulk carriers. When this segment of the market became depressed, owners of large bulk and combination carriers began soliciting part cargoes, which depressed rates for the next smaller class of bulk carriers. These, in turn, began seeking smaller shipments. This cascading process of larger-sized vessels soliciting part cargoes away from smaller-sized vessels continued until the entire rate structure for all bulk carriers, regardless of size, was wrecked.

At one time, some bulk carrier owners were proud they were not involved with tankers except for the iron ore and coal shipments generated by the large amount of steel consumed in tanker construction.

Now the existence of a large combination carrier fleet of 50 million dwt ties the bulk carrier and tanker owner together for all time. Bulk carrier owners no longer ignore the swing factor of combination carriers shifting employment between the crude and dry bulk trades. The prospects of large bulk carrier owners depend as much on the state of the tanker market as they do on the level of European and Japanese steel production.

6

Liquefied Gas Carriers

Petroleum gas is usually pipelined between where it is found and where it is consumed. When petroleum gas is cooled to a liquid, its volume is reduced by over 600:1. In this form, petroleum gas can be traded in the international marketplace and transported from the seller to the buyer in liquefied gas carriers. The two principal types of liquefied gas vessels are liquefied natural gas (LNG) and liquefied petroleum gas (LPG) carriers.

The fivefold expansion of the world LNG carrier fleet and the doubling of the world LPG carrier fleet were concentrated in large-capacity vessels. It resulted from forecasts by those involved in the international gas business at the time the vessels were ordered. On the one hand, there were the vast, partly developed gas reserves in Algeria and Iran and the wasteful practice of flaring (burning) gas associated with crude oil production throughout the Middle East. On the other, there was the growing inability of the United States to satisfy its petroleum gas needs from domestic sources. For all those shipowners, shipping companies, shipping subsidiaries of oil and gas companies and public utilities, and the gas producers themselves who ordered large liquefied gas carriers, the only missing ingredient was oceanborne transportation capacity.

TABLE 6.1
LNG/LPG FLEET EXPANSION, 1975–1979

LNG carrier fleet

Total cubic meter capacity of fleet in 1974	Existing vessel size range, cubic meters	Cubic meter capacity of vessels on order	Most common size of vessels on order, cubic meters
900,000	25,000–90,000	4,600,000	125,000

LPG carrier fleet

Total cubic meter capacity of fleet in 1974	Existing vessel size range, cubic meters	Cubic meter capacity of vessels on order	Most common size of vessels on order, cubic meters
1,300,000	1,000–75,000	1,700,000	50,000 and 75,000

1974 Liquid Gas Carrier Register, H. Clarkson and Company, London

Natural Gas

Natural gas is a mixture of petroleum gases whose constituents vary among gas fields. Overall, methane is the predominant gas (90%) plus ethane (5%), propane, butane, and trace amounts of other gases. Natural gas is found in gas fields, such as those in southwestern United States, the Soviet Union, Algeria, Iran, and the North Sea. Natural gas is also associated with crude oil production and is called associated gas. Associated gas is separated from the crude oil and is either fed into natural gas pipelines, injected back into the oil field to maintain its pressure, or flared.

Natural gas is the cleanest-burning fuel available. Its residue is carbon dioxide and water. Coal and heating oils leave ash and nitrogen and sulphur oxides. In the United States, natural gas is distributed through a million miles of pipelines connecting gas fields in the South and Southwest to consumers in the Midwest, the Northeast, and the Pacific Coast. The West is also connected by pipeline to gas fields in western Canada. Natural gas heats millions of buildings, dries crops, supplies energy for electric generating plants, and is a raw material in the production of ammonia, a feedstock for the chemical and fertilizer industries.

In 1954, the pricing of natural gas in interstate commerce in the United States became subject to the jurisdiction of the Federal Power

Commission (FPC), now called the Federal Energy Regulatory Commission (FERC). By legal mandate, FERC is responsible to the American people for a low cost and reliable supply of natural gas as a source of energy. No one can criticize FERC for not fulfilling half its mandate of keeping the wellhead price of natural gas, which is the price paid to the gas producer, low. Looking at the situation as it was, the intrastate price of gas reflected market realities while the interstate price was an artificial price set by a government regulatory body. The disparity between the two indicates the success of the FPC/FERC in suppressing the cost of natural gas to the overwhelming majority of consumers who pay interstate rates for their gas.

TABLE 6.2
DOLLARS PER THOUSAND CUBIC FEET OF NATURAL GAS, 1974/75

Wellhead priced of natural gas paid to U.S. gas producers for interstate use (subject to FERC control)	$0.20–0.50
Wellhead price of natural gas paid to U.S. gas producers for intrastate use (not subject to FERC control)	$0.70–2.00
Anticipated delivered price of LNG import projects under negotiation	$2.00–4.00

The interstate rate includes both the wellhead price of gas and the cost of distribution through an already existing, largely amortized natural gas pipeline system. If one nets out the financing, operating, and transporting costs of LNG projects, the wellhead price of gas demanded by foreign gas exporting nations is equivalent to crude oil on an energy content basis, a price far in excess of what U.S. domestic gas producers receive for interstate gas.

The pricing policies of the FPC/FERC have predictably led to an enormous growth in the consumption of natural gas encouraged by its low cost relative to alternative sources of energy. This was aggravated by the legal requirement of state-regulated public utilities to burn the cheapest source of available energy. The policies also resulted in a sharp drop in natural gas exploration activity and a decline in "known" reserves. Shortages of natural gas during the peak winter months were becoming more severe, forcing layoffs in 1977 of thousands of workers. Crop drying was suffering from shortages of natural gas, and ammonia and ammonia-based fertilizers such as urea were being imported as a consequence of natural gas curtailments to the ammonia producers.

Government regulatory policy in the mid-1970s was to keep the lid on the wellhead price of domestic gas sold in interstate commerce and to mix in a little high-priced gas to make up for shortfalls. The average price of gas is marked up according to the mix of high-priced and low-priced gas. The sources of high-priced gas are spiking or injecting LPG into a natural gas stream, producing synthetic natural gas (SNG) or methane from LPG, gasifying crude oil and coal, and importing natural gas in a liquefied state (LNG).

SNG produced from the gasification of crude oil would purify the least desirable grades of crude oil. Pollution-free methane would be fed into existing natural gas pipelines with the crude oil impurities (sulphur, vanadium) left behind for sale or disposal. Crude oil gasification projects were proposed by consortia of natural gas pipeline companies, oil companies, public utilities, and shipowners who had their eye on the tanker requirements. The repricing of crude oil in 1973 and the impact of crude oil gasification plants on U.S. dependence on foreign crude sources have placed further consideration of crude oil gasification projects in abeyance. Of greater promise is the gasification of the abundant supplies of domestic coal. However, large-scale coal gasification plants could not be completed in time to bridge the ever-widening gap that was occurring in the mid-1970s between the supply and

TABLE 6.3
PRINCIPAL LNG PROJECTS, 1978*

Trade	Contract initial delivery	Contract term, years	Gas volume, (MMcfd)
Algeria-France (Sonatrach)	1964	25	50
Algeria-Britain (Sonatrach)	1964	15	100
Alaska-Japan (Phillips)	1969	15	135
Libya-Italy (Exxon)	1969	20	235
Libya-Spain (Exxon)	1969	15	110
Algeria-U.S. (Distrigas I)	1971	20	43
Algeria-U.S. (Distrigas II)	1978	(a)	115
Algeria-France (Sonatrach)	1972	25	350
Brunei-Japan (Brunei LNG)	1972	20	737
Algeria-Spain (Sonatrach)	1974	15	50
Algeria-Spain (Sonatrach)	1979	(a)	450
Indonesia-Japan (Pertamina)	1977	20	1050
Abu Dhabi-Japan (Das Island LNG)	1977	20	320
Algeria-U.S. (El Paso I)	1978	20	1000

*Sources of data are the *Petroleum Times* and the *Oil and Gas Journal*, 1978.
(a) The contract is an extension or modification of the existing contract.

demand for natural gas. Only LNG import projects provided the timely means of obtaining sufficient quantities of high-priced gas to roll in with low-priced domestic gas.

The throughput of natural gas in millions of cubic feet per day is measured under standard temperature and pressure (atmospheric) conditions. One million cubic feet of gas is equivalent to 165–170 barrels of crude oil on a heat content basis. When transported in a liquefied state, the volume is less than one six-hundredth of that indicated in Table 6.3.

The Distrigas I LNG project was approved by the FPC to meet peak shaving needs during the winter. The receiving terminals are at Everett (near Boston) and on Staten Island (now inoperative). Distrigas II and El Paso I are base load projects that receive regularly scheduled LNG shipments year round. The receiving terminals for the El Paso I project are at Cove Point, Maryland, and Savannah, Georgia. FERC has also approved Panhandle Eastern's LNG proposal to import LNG from Algeria to its receiving terminal under construction at Lake Charles, Louisiana. Other projects that may receive FERC approval are additional El Paso proposals for importing LNG from Algeria to U.S. East Coast destinations and Pacific Lighting's proposal to import Indonesian LNG to the U.S West Coast. Other LNG projects under negotiation involve Algerian exports to Spain, France, Belgium, the Netherlands, and West Germany.

More remote possibilities for U.S. LNG import projects involve Iran, the Soviet Union, Nigeria, and Chile. One other proposal that has been before FERC is moving LNG from Alaska to gas utility companies on the Pacific Coast. This is a logical project because LNG is already being exported from an Alaskan liquefaction plant to gas utilities in Japan, and domestic U.S. production of natural gas is declining in the West. Moreover, Canada has unilaterally repriced and partially curtailed its pipeline exports of natural gas to the western states. However, FERC has ruled that U.S. consumers on the West Coast are not to be exposed to such exorbitant rates for LNG from Alaska as those paid by Japanese consumers. A similar fate originally befell a proposed Mexican gas pipeline export project to California, which was finally approved in 1979. The fact that Japanese utilities are willing to pay a fair market price for their energy imports is the primary reason behind all the progress made by LNG projects associated with Japan.

FERC is caught on the horns of a dilemma. Its policy of ensuring a low-cost, reliable source of natural gas by rolling in some high-priced gas from foreign sources is contradictory. Foreign gas exporters will not be bound to 20-year fixed price contracts with guaranteed deliveries of

LNG at the low prices demanded by FERC. In other words, the source of incremental gas supplies from overseas is neither low cost nor reliable as mandated by law. Herein lies the reason why the FPC/FERC procrastinates 5–10 years after the initial submission of an LNG proposal before reaching a final decision on whether to approve or disapprove the proposal.

The concept of rolling in a little high-priced gas with low-priced domestic gas has been bitterly attacked by the domestic gas producers who have been lobbying for deregulation of interstate gas. They argue that artificially low wellhead prices for their finite resources encourage wasteful consumption, jeopardize national security by increasing U.S. reliance on foreign energy sources, and cause economic dislocations from natural gas curtailments. By marking up the price of natural gas, wasteful practices would be discouraged and exploration would be encouraged, eliminating the need for costly LNG and SNG projects. Domestic gas producers claim that windfall profits derived from deregulation of the price of interstate natural gas would at least be subject to U.S. taxes, whereas profits made by foreign gas suppliers remain outside the jurisdiction of U.S. tax authorities.

The Natural Gas Policy Act of 1978 imposed a complicated set of escalators for determining the future wellhead prices for natural gas sold in interstate commerce, regulated for the first time the price of gas sold intrastate, and dumped the full cost of high-priced incremental supplies of natural gas into the laps of industrial boiler fuel users. The anticipated effect of this legislation was to encourage industrial boiler fuel users to switch to alternative fuels such as coal and residual fuel oils. This has alleviated shortages of natural gas by reducing its demand rather than increasing its supply. The Natural Gas Policy Act has not solved the natural gas crisis, it has postponed it for a few years. In the meantime, LNG carriers are being built at a cost of $70–130 million or more each, some of which depend on favorable FERC rulings for the recoupment of their capital investment. The nightmare for these owners is to pace the corridors of FERC for another five years awaiting its decisions.

LNG Carriers

LNG projects consist of gas gathering and liquefaction plants in the exporting nation which collect, cool, and liquefy natural gas; the LNG carriers, which may represent half the total investment depending on the shipping distance; and the LNG receiving terminal and gasification facilities in the importing nation. Gasification is a straightforward heat exchange process which could be cooling the same river water that had been previously heated by an upstream electric generating plant.

Natural gas liquefies at −260°F. At this low temperature, conventional steel tanks become subject to brittle fracture; they can literally split apart when stressed. For this reason, LNG cargo tanks are constructed of nickel steel or aluminum alloys, requiring special welding techniques. The cargo tanks are the largest single cost component of an LNG carrier because of the value of the alloys and the need for highly qualified welders.

The cargo tanks may be independent and free-standing of spherical (Kvaerner-Moss) or prismatic (Conch) design, which are isolated from the stresses and strains borne by the vessel's hull.* They may also be of membrane or semimembrane design where special barriers and the tank insulation reduce the transfer of stresses from the outer vessel hull to the flexible inner plates of the cargo tank. The insulation, which is installed outside the cargo tank, is critical in maintaining the cargo temperature at −260°F. Various types of cargo insulation are balsa wood, polyurethane and polystyrene foams, and perlite. No matter how well the insulation is designed and applied, some heat will be transferred to the LNG cargo. Although it is possible to add a reliquefaction plant to convert the buildup in vapor pressure (boiloff) back to a liquid, the boiloff in LNG carriers is usually fed into the ship's boilers as fuel for the propulsion plant. A design boiloff rate of less than 0.25% per day can keep the cargo at −260°F at ambient (atmospheric) pressure, while simultaneously supplying about half the fuel for propulsion. Reliquefaction plants have not been installed on LNG carriers because the price differential between LNG and Bunker C on an energy content basis has not been large enough to justify the additional capital and operating costs of an onboard reliquefaction plant. Following sharp rises in bunker prices, LNG is sometimes less expensive than Bunker C as a propulsion fuel.

Not all LNG is pumped ashore at the receiving terminal; a small amount is retained onboard to boil off during the ballast voyage to keep the cargo tanks at −260°F. If the cargo tanks warm up during the ballast voyage, loading must be delayed to prevent cold-shocking the tanks. In addition, minimizing the number of thermal cycles extends the useful life of the LNG tanks.

---

*"LNG Carriers" and "LPG Carriers," Fairplay International, London, contain technical descriptions of liquefied gas carriers.

LNG carriers also require extensive leak detection systems, nitrogen inerting systems for drydocking and tank maintenance, cargo measuring and pressure relief systems, and other features which make them costly to build and operate. Their sophisticated systems and the importance of ship safety in their operations require highly trained and properly motivated crews who must be handsomely compensated for their services. It is interesting to note that the critical factor in LNG carrier transportation cost is the nature of the financing of these vessels and not the cost of operation.

One recent development in LNG carrier technology is internal tank insulation, which reduces the cost of construction because the cargo tanks are no longer in contact with the low-temperature cargo. Building LNG carriers from reinforced concrete has been proposed. Concrete becomes stronger at low temperatures, is a self-insulator, and can more safely withstand collisions and groundings.

Natural gas can also be converted to methanol (wood alcohol) at the exporting nation and transported as a less-hazardous liquid cargo in conventional tankers. However, methanol conversion plants are more costly to build than liquefaction trains, require more qualified operating personnel, and are energy inefficient, i.e., more energy is consumed converting natural gas to methanol than to a liquefied state. In the importing nation, methanol can be fed directly into boilers as fuel or converted back to methane, which is again a costly and energy-inefficient process. The economics work against methanol conversion plants except on the longest haul trades where the substitution of inexpensive tankers for costly LNG carriers has the greatest impact.

LPG Carriers

Liquefied petroleum gas (LPG) carriers transport propane and butane, either singly or combined, in a liquid state. LPG is a feedstock for the petrochemical industry and a source of energy for industry, homes, and vacation trailers. Butane is a blending agent in gasoline production and propane is used to dry crops and fuel vehicles (tractors, buses, and forklifts). LPG is obtained from stripping natural gas of its propane and butane content and is a byproduct of refining. Carriers transport LPG in intra-European trade from refineries in Italy and northern Europe, which produce a surplus of LPG, to LPG-deficient nations such as France, Spain, Portugal, Greece, and Turkey. The source of LPG in the North Africa/southern Europe trade is the propane and butane stripped from natural gas fed into LNG liquefaction trains. The source of LPG in the Persian Gulf/Japan trade, the largest movement in the world, is propane and butane stripped from associated gas. Butane is sometimes spiked into crude oil and transported in crude carriers and is recovered during the refining process.

In the United States, LPG production from stripping has been falling, both from declining natural gas production and from a decreasing concentration of propane and butane in natural gas flowing from aging gas fields. In the mid-1970s, most LPG imports were from Venezuela; most forecasts made at that time stated the Middle East would again emerge as the ultimate source of supply to satisfy the projected LPG import needs of the U.S. This was the underlying reason for ordering the large number of 50,000 and 75,000-cbm LPG carriers at that time.

LPG carriers are much easier to build than LNG carriers. The minimum temperature of an LPG cargo of $-50°F$ allows conventional tank design, construction, and insulation. Refrigeration plants are installed on LPG carriers to keep the cargo in a liquid state at ambient pressure. With some adaptation, LPG carriers can participate in the ammonia, butadiene, vinyl chloride, propylene, and other liquid gas and chemical trades. A few liquid gas carriers are built specifically for transporting ethylene and ethane, whose liquefying temperatures are too low for conventional LPG carriers. Although LPG carriers are prohibited from carrying LNG cargoes, some LNG carriers have been fitted with a refrigeration plant to participate in the LPG trades. This has been unsuccessful because there are few trading opportunities of LPG in size lots of 125,000 cubic meters.

Many 50,000 and 75,000-cbm LPG carriers built during the 1970s comply with the U.S. Coast Guard regulations in anticipation of a growing U.S. LPG import trade. Since these regulations are the most stringent in the world, an LPG carrier with a certificate of compliance from the U.S. Coast Guard has worldwide trading privileges, whereas those vessels built in compliance with other nations' standards cannot enter U.S. ports. Naturally, there is no need for an LPG vessel built for the Persian Gulf/Japan trade to comply with U.S. regulations.

During the mid-1970s owners who ordered 75,000-cbm LPG vessels gibed at those who ordered 50,000-cbm vessels for building ships that could not compete against the economy of scale of a vessel with a 50% greater cargo-carrying capacity. The latter retorted that a vessel whose draft was too deep to enter U.S. ports and whose cargo exceeded the storage capacity of most terminals in U.S. ports was of questionable value. Owners of both types of vessels suffered during the late 1970s when projected LPG imports into the U.S. failed to materialize because of conservation efforts and the switching to alternative forms of energy by consumers and industrial users. Meanwhile, there are large-scale LPG export-oriented production plants coming onstream in the Middle East, which will be underutilized if the LPG export market does not develop in the interim.

With these export plants in mind, it is interesting to speculate on the consequences of the National Gas Policy Act of 1978 on LPG production in the United States. If new gas increases in price to reflect the international price for energy, depending on the relative price of natural gas versus LPG, it may be more profitable for gas producers not to strip out the LPG content from a new gas stream. If this occurs, U.S. domestic production of LPG from stripping will decline as new gas displaces old. Falling domestic production could spur LPG imports and provide the market for the output of the Middle East LPG plants and cargoes for large LPG carriers. Curtailments of crude exports by the OPEC producers would also encourage the international trade of LPG and other alternative energy sources such as LNG and coal. Owners of LPG carriers are more than disinterested spectators as the world wrestles with its energy problems.

7

General Cargo and Container Vessels

General Cargo Vessels

Break-bulk, or general, cargoes are goods packed in boxes, cartons, drums, and bags sized in volume and weight for handling by longshoremen and stevedores. Longshoremen in the vessel's holds load the cargo into a sling which is positioned by the ship's booms. A winch operator hoists the sling through the open hatch, swings it around, and lowers it to the pier where stevedores transfer the cargo to a forklift truck that takes it to a warehouse. The cargo is manually stacked there, awaiting further distribution by truck or boxcar. Checkers at every point of the transfer tally the consignments, attempting to keep them together as they are transferred.

One critical function in the cargo business is proper planning and stowing of individual consignments in a vessel in sequential order of ports of call for accessibility. In addition, the cargo must be loaded so it keeps the vessel trim and stable at sea and so it will not break loose and become damaged in transit.

Most general cargo vessels are 2,000–15,000 dwt with one or more decks within each hold, called 'tween decks, for storing break-bulk cargoes. A general cargo vessel, or 'tween decker, has a greater cubic capacity than a bulk carrier of the same deadweight to accommodate a large number of individual consignments of less dense break-bulk cargo plus an allowance for dunnage ("padding" materials for securing cargo) and unusable space. 'Tween deckers may have deep tanks located in the bottoms for vegetable oils, chemicals, lubricating oils (lubes), latex, and other liquid cargoes and refrigerated space for fresh and frozen fruits, vegetables, fish, and meat. Some also have a few passenger cabins.

The general cargo business is a service operation where freight agents, brokers, and forwarders represent the shipping public in dealing with warehouse and terminal operators, longshoremen and stevedore firms, vessel operators, customs inspectors, and cargo insurers. In a similar fashion, port agents represent the owner's interest when a vessel calls at a port. They deal with freight forwarders, port authorities (for clearance to enter and leave a port), public health and customs authorities, tug boat operators, pilots, ship chandlers and bunker suppliers. Ship chandlers supply food, stores, and other items for vessel operations. Port agents also arrange for vessel repairs and crew transfers.

The break-bulk business is labor intensive and is a major source of employment in many ports of the world. Even with gangs of longshoremen and stevedores handling cargo, only a few hundred tons of cargo are transferred from ship to shore or shore to ship in a working day. A 'tween decker leaving Europe, calling at ports in the Mediterranean, passing through the Suez Canal (or calling at ports around Africa) on to Bombay, Calcutta, Singapore, Hong Kong, Japan, and returning to Europe via the Panama Canal, calling on ports in North or South America, has spent half its round-the-world voyage of many months in port. This was the lure of the sea, which, in the past, attracted seafarers. It is quite unlike the modern life of a merchant seaman onboard a large crude carrier who spends a day at the end of an oil pier in the middle of nowhere after a one-month voyage.

General cargo vessels may trade between two areas of the world where the cargoes are fully transferred at each end of the voyage, or they may encircle the world, stopping at many ports to transfer only a small portion of their cargo at each call. If these vessels maintain a scheduled service with published rates, they are said to be in liner service. Not all general cargo vessels are in liner service maintaining a schedule of sailings and published shipping rates. Some trade in nonliner, or tramp, service. A tramp operator employs his vessel on the trade that maximizes his earnings.

It is vital for the commerce between nations that some vessels trade as tramps. A tramp operator satisfies transient demand for shipping capacity which cannot be handled by vessels in liner service, which does not fit liner service trading patterns, or which isn't served by liner service vessels. Tramps may be chartered-in by liner service companies to add temporary capacity and may carry hundreds of individual consignments. Alternatively, tramps may be chartered to bulk parcel firms, which specialize in organizing large consignments for a few shippers. The rates received by tramp operators depend solely on market forces related to the supply and demand for vessels at a point in time, whereas liner service vessels operate under a fixed tariff structure where profitability is primarily a function of the volume of business.

Much of the world trade of finished and semifinished goods is carried by vessels in liner service. An operator of a liner service vessel may be a member of a conference. The conference system plays an important role in international trade because most liner operators are members.

To understand the conference system, consider a person wishing to fly between New York and Chicago. Usually he contacts an independent travel agent who provides the necessary information on the approximately seventy flights flown each day by various airlines. The travel agent advises his client on the flight and airport (LaGuardia, JFK, or Newark) that best suit his needs, giving consideration to airline preference, type of aircraft, or other matters except fares. Fares from New York to Chicago are regulated by the Civil Aeronautics Board (CAB), so a travel agent can do little except point out potential savings which apply to special groups (military servicemen, senior citizens, clergymen, children), priority (standby fares), or departure time (night and weekend fares). Acting as agent for the traveling public, the agent inquires about seat availability on a desired flight, reserves a seat in his client's name, confirms the reservation, issues a ticket, and collects the fare, which is forwarded to the airline less his commission. An individual may book directly with the airline, paying the same amount as he would pay an independent travel agent. Since it is not realistic to expect an airline to endorse tickets for competitors, travel agents maintain the public is better served by those who provide impartial advice. In shipping, the role of independent travel agent is fulfilled by freight forwarders, agents, and brokers who physically handle a shipment, process a great amount of paperwork, and deal with customs inspectors, cargo insurers, and terminal operators.

The CAB decides which airlines will fly on the New York/Chicago route and sets a rate that is "attractive" for passengers and provides an "adequate" rate of return on the capital investment of the airlines.* Once given the right to fly New York/Chicago with a set fare structure,

---

*In 1978, the CAB relaxed its regulations on fare reductions and route assignments.

each competing airline decides its own schedule of flights. The wish to capture the largest market share by offering as many flights as possible is tempered, and ultimately controlled, by the average load factor on all the flights.

Since an airline must comply with its own published schedule whether a plane is empty or full, its profitability depends on the average level of occupancy of the available seats, or the load factor, over time. An airline with a break-even load factor of 55% will generate just enough revenue to meet its operating and financing expenses when 55% of its available seats are occupied with fare-paying passengers. The incremental fare collected for each passenger above the break-even load factor is essentially all profit because of the miniscule incremental cost of carrying one extra passenger on an already scheduled flight. For a given rate structure, the profitability of an airline is strictly a function of passenger volume.

Airlines suffer from financial losses if there are too many flights on route for the level of passenger volume. Overcapacity may be caused by either a downturn in economic activity, decreasing the volume of passenger traffic, or by assigning too many aircraft on a route that could be experiencing an expanding volume of passenger traffic. Under either condition, the losses can only be stemmed by the airlines "rationalizing" their services; i.e., cutting back on the number of scheduled flights by reassigning aircraft to other routes or by taking them out of service.

The CAB's role in the airline industry is analogous to the conference's role in liner service: it maintains a schedule of sailings at published rates (tariffs) regardless of the amount of cargo onboard the vessel at departure time. A conference is a voluntary association of independent vessel operators without direct government participation other than some members are state-owned or controlled shipping companies and many dealings involve government maritime agencies. Each conference establishes its own rules of conduct regulating the performance of services and the relationship among the members, including the amount of tonnage committed to a trade and the tariff structure. As a conference member, an independent liner operator pledges to comply with the conference rules and to charge the conference tariffs for his services rendered to the shipping public. The conference monitors its membership for compliance and acts as spokesman for all the members on shipping matters. The chairman must conciliate, placate, and negotiate external differences with government maritime agencies and shippers' associations and internal differences with conference members.

However, the conference system lacks the power to keep its members in tow or even to force all liner service vessel operators serving a trade to join the conference. Nonconference liner companies exert a strong competitive pressure on conferences because their published rates often offer a discount on conference tariffs.

Some conferences are closed, prohibiting the admission of new members; others are open. Conferences serving the United States must by law be open and must file their tariffs with the Federal Maritime Commission (FMC). The FMC does not have the authority to regulate conferences, just as the CAB does not have the authority to regulate international flights. U.S. flag liner operators who are conference members are exempt from the provisions of anti-trust legislation (the Sherman Act), which prohibits fixing rates and establishing conditions of trade with competitors. The basis of the conference system is interpreted by U.S. law as being in restraint of trade.

Conference spokesmen argue that a conference is not a cartel organized to maximize profits; rather, it is a defense against ruinous losses. They maintain that it is in the long-term interests of the shipping public to know that their goods, regardless of the size and timing of their shipments, will be transported by reliable and dependable carriers maintaining a schedule of sailings at published rates that cover operating costs and provide a fair and reasonable return on capital. "Fair and reasonable" is often a point of contention between shippers and carriers.

As far as shippers are concerned, the members of a conference speak with one voice. Behind the monolithic facade, however, is a continual struggle by those who wish to enhance their profits by raising tariffs even at the risk of losing some volume of trade and those who wish to enhance their profits by lowering tariffs in the hope of increasing the volume of trade. The advocates of lowering tariffs point out that the cost of transportation plays a role in the comparative price advantage of, say, Far Eastern goods in the European and American markets. Lowering the shipping rates on these routes may encourage further penetration of Far Eastern goods in these markets, thereby increasing the volume of shipments, load factors, and profitability.*

If the proponents for higher tariffs win, the nonconference liner operators may attempt to increase their market share by not raising

---

*In the late 1970s, lowering tariffs was not the immediate issue of concern. The question was to what degree rate hikes were providing coverage for escalating vessel operating and bunker costs plus protection against adverse foreign exchange rate fluctuations.

their rates and adding more vessels to the trade. If the proponents of lower tariffs win and the subsequent increase in trade is less than anticipated, if too many vessels are working a trade which may not allow operating at breakeven load factors, or if the volume of shipments declines, the conference system can collapse. One member may try to enhance the load factor on his vessels at the expense of fellow members by arranging for shippers, who direct their shipments to his vessels, to receive a secret rebate. Since there is no way to keep this a secret, rebating signals a rate war, which can ruin a conference as other members underbid one another by offering larger rebates or they quit the conference and charge market rates. Remaining members try to rationalize the trade by reassigning or laying up vessels to increase load factors. They attempt to restore the conference system with members abiding by the conference rules and charging conference tariffs. The advocates of rationalizing the trade usually win in the end—not so much by their powers of persuasion as by a subsequent upturn in world trade.

Conferences have a long history in shipping. The first was the Far East Freight Conference formed in 1879 to combat the losses sustained by liner operators in the tea trade between India and Britain. Today there are about 350 individual conferences in the world with the most important linking the U.S. with Europe, the U.S. with Japan, and Japan with Europe. The system is quite complex; for example, the North Atlantic conference system has 14 individual conferences connecting various areas of North America and Europe. Nigeria is served by four independent conferences: the Continental West Africa Conference and the UK West Africa Lines linking it and Europe, the American West African Freight Conference for the U.S., and the West African Far East Freight Conference for trade with the Far East. A shipper on any of these routes may deal with a conference or a nonconference liner company. For shipments between Nigeria and South America, shippers depend on the services of tramp operators or liner operators who have not organized a conference.

Just as a conference spokesman speaks for all members of a conference, shippers unite to exert their views on shipping matters more forcefully. The rubber companies act through a single entity in negotiating with conferences and vessel operators on rates and terms for shipments of rubber and latex. The European Shippers' Council represents the interests of European importers and exporters on public matters and deals with conferences serving Europe. In turn, liner operators express their views and pursue their interests through the Council of European and Japanese National Shipowners' Associations (CENSA). Owner and shipper organizations are a way for suppliers and users to air grievances and make suggestions for improving service.

Container Vessels

The U.S. Armed Forces first used containers for shipping valuable and pilferable military cargoes during World War I. One of the first commercial uses of containers was in Europe in 1949 when John Woolam, a shipper (not a shipowner), packed his sporting goods into a large container for shipment as a single unit rather than as a consignment of individual packages. In the early 1950s, Malcolm McLean, an owner of a large trucking firm, acquired two U.S. flag tankers with contracts to haul oil from the U.S. Gulf to the U.S. Northeast, a route that paralleled his trucking activities. The revenue from the oil cargoes covered the direct costs of the operation but offered little profit. McLean recognized the potential of enhancing the profitability of the vessels if he could combine his tanker and trucking activities. He invested in container-handling equipment and modified the main decks of the tankers to hold containers. The tankers could then shift berths at both ends of the crude oil voyage to on- and off-load containers that were stacked on the main decks. The containers earned revenue comparable to driving tractor-trailers up and down the eastern seaboard. The incremental costs associated with modifying the decks of the tankers and acquiring the containers and container-handling equipment and the cost of time and expenses associated with transferring the containers between flatbed trucks and the tankers were small compared to the incremental revenue. McLean expanded the business by converting excess war-built general cargo, bulk carrier, and tanker tonnage into container vessels to serve ports along the eastern seaboard including Puerto Rico. This was the beginning of Sea-Land, the world's largest container vessel company. About the same time, Seatrain and Matson Navigation inaugurated container services.

Containerization on the North Atlantic began with the Scotch whiskey trade between Glasgow and the United States. The containers were stuffed with cases of Scotch at the exporters' warehouses, sealed for transit, and emptied (stripped) at the importers' warehouses. The entire investment of substituting a high-capital, low-labor cost system of containerized cargoes for the high-labor, low-capital cost system of break-bulk cargoes was justified by the reduction in pilferage of cases of Scotch handled as break-bulk cargo on the U.S. waterfront. Except for a hijacked container or two, the savings from reduced "inventory shrinkage" economically sustained the start of the transformation of the international trade of goods from break-bulk to containerized cargoes.

The first container vessels associated with the Scotch trade were conversions of other types of vessels, such as general cargo vessels, tankers, and bulk carriers. They had a speed of about 15 knots and had container-handling gear installed on the main deck to transfer containers on and off the vessel and to stack the containers in the holds of the vessel and topside on the main deck. The containers were secured individually to the vessel to prevent shifting below decks and toppling overboard topside. Today, these vessels are called geared or self-sustaining noncellular container vessels.

In the commercial world, the intentional underutilization of capital assests was and is an unnatural act. As long as there was any possibility of enhancing revenues with backhaul shipments of goods, returning empty containers to Scotland for another shipment of Scotch was doomed. However, the volume of high-value and pilferable goods shipped to Scotland was small compared to the opposite movement of Scotch. Container vessels had to call on London where the volume of goods being shipped from the U.S. could fill the empty containers. After off-loading containers in London, a container vessel would then call on Glasgow for containers stuffed with cases of Scotch; after the containers were stripped of their contents in London, they were transported to Scotland by truck, rail, or container vessel for stuffing with Scotch whiskey. Once container vessels began calling on London, the commercial temptation to return to New York with containerized shipments was too strong to resist. Container vessels began shuttling between New York and London without bothering to call at Glasgow. After the London/New York container trade was established, the incremental cost of calling on other ports along the U.S. eastern seaboard and on other European ports was small compared to the incremental revenues. The containerized traffic on the North Atlantic trade grew rapidly until the Scotch whiskey movement, the initial mainstay of the business, was just a small fraction of all containerized shipments.

The traditional break-bulk liner service shipping companies closely watched the early development of containerization along the U.S. eastern seaboard and between California and Hawaii. The Scotch movement convinced them that containerization was the wave of the future. By the mid-1960s, the conversion from break-bulk to containerization on all the routes linking North America, Europe, and Japan was in full swing.

Since the traditional wharfs and warehouse terminals for break-bulk cargoes were not designed to handle large numbers of containers, specialized container terminals were built on empty tracts of land to provide ample storage space for containers. New York is still the world's busiest port. Much of its waterfront activity has shifted from the Manhattan wharfs and piers, which are now largely abandoned, to publicly and privately owned container terminals at Staten Island and nearby New Jersey. These terminals have the necessary space for container storage and have easy access to the nation's highways. Large, costly ship-to-shore cranes serve the needs of all container vessels rather than requiring each vessel to be geared or self-sustaining. A crane operator can off-load a container from ship to shore and on-load another container from shore to ship in less than two minutes. He can transfer as much cargo in fifteen minutes as a gang of longshoremen and stevedores can do in one day.

Container ports multiply. Once the transition to containerization started in one port, authorities in nearby ports were forced to follow suit if they wished to preserve their share of the volume of international trade. When the Japan/Europe route was containerized, Hong Kong, Singapore, Australia, and New Zealand had to build container ports because their European goods were carried as topping-off cargoes on the same vessels serving Japan. Container terminals in the Far East which served the deep-sea container operators in the European trade encouraged the containerization of the Far Eastern regional trade between Japan, Australia, New Zealand, Hong Kong, and Singapore, which is handled by short-sea container vessel operators. Short-sea container vessel operators also handle a large volume of containerized shipments between various European container terminals. Container terminal operators welcomed the development of the short-sea container vessel because of the incremental fee income of intraregional container traffic. For the same reason, they welcomed the advent of the container feeder vessel, which expanded the geographic area served by a container terminal. The services rendered by container feeder vessel operators have allowed Singapore to become a central staging point for much of Southeast Asia.

There are now about 175 container ports located throughout Europe, the U.S., Japan, Australia, New Zealand, the Soviet Union, Hong Kong, and Singapore. In the late 1970s, new container ports were built in the Persian Gulf, South Africa, and the Caribbean.

The tremendous demand for capital for container vessels, containers, container-handling facilities and terminals was satisfied, in part, by the formation of joint ventures or consortia which pooled the

TABLE 7.1
LEADERS OF WORLD CONTAINER TRAFFIC, 1978

Country	%
United States	23
Japan	11
Great Britain	7
the Netherlands	6
Hong Kong	5
West Germany	4
Puerto Rico	4
Taiwan	4
Australia	3
Italy	3

Containerisation International Yearbook (1980), National Magazine Company, London.

managerial and capital resources of several independent liner shipping companies for the ownership and operation of container vessels and the common use of container terminals. The ownership interests of the principal firms in the North Atlantic conference system illustrate the structure of container vessel-owning companies. It is quite unlike the situation in tankers where individuals own an important share of the world fleet:

TABLE 7.2
TOP CONTAINER PORTS, 1978

Port and country	%
New York, United States	8
Rotterdam, the Netherlands	6
Kobe, Japan	5
Hong Kong, Hong Kong	5
San Juan, Puerto Rico	4
Oakland, United States	3
Seattle, United States	2
Hamburg, West Germany	2
Bremen/Bremenhaven, West Germany	2
Kaohsiung, Taiwan	2

Containerisation International Yearbook (1980), National Magazine Company, London.

Sea-Land	Unsubsidized U.S. flag liner service shipping company that is part of larger publicly traded corporate entity.
U.S. Lines	Unsubsidized privately owned U.S. flag liner shipping company.
Seatrain	Publicly traded subsidized U.S. flag liner shipping company. Sold its North Atlantic service to an Australian firm in 1980.
Lykes Lines	Subsidized U.S. flag liner service shipping company that is a part of a larger publicly traded corporate entity.
Baltatlantic Line	State-owned Soviet liner service shipping company. Temporarily withdrawn from North Atlantic trade in 1980.
Polish Ocean Lines	State-owned Polish liner service shipping company.
Atlantic Container Line (ACL)	A consortia made up of three Swedish, a French, a British and a Dutch liner shipping company.
Dart Line	A consortia made up of a Belgian, a British, and a Hong Kong liner shipping company.
Hapag Lloyd	A publicly traded West German liner shipping company.
Manchester Liners	A subsidiary of a publicly traded British shipping company.
C P Ships	A subsidiary of the publicly traded Canadian Pacific Railroad.

Whereas 40% of all tankers are registered under flags of convenience/necessity and only 5% are under the U.S. flag,* 20% of the world container fleet,** in terms of container-carrying capacity, is under the

*Data taken from the *Tanker Register* (1980), H. Clarkson & Company, London.
**Data taken from *Containerisation International* (April 1980), National Magazine Company, London.

U.S. flag and 13% is under flags of convenience/necessity. The combined U.S., British, Japanese and West German flag fleets account for 57% of the carrying capacity of the world container fleet.

TABLE 7.3
CARRYING CAPACITY OF WORLD CONTAINER FLEET

Carrying capacity (TEU)*	Number of vessels
400-699	75
700-999	80
1,000-1,499	155
1,500-1,999	89
2,000-2,999	34
3,000 and greater	7
Total	440

Courtesy *Shipping Statistics and Economics* (August 1980), H.P. Drewry, London.
*TEU or TFE stands for twenty foot equivalent. A 20′ long container is 1 TEU and a 40′ long container is 2 TEUs.

Modern container ships have speeds of 20–25 knots. They are gearless, relying on shore-based cranes to transfer containers. Cellular structures are constructed within the vessel, in which containers are stacked without having to be secured. The world's largest container vessels can carry 3,000 TEU of containers. This may be 3,000 20-foot containers, 1,500 40-foot containers, etc. The containers are stacked in the cellular structures and are stowed topside almost to the height of the bridge.

Sea-Land's eight SL-7 container vessels are unique in the trade for the size of their propulsion plant and, consequently, their speed. An SL-7 carries about 900 35-foot and 200 40-foot containers and has the same deadweight (28,800 tons) of a small tanker; but it is not a small tanker. The gross registered tons, a measure of the internal volume of a vessel, are a far better gauge of the actual size of the SL-7 than deadweight. This is why shipbuilders often express their building programs in terms of gross registered tons rather than in deadweight tons. A fully loaded 28,800-dwt tanker sits low in the water with only 12 feet of free board, which is the difference between the depth (45 feet) of the vessel with its fully laden draft (33 feet). The SL-7 has 58 feet of height above the waterline, made up of 34 feet of free board and 24 feet of height from the three-high stacking of containers on the main deck.

TABLE 7.4
COMPARISON OF SL-7 AND TANKER

	28,000-dwt SL-7	28,800-dwt tanker
Length	950 ft	630 ft
Beam	105 ft	80 ft
Depth (distance from the main deck to the keel)	68 ft	45 ft
Draft (distance from the waterline to the keel when the vessel is loaded to its full deadweight capacity)	34 ft	33 ft
Propulsion plant shaft horse power capacity	120,000	9,000
Speed	33 knots	14 knots
Gross registered tons	41,555	18,000

A tanker is a slow tub compared with a fast container ship designed with the long, sleek lines of an aircraft carrier.* The unusually high speed on the SL-7 container ship was originally seen as a marketing device. Shippers could reduce their inventory carrying charges because of the shorter duration of trans-Atlantic and Pacific crossings. However, after the 1973 oil crisis, the fuel bill for the estimated 500 tons of fuel consumed each day by an SL-7 at full steaming speed jumped to over $40,000 per day. This cost forced a reduction in the speed of the SL-7s to 22–25 knots in line with other modern container vessels, with the savings in fuel costs more than compensating for the loss of revenue-generating capacity from slow steaming. Slow steaming for the SL-7s is not without its benefits, since the vessels can react to an increased volume of trade or make up for port or weather delays by increasing their speed. Scheduling difficulties among the various vessels can also be resolved through speed adjustments. The economic burden of inefficient fuel consumption of the SL-7s became too much to bear when bunker prices doubled in 1979. Sea-Land proposed that the U.S. government take over the vessels for national defense purposes in return for Sea-Land ordering replacement vessels from U.S. yards.

At first, containerization did not seriously affect the livelihoods of longshoremen and stevedores. Most of the stuffing and stripping of containers was done in the same warehouses serving break-bulk cargoes.

*Fairplay International has published articles on the possibility of converting container ships to auxiliary aircraft carriers during national emergencies.

The advent of the modern container terminal made it more practical to transfer the container to a flatbed truck or railroad car rather than transfer its contents to a trailer, van, or boxcar for further distribution. When the container was finally stripped of its contents at an inland point, it made more sense to transport the empty container to a nearby origin of another shipment. This was less costly than transporting the empty container back to a container terminal and making a separate shipment of goods to the same terminal for stuffing. Spurred by the desires of shippers to minimize costs, the practice of stuffing containers at the origin of a shipment and stripping them at their final destination (intermodalism) grew. An early form of intermodalism was truck trailers riding "piggy-back" on railroad flatcars.

Intermodalism eliminated nearly 90% of all intermediate labor requirements between stuffing and stripping. This drastic reduction in labor demand created an intense struggle between labor, which wanted job security, and shippers, who wanted the low-cost benefits of intermodalism. The actual battle was fought by container vessel operators. Though residual flarings still erupt from time to time, labor peace has been purchased, by and large, through guaranteed wage and pension funds supported by fees charged to every container entering or leaving a port.

Most containers are 8 feet or 8½ feet high by 8 feet wide by 20 feet or 40 feet long, capable of carrying 20 or 30 tons of cargo, respectively. The main exceptions are Sea-Land's 35-foot and 10-foot containers, which are more compatible with the highway and rail facilities serving certain Far Eastern ports. The ubiquitous container is made of steel, or an aluminum covering over a steel frame, with standardized fixtures for easy handling between any mode of transport. The number of containers that enable a container ship to shuttle between ports without waiting for containers to be stuffed or stripped is approximately three times the number of container slots onboard the vessel. With an ample number of containers to serve the needs of shippers at each end of a voyage, port time is solely dedicated to transferring containers on and off the vessel. This maximizes the utilization of the capital invested in containerization.

In the early days of containerization, container vessel operators owned their containers and proudly displayed their corporate logos on the sides of the containers. This discouraged the free exchange of containers among vessel operators because of the natural reluctance to carry containers emblazoned with a competitor's logo. The end result of this was vessel operators transporting empty containers, called deadheading, in opposite directions between ports to meet their respective customers' needs. Deadheading expenses would have been reduced if there were a free exchange of containers among vessel operators. This led to the emergence of container leasing companies specializing in neutral containers that could be freely exchanged among operators to meet their transient needs. Container leasing companies are to container vessel operators what tanker owners are to oil companies: they reduce the amount of capital that container vessel operators must raise to acquire containers and let them decide what portion of their containers will be owned or leased (chartered-in) through a portfolio of short-, medium-, and long-term leases (charters). Container leasing companies have container depots or pooling areas conveniently located for their customers: vessel operators, freight forwarders or consolidators acting as nonvessel-owning common carriers (NVOCCs), and shippers' manufacturing plants.

Regardless of the type of lease arrangement concluded, lease rental payments continue until the leased container is returned to an authorized container depot. Container leasing companies do not really care if one of their containers, at any given moment, is on the Trans-Siberian railroad, on a barge on the Mississippi River, in an aircraft over Brazil, in a truck in Paris, resting comfortably at the bottom of the Atlantic, or being converted into a housing unit in the Philippines or a chicken coop on Christmas Island. The lessor must continue making his payments until the container is returned to the lessee's depot. This worldwide dispersal of containers does not always work in favor of the container leasing companies. Representatives of container leasing companies joined shippers scouring the waterfront of Lagos and other West African and European ports when a container vessel operator serving these areas failed in 1975. Lenders have sometimes questioned the collateral value of mortgages on containers that are dispersed like water droplets around the world.

Some container vessel operators do not lease containers at all. Others have a mix of owned and leased containers. The ownership of the estimated 2–3 million containers in existence is about evenly split between container vessel operators and leasing companies. All have made significant investments in computer facilities to monitor and mobilize containers to meet shippers' demands in addition to performing routine accounting and billing functions.

From time to time, container leasing companies find that container vessel owners take advantage of their leasing terms to reduce their deadheading expenses. Suppose that a container leasing company has depots in Japan and Europe and leases containers on a day rate basis which can be returned to either depot without a punitive charge. Further suppose that there is more container traffic from Japan to Europe. Ordinarily, the container vessel operator would bear the deadheading expenses of repositioning empty containers to Japan. He could reduce this expense by leasing containers in Japan and returning them to Europe. The container leasing company would then find itself with a growing shortage of containers in Japan to satisfy demand and a growing surplus of containers in Europe with little or no demand. Sooner or later, the container leasing company will have to pay a container vessel operator to reposition the empty containers from Europe to Japan. Normally, the container leasing companies are wise to this practice and set the terms of their leases to prevent container vessel operators from transforming an expense (deadheading) into a source of revenue; they can only minimize, not eliminate, deadheading or repositioning costs.

The container leasing companies contend worldwide dispersal of containers leased out on a day rate basis is a long-term commitment on the part of the lessor because of the difficulty of identifying, isolating, and returning containers. This did not hold up during a contraction of world trade in 1975: container vessel operators shifted through their excess container inventories and returned leased containers to their rightful owners. Even though most container leasing companies' utilization rates plummeted in 1975, they quickly rebounded in 1976 when world trade recovered. Overall, their investments in containers and related equipment have been more profitable than liner shipping company investments in container vessels.

Although the concept of containerization is epitomized by the standard container, there is specialization of containers to particular trades. Insulated containers, some with self-contained refrigeration plants and others depending on outside sources for refrigeration services, have taken over much of the Australian and New Zealand meat trade to Europe. Containers fitted with tanks (tanktainers) are used in the liquid chemical and vegetable oil trades. Rubber interiors in conventional containers have been proposed for carrying liquid cargo shipments. Some containers open at the top or side rather than the end; others are constructed without a top or side.

Wide-bodied jets have attracted highly valued lightweight cargoes away from container vessels. A European women's apparel manufacturer hangs finished coats on racks that fit securely inside a container constructed of a lightweight aluminum alloy for transport by aircraft.

After landing in the U.S., the container is trucked to the retailer who wheels out the racks of coats ready for immediate display and sale. Container air/sea service is an optimizing transportation technique which blends the shorter shipping time and higher cost of aircraft with the longer shipping time and lower cost of container vessels. Highly valued containerized shipments entering Vancouver by vessel from the Far East are flown to London on Air Canada. Manchester Liners moves containers on vessels from Great Britain to Montreal and then has them flown throughout North, Central, and South America on a single bill of lading. Atlantic Container Line, Eastern Airlines, and American Airlines provide a single service for shippers where the containers are transferred between sea and air modes of transport at Newark.

Although containers are usually associated with high-value goods, a European short-sea container vessel operator moves relatively low-valued grain directly from farms in France to flour mills in Ireland. The collapsible container has been proposed for reducing deadheading expenses. Several folded containers could be transported from one port to another port, taking up the space of one conventional container onboard the container vessel.

There are five alternative routes for moving containers between Europe and Japan. The three all-water routes are via the Cape of Good Hope, the Suez Canal, and the Panama Canal. The U.S. land bridge system involves trans-Atlantic and trans-Pacific crossings by container vessels coupled with the transcontinental railroads. Unit trains, dedicated only to hauling containers, cross North America regularly. In the Soviet land bridge system, small container vessels operate between Japan and the Pacific terminus of the Trans-Siberian railroad at Vladivostok and nearby Nakhodka. Containers are then distributed by rail to Iran and throughout eastern, central, and western Europe. The Soviet land bridge Atlantic terminal is Leningrad. Although container leasing companies may not care whether their containers in the Europe/Japan trade are on the Trans-Siberian railroad or on vessels belonging to the Far Eastern Freight Conference (FEFC), FEFC members whose investments are in container ships do care. The Trans-Siberian land bridge system is a reliable service for shippers and offers discounts on FEFC tariffs. It has drained a fair amount of traffic from the world's longest container vessel trade.

In 1975, while FEFC members worried about doubling the track on single track stretches of the Trans-Siberian railroad, North Atlantic conference members worried about the expansion of the Soviet liner shipping company Baltatlantic Line, which threw vessels into this trade, slashed rates, and made a nuisance of itself. By promising to stop this disruptive behavior and abide by conference rules as negotiating tactics on establishing the conditions of membership in the North Atlantic conference, Baltatlantic Line became a law-abiding member in 1976. Conference members greeted this with relief, many of whom had attained their membership in the same capitalistic fashion.

Until 1972, Seatrain served between Europe and the U.S. Atlantic coast and between Japan and the U.S. Pacific coast, but not between Europe and the U.S. Pacific coast nor between Japan and the U.S. Atlantic coast. That year, Seatrain inaugurated the U.S. minibridge system where the latter services were offered on a single bill of lading. Seatrain coupled its regular trans-Atlantic and trans-Pacific sailing with unit trains to haul containers across the continent. The U.S. minibridge system was a new, competitive alternative for shippers. It quickly came under attack by U.S. port authorities and U.S. port labor unions who discovered that the minibridge system reduced shipping costs by avoiding ports with high container transit fees that supported local dockworkers' guaranteed pension and income funds. While these suits are still pending in U.S. courts, more liner shipping companies are offering U.S. minibridge service to their customers. Another minibridge system is in the Middle East where containers destined for Persian Gulf ports are shipped to eastern Mediterranean ports for overland movement by truck and rail.

Intermodalism does not exactly fit the world as perceived by U.S. regulatory authorities. Railroad, truck, and barge operators acting as common carriers (offering their services to the public) in interstate commerce are regulated and are required to file tariffs by the Interstate Commerce Commission (ICC). Liner service vessel operators are required to file their rates with the Federal Maritime Commission (FMC) and abide, along with other carriers, with the regulations of the U.S. Customs Bureau. The number of rates filed in Washington by type of shipment and by mode of transport between any two points within, or in and out, of the U.S. runs into hundreds of thousands. This legally mandated system works well, in principle, for shipments that are manually transferred from one mode of transport to another where separate bills of lading are issued at each point. However, intermodal shipments of containerized freight are more amenable to an administrative system where one bill of lading is issued for a shipment between two points, independent of which mode(s) is used to transport the container. The actual mode of transport is of little importance to the shipper as long as his goods are delivered on time, undamaged, and at known costs. Each government agency (the ICC, CAB, FMC) has publicly declared its support of intermodalism as long as it falls under its jurisdiction.

Commerical organizations must be more responsive to change than goverment agencies if they wish to survive. The break-bulk cargo conference system, with certain modifications for containerized shipments, was adopted by container vessel operators. Cargo insurance underwriters faced a more difficult challenge; they had to identify the carrier responsible for damaging a containerized shipment of goods. They also had to adjust to a more restricted interpretation on the limitation of liability of ocean carriers of containers.

When a shipper insures a consignment of goods against damage or loss, he or his freight forwarder or agent acting on his behalf works through a cargo insurance broker who arranges for the insurance from underwriters. All validated claims for damage or loss are paid out of the premium income and the reserves of the underwriters. If it can be substantiated that a particular carrier has been negligent, underwriters—after honoring the shippers' claims—and uninsured shippers can seek restitution from the carrier. In the break-bulk trades, it is relatively easy to identify the offending carrier because of the continuous inspection of a shipment as it is manually transferred from one carrier to another. A separate bill of lading is issued at each transfer, noting any irregularities or apparent damage to the shipment. A container, however, is sealed at the origin of the shipment and is opened at its ultimate destination. If the shipment is discovered damaged at its destination, it is difficult to identify which carrier is responsible. Unable to identify the responsible carrier, underwriters cannot press a claim.

Even if a cargo insurance underwriter can identify the ocean carrier responsible for damaging the goods, the Hague Rules, an international convention dealing with the conduct of international trade, limit the maximum liability of the carrier to $500 per package for prescribed acts of negligence. The limitation of maximum liability has been historically associated with shipping to induce individuals to risk their capital in ships. This longstanding tradition was incorporated in the Hague Rules.

The Hague Rules were codified in the 1920s long before containerization. After containerization made its mark in world trade, the courts ruled that a container, from the point of view of the Hague Rules, was a single package. If one hundred packages are shipped as break-bulk cargo, the maximum liability of the vessel operator would be $50,000. If all the packages are stuffed into one container, the maximum liability of the vessel operator is $500.

The underwriters adapted quickly to the new environment by adjusting their rate structure. The United Nations Conference on Trade and Development (UNCTAD) wants to enlarge the extent of the ocean carrier's liability, both in dollar amount and the stipulated conditions of negligence. If the UNCTAD succeeds in its efforts, cargo insurance rates should decline because cargo insurance underwriters will have greater access to vessel operators to recoup their losses. However, vessel operators will have to raise their freight charges for the additional risk of doing business. From a practical standpoint, shippers, who pay both cargo insurance premiums to underwriters and freight charges to vessel operators, should see little change in their total costs regardless of the outcome of the UNCTAD deliberations.

Despite all impediments to change, containerization and intermodalism are here to stay simply because of their proven record of lowering the cost of shipping goods. Little, if any, of what exists today was foreseen by the merchant who stuffed his sporting goods into a large box to save some money in shipping charges and by an owner of a trucking firm who wanted to make more money by carrying containers on his tankers.

Lash Vessels

U.S. flag subsidized shipping companies involved in foreign commerce must modernize their fleets in return for receiving operating subsidies from the U.S. government. During the late 1960s, U.S.-subsidized operators of 20-year-old general cargo vessels had to choose the best type of replacement vessel. The container vessel was the obvious choice for shipping break-bulk cargoes to Europe and Japan. Yet some types of cargoes handled by general cargo vessels did not lend themselves to containerization, such as iron and steel products, bagged fertilizer, cement, bulky and heavy industrial goods, machinery, and machinery parts. Other operators served areas of the world where port, highway, and rail facilities did not support containerization. An analysis of the types of cargoes and the transportation infrastructure of nations served by these routes convinced a marine architect, J. L. Goldman, that the best replacement was a barge-carrying vessel. Goldman's achievements in shipping are threefold: the origination of a new concept, the design of the vessel, and his success in persuading U.S. flag operators to order an untried vessel.

A container vessel carries thousands of 8 × 8 × 40 containers, each with 20–30 tons of cargo. A Lash (Lighter Aboard SHip) vessel carries

80–90 lighters, or barges, measuring 13 feet high, 30 feet wide, and 60 feet long, each with a capacity for 375 tons of cargo. Lash barges are fitted with large, watertight hatches and can be towed or pushed by tugs on inland, interisland, and coastal waterways. They are pushed by a tug or work boat into position at the stern of a Lash vessel, which may be moored alongside a pier or anchored in protected waters. They are lifted up and stowed in the vessel's holds and two high along the main deck by a track-mounted gantry crane.

Lash vessels form a connecting link between coastal and inland waterway systems and island nations. They are collected and distributed along inland and coastal waterways and between islands by conventional tug tows. Central staging areas are set up near mouths of rivers or along key points of coastal waterways for Lash vessels to pick up and drop off Lash barges. The most important inland and coastal waterway systems that were once hoped to be linked up by Lash vessels are the U.S. (the Mississippi River system and the Atlantic coastal inland waterway), Europe (the Rhine and other rivers and the European coastal waterway system), the Soviet Union with its well-developed inland waterway system, and the water highways of Brazil (the Amazon River) and Mainland China (the Yangtze River). These waterways were hoped to be eventually linked to the island nations of the Philippines, Indonesia, and Malaysia where small vessels and barges are the chief mode of transport.

The open water operation of Lash vessels to pick up and drop off barges and the warehouse capacity of the barges to store goods without the need for berths and shoreside storage facilities were ideal for shipping goods to the congested Persian Gulf ports after the 1973 oil crisis. Lash vessels have been built to enlarge the geographic area served by a central staging point. Small-capacity Lash feeder vessels serve between Scandinavia and a central Lash vessel staging area near Rotterdam. However, the Lash system has not made as much progress as anticipated by its supporters.

Roll-on/Roll-off Vessels

Roll-on/roll-off (Ro-Ro) vessels are multidecked ferries for hauling truck trailers, automobiles, or an assortment of unitized cargoes. Ramps connect each deck, which permit driving the trailers, automobiles, or forklift trucks and straddle carriers with unitized cargoes to move between decks. Stern or side ramps allow them to move on and off the vessel. U.S. flag Ro-Ro carriers, with rows of trailers on each deck, have served the U.S. East Coast/Puerto Rico and the U.S. West Coast/Hawaii and Alaska trades; European flag Ro-Ro carriers have served the Great Britian/Scandinavia/Northern Europe trades for many years.

The market for Ro-Ro vessels exploded after the 1973 oil crisis because of the commerical value of their short port turnaround time and their need of only a berth and a parking area for discharging cargoes. As Ro-Ro vessels arrived in Persian Gulf ports, they were immediately put ahead of general cargo vessels which had been waiting months for a berth because their entire cargo could be driven off the vessel in less than a day. Berth space was so critical in these ports that stern-loading Ro-Ro vessels, which take up berth space equal to the width of the vessel, were preferred to side-loading Ro-Ro vessels, which moor lengthwise to a berth. Besides, the Ro-Ro vessel is best for handling the massive imports of tractor-trailers, trucks, vans, construction and cargo handling equipment, and wheeled units. They may not be the most economic form of ocean transport because they carry fewer 40-foot trailers than 40-foot containers on an equally sized container ship. Trailers parked on decks have wasted (nonrevenue-earning) space above and below the trailer that does not exist when containers are stacked.

A Ro-Ro vessel may be designed primarily as a floating warehouse. Unitized and palletized cargoes are moved by forklift trucks and straddle carriers which are carried onboard as part of the ship's gear. An example of a unitized cargo is a stack of lumber bound by steel bands. Palletized cargoes are drums or cartons secured to a portable platform, or pallet. A floating warehouse-type Ro-Ro may also carry trailers and containers that are moved by forklifts. If a crane is installed onboard the vessel to transfer containers between ship and shore, the Ro-Ro vessel has lift-on/lift-off (Lo-Lo) capability, not to be confused with a Wo-Wo vessel. A Wo-Wo vessel is a livestock carrier whose cargo walks-on/walks-off.

Ro-Ro vessels built for carrying automobiles are called pure car carriers. These vessels may have up to 13 completely enclosed decks capable of carrying 1,500–4,000 automobiles. The largest carries 6,000 automobiles at a time. Pure car carriers offer the lowest cost of ocean-borne transportation for automobiles over other vessel types. Their economy of transport is brought about by the large number of automobiles carried at one time, their speed, and the short port turnaround time where automobiles are driven on and off the vessel at a rate of 300 cars per hour. Pure car carriers handling Japanese and European exports to the United States and Japanese exports to Europe usually return empty for another cargo of automobiles.

Owners often tailor their vessels to the needs of a trade, which may result in hybrid ship designs. Many early container vessels were part containers/part break-bulk vessels. Some holds were designed for containerized and others for break-bulk cargoes. A Seabee vessel is part container/part Lash. Atlantic Container Lines vessels in the North Atlantic trade are part container/part Ro-Ro. The BORO is a new type vessel that can combine the dry bulk, oil, general cargo, container, and Ro-Ro trades. An example of its versatility is carrying Scandinavian lumber to the Persian Gulf and returning with a cargo of crude oil. The *Capricorn* is a proposed Lash/container/Ro-Ro vessel. Lash barges are pushed by a work boat into the partially flooded main hold of the vessel through a swing-away bow. Trailers and containers are carried on the main deck.

Multipurpose Cargo Ships

One might conclude that container, Lash, and Ro-Ro vessels have so taken over world trade that longshoremen and stevedores working general cargo vessels can only be seen on late-night TV showings of *On the Waterfront*. Nothing could be further from the truth. Over 20,000 general cargo vessels of every description ply the world's trade routes. While containerization has and continues to capture an ever-increasing share of the world trade in break-bulk cargoes on all major routes since the mid-1960s, this period has also been marked by a massive growth in the volume of world trade. Moreover, there are many ports without container terminals and many cargoes which cannot be boxed. There has been no change in cargo handling practices in the break-bulk trades except for some palletized shipments that require flat and obstruction-free 'tween decks for forklift trucks. Some shipments of canned foods are handled by conveyor belts between ship and shore. Palletized shipments and conveyor belt systems call for concentration of shipments of a particular type of cargo, investments in cargo handling equipment, and some degree of specialization on the part of the shipowner.

In the mid-1960s, in spite of the rapid conversion of break-bulk to containerized shipments, two shipbuilders decided that the time was ripe to build a long series of identical vessels as replacements for the general cargo fleet. The Japanese shipbuilder Ishikawajima-Harima Heavy Industries (IHI) began constructing the Freedom class, and the British shipbuilder Austin and Pickersgill started building the SD-14 class of multipurpose cargo vessels. Both classes are about 15,000 dwt and have been standardized as much as possible to reduce building costs. A shipowner has a wide choice of options on engine size, design of 'tween decks and hatch covers, type and lifting capacity of ship's cargo-handling gear, and degree of automation in the engine room and on the bridge. The Freedom and SD-14 vessels are not identical. Each has a different number of holds, different 'tween deck arrangements, and a host of other characteristics that make one class or the other more

From	To	Cargo or employment
Maine	Northern Europe	Rolls of newsprint and lumber in the holds and 'tween deck spaces with containers topside
Northern Europe	Great Lakes	Steel products in the holds
Great Lakes	Japan via the Panama Canal	Bulk shipment of grain in all holds and 'tween deck spaces
Japan	Western U.S.	Pipe in the holds and automobiles on the 'tween deck
Western U.S.	Western Canada	Ballast voyage
Western Canada	Eastern U.S. via the Panama Canal	Lumber in all holds, 'tween deck space, and topside
Florida	Japan via the Panama Canal	Bulk shipment of phosrock
Japan and Korea	Persian Gulf	Trucks from Japan on the 'tween deck and bagged cement from Korea in the holds
Persian Gulf	Northern Europe via the Suez Canal	Bulk shipment of sulphur
Northern Europe	West Africa	Eight months under time charter to a
West Africa	Northern Europe	liner service shipping company on the West African trade carrying break-bulk cargoes
Northern Europe	South America	One-trip charter to a bulk parcel operator who has assembled three consignments to fill the vessel: bagged fertilizer, bagged cement, and industrial machinery
South America	United States	One-trip charter to a liner service operator who needs additional temporary capacity; cargo includes bags of coffee in the holds and containers topside

desirable for a particular owner. In the 1970s the Spanish yard Astilleros Espanoles started building the 21,000-dwt Santa Fe 77 class. IHI also started production of the 21,500-dwt Fortune and the 32,700-dwt shallow draft Future-32 class of multipurpose cargo vessel. Shipyards in Argentina, Brazil, Greece, and Singapore are building multipurpose cargo vessels under licensing arrangements with IHI or Austin and Pickersgill. Shipyards in West Germany and South Korea are building multipurpose cargo ships of their own design.

A liper is similar to a multipurpose cargo vessel. It is built with the flexibility to trade as a liner service vessel in the break-bulk trades and as a tramp in the bulk commodity trades. Its 'tween decks are level and obstruction-free for the use of forklifts and can be folded to the sides of the vessel for bulk cargoes. Its hatches are wide, flush with the main deck, and strengthened to hold topside cargoes of lumber and containers. The itinerary on p. 109 illustrates the versatility and flexibility of a suitably geared multipurpose or liper cargo vessel.

Another area of specialization in the general cargo business is the heavy lift vessel. These vessels can handle individual items (locomotives, large electric generators, large subassemblies of refineries, chemical and other industrial units) weighing up to 1,200 tons. A specially designed counterweight or water ballast system keeps the vessel trim while transferring the cargo from ship to shore and from shore to ship. The Multiflex 12,600-dwt class omnipurpose vessel has a heavy lift capability and can participate in Ro-Ro, general cargo, bulk, and container trades.

There are many general and multipurpose cargo vessels of all types, sizes, and characteristics on order or under construction as replacements for the large portion of the existing fleet of 20,000 vessels built before 1960. The 1979 shipyard price of a 15,000-dwt general cargo vessel was over $10 million, nearly triple the original mid-1960s price. The move toward the larger Fortune, Santa Fe, and Future classes of multipurpose vessel is an effort to introduce greater revenue-generating potential to support higher capital costs.

In the midst of all these trends are the owners of thousands of older, fully amortized general cargo vessels who conduct their business today just as they did in the past. These owners are in a race against time with their future earnings' potential squeezed between the remaining years of serviceable life on the one hand and the level of rates on the other. The rate structure is primarily determined by anticipatory changes in the supply and demand for vessel capacity. Demand is linked to the overall rising level of world trade less the growing portion lost to container, Ro-Ro, and specialized vessels. The present worth of older general cargo vessels is the discounted value of the future earnings stream (revenues less costs) over the remaining years of their useful lives plus their discounted scrap value. A massive amount of data would be required and many important assumptions on world trade and other matters would have to be made to assess the value of these vessels. Yet their value is determined by the market every time owner-ship changes.

8

Single-Purpose Vessels

A versatile multipurpose vessel lets an owner select any facet of the break-bulk, dry-bulk, or unitized cargo trades, in liner or tramp service, which maximizes the vessel's earning capacity. Some owners prefer to establish their niche by deliberately sacrificing flexibility. Single-purpose vessels are built for a particular trade. Their economic viability depends on maintaining a competitive edge over multipurpose vessels in just one sector of the general cargo business. Single-purpose vessels have been built for the principal high-volume, long-haul trades in forest products, liquid chemicals, vegetable oil, fresh and frozen foodstuffs, automobiles, cement, sugar, rice, salt, fish meal, molasses, and wine. Single-purpose and general-purpose vessels do not usually compete with one another on the low-volume, short-haul trades where the economic benefits of specialization cannot be fully realized.

The world's largest tankers are single-purpose vessels trading between a few terminals on a small number of long-haul, high-volume crude oil trades. Large LNG carriers are also single-purpose vessels whose economic value is based on being part of an ongoing LNG project. Other specialized vessels include ice breakers, dredges, cable and pipelaying ships, and floating factories. Fish processing plants accompany the Soviet and Japanese fishing fleets, and lumber mills on the Amazon go to the source of the logs rather than taking the logs to the mill. At one time, vessels were to be converted to ammonia and urea production plants that could shift sources of raw materials (natural gas) in Indonesia. Recent proposals for floating plants have involved paper mills on the Amazon and LNG liquefaction plants towed from Norway to offshore sites in the Persian Gulf. Another example of vessel specialization has been a proposal to build large barge-carrying vessels that would carry large subassemblies of processing plants and refineries. The large subassemblies would be loaded on barges at manufacturing sites in Europe, the United States, and Japan. They would then be pushed aboard a partially flooded vessel. The vessel, similar to a floating dry dock, would deballast itself, sail to the plant site in the Middle East, and flood down so the barges could be towed out. The economic basis of this scheme is the savings in labor costs of assembling as much of the plant as possible at the manufacturing site rather than at the plant site where skilled labor is less available and more expensive.

Forest Product Carriers

TABLE 8.1
MAJOR FOREST PRODUCT MARKET SEGMENTS

	Approximate percentage of movement*
Logs	40
Lumber, plywood and wood panels	30
Wood chips and wood pulp	20
Rolls of newsprint, paper, and paperboard	10

*Over 130 million tons of forest products were carried on the high seas annually during the 1970s.

Single-purpose vessels have been designed for each segment of the forest products trade. A 15,000-dwt general purpose cargo vessel has a 'tween deck in each of its four or five holds and is equipped with shipboard gear designed to handle a wide variety of cargoes. A single-purpose log carrier of the same deadweight has two holds, no 'tween decks, and long, wide hatches to expose as much of the area of the holds as possible. Specialized shipboard equipment loads and unloads bundles of logs, which have been unitized to reduce port turnaround time by speeding up cargo-handling rates. One of the fastest cargo-handling methods has been devised for a log carrier operating in Canadian waters. Logs are carried only on its main deck. At the receiving terminal, the vessel is lowered in the water, then listed up to 40° by a uniquely designed ballast system until the entire cargo slides off the vessel in a matter of seconds.

Log carriers serving the Malaysia, Indonesia, and the Philippines/ Japan trades are shallow draft, enabling them to leave the backwater log-exporting ports loaded. Japan has insisted on importing much of its forest product needs as logs from northwestern United States and Southeast Asia for its domestic lumber mills and to minimize its foreign exchange expenditures for forest products. In recent years, the log-exporting nations in Southeast Asia have built lumber mills and plywood plants to divert the "value-added" economic benefit of processing logs from Japan to their domestic forest products industry. As these plants were constructed, the mix of types of vessels serving the forest products trades in the Far East changed. While log carrier owners suffered, lumber carrier owners benefited as the log-exporting nations sought to aid the development of their domestic lumber and plywood industry.

Specialized lumber carriers are not generally found on the world's largest lumber (sawn timber) movement from Scandinavia and western Soviet Union to northern Europe nor, for that matter, on the smaller movement between eastern Soviet Union and Japan. These trades are too short to justify the capital investment in specialization and are more economically served by square-hold, general-purpose vessels. Square-hold vessels have a flat surface at the bottom of their holds for stacking unitized shipments of lumber rather than a curved surface which follows the contour of the hull as in bulk carriers. The Scandinavia northern Europe trade is also served by small Ro-Ro carriers where the lumber is handled by forklift trucks.

Large single-purpose 25,000–50,000-dwt lumber carriers have square holds, no 'tween decks, wide hatches flush with the main deck for topside loading, and large, costly gantry cranes for efficient and fast cargo handling. Specialized lumber carriers trade from western Canada (Vancouver) to both coasts of the United States and from northwestern United States to Europe and Japan. Eastern U.S. forest products needs are satisfied by imports from eastern and western Canada, not from northwestern U.S. sources. This avoids employing U.S. flag tonnage, mandated by the Jones Act, for all shipments between U.S. ports. The arrangement of exporting North American forest products from northwestern U.S. ports and supplying eastern U.S. forest products needs from Canada is not deliberately done to rob Americans of seafaring jobs.

Rather, it is a consequence of a loss of competitive position for any firm that decides to pay the extra freight charges to "ship American."

Large lumber carriers can generate further cost savings if shipments are concentrated at fewer terminals. Lumber shippers must bear the extra cost of concentrating their shipments at a few terminals but are compensated by the savings in transportation costs. One European shipping company has adapted its lumber carriers for backhaul cargoes of automobiles to the U.S. West Coast and another has designed its lumber carriers to fit into the container trades. Combining the forest products, automobile, and container trades enhances the competitive position of an owner and simultaneously lowers the cost of transportation for shippers. Independent shipowners have pooled their technical, marketing, managerial, and capital resources to bid for large shipments of lumber. This has enabled them to acquire the costly vessels necessary to handle these shipments. Pooling has also strengthened their bargaining position in dealing as a group rather than as individuals with the few large forest products companies.

Pulpwood (sawn-off logs) is mechanically reduced to wood chips, which are then treated with sulphuric acid to produce either sulphate or sulphite pulp, depending on the paper-making process. Paper-making plants located in areas of insufficient raw materials import pulpwood in general-purpose vessels or wood chips in wood-chip carriers. Wood chips are a low-density cargo of about 100 cubic feet per ton. A conventional 25,000-dwt bulk carrier with 1,250,000 cf of cargo-carrying capacity will cube out with a shipment of only 12,500 tons of wood chips (1,250,000 cf divided by 100 cf/ton of cargo). Wood chip carriers of 20,000–60,000 dwt are built with a large cubic capacity to enable them to be loaded to their marks. They are also fitted with modern cargo-handling gear employing pneumatic (air) conveyor belts or specially designed buckets for efficient handling. Most of the world's wood-chip carrier fleet is owned by or under long-term charter to Japanese shipping companies which, in turn, operate the vessels under long-term transportation contracts to Japanese paper manufacturers. Japan imports most of its wood chips from Malaysia, Indonesia, and the Philippines. Brazil is an emerging major exporter of forest products spurred, in part, by the development of the world's largest pulpwood plantation by tanker owner D. K. Ludwig.

Sulphate and sulphite pulp are also traded internationally. One sophisticated vessel transports sulphate pulp from Brazil to Norway, returning with a cargo of sulphuric acid. The next step in this process would be a vessel that takes on a cargo of wood pulp or wood chips and delivers a cargo of sulphate or sulphite pulp. Single-purpose, twin hold, wide hatch, 8,000-dwt newsprint carriers transport rolls of newsprint from North America or Scandinavia to northern Europe. A shipper of newsprint between eastern United States and Europe can use specialized newsprint, Lash, Ro-Ro, general, or multipurpose carriers. The growth of vessel specialization has widened the number of options available to shippers, who make their final selection on the basis of which owner provides the best service at the least cost.

Car Carriers

The few U.S. automobile imports in the early post-war period were easily handled by general cargo vessels. The growth in U.S. automobile imports in the 1950s and 1960s spurred the development of first the car-bulk and then the pure car (Ro-Ro) carrier by owners who specialized in this trade.

The first car-bulk carrier was a conventional geared-bulk carrier that was altered to carry hoistable car decks. The car decks were stowed on the main deck when the vessel was carrying bulk cargoes of grain, phosrock, coal, and other commodities from the U.S. to Europe or Japan. After discharging the bulk cargo, the bottom deck was lowered and cars were loaded, one at a time, by the ship's gear and secured to the deck. As each deck was filled with automobiles, the next deck was lowered in place until the entire hold was filled with car decks loaded with automobiles. The adaptation of the geared-bulk carrier to the automobile and steel products trades raised the effective utilization of these vessels from 50% to 100%, making them very competitive for handling U.S. commodity exports and automobile and steel products imports.

As foreign automobile manufacturers were carving out their 20–25% share of the U.S. market, car-bulk carriers were built specifically to combine the dry bulk and automobile trades. They ranged from 20,000–40,000 dwt and could carry 1,500–3,000 automobiles. The largest car-bulk carrier is a 63,000-dwt vessel which carries 4,000 automobiles on its ten decks. Modern car-bulk carriers have decks that can be hoisted and stowed in the holds or folded to the sides of the hold prior to loading. The volume capacity is reduced somewhat by the space taken up by the car decks and their supporting structures.

Single-purpose, pure car (Ro-Ro) carriers with fixed decks transport automobiles more economically than car-bulk carriers because of their larger automobile-carrying capacity, higher speed, and shorter port turnaround time where several thousand automobiles can be driven on or off in a day. The higher the state of the bulk carrier market, the less the differential dollars/automobile freight charge between the two types of vessels because car-bulk carriers return to Europe or Japan with back-haul bulk cargoes while pure car carriers usually return in ballast. Pure car carriers dominate the Japan/Europe automobile trade as there are few backhaul bulk cargoes in the 20,000–40,000-ton range for car-bulk carriers.

Although pure car carriers return in ballast, combining automobile trades increases the loaded legs of a voyage relative to the ballast legs. For example, a pure car carrier combining Japanese automobile exports to the U.S. East Coast with European automobile exports to the U.S. West Coast can raise its utilization rate to 67%.

	Voyage distance of loaded leg	Voyage distance of ballast leg
Northern Europe/U.S. West Coast	7,700	—
U.S. West Coast/Japan	—	5,100
Japan/U.S. East Coast	9,900	—
U.S. East Coast/northern Europe	—	3,500
Total	17,600	8,600
Distance		
Loaded Legs	17,600	
Round-Trip Voyage	26,200	
Vessel Utilization	67%	

In addition to pure car carriers shortening the effective ballast voyage by combining European exports to the U.S. with Japanese exports to Europe, pure car carriers hauling Japanese exports to Europe can achieve the same objective by taking on a return cargo of automobiles from Europe to South Africa, the Persian Gulf, Australia, or, best of all from an owner's viewpoint, Japan. However, Japan does not presently permit large-scale imports of automobiles.

Pure car carriers fill the base or core needs of automobile cost of transportation, while car-bulk carriers, with their flexibility to shift trading patterns, satisfy the exporters' marginal needs. An owner of a pure car carrier accepts the risk of a single-purpose vessel, hoping it will be employed as long as there are any car-bulk carriers trading in automobiles. The risk of being forced to lay up the vessel becomes real when there are no more car-bulk carriers to relet to the bulk commodity trades. On the other hand, owners of car-bulk carriers feel more comfortable with a vessel with a wide range of trading flexibility that compensates for the risk of being the first to be laid off in times of excess shipping capacity in the automobile trades.

Parcel Tankers

Necessity is the mother of invention. Owners developed the forest products and car carrier businesses to employ their liquid capital assets profitably. The parcel tanker business was started by owners seeking a means to employ their fixed capital assets profitably.

During a depressed tanker market in the early 1960s, a few owners of small tankers with segregated (independent) tank systems, supported by their brokers, canvassed the chemical and petrochemical companies for cargoes. The marketing managers of these companies did not ignore the possibilities of expanding foreign sales. However, there was hardly any incentive to do so if a chemical sold for $200 per ton in the U.S., $250 per ton in Europe, and an owner of a general cargo vessel wanted $60 per ton to transport 300-ton lots or parcels of the chemical in his deep tanks. The picture would be different if an owner of a tanker with segregated tanks approached the marketing manager with an offer to transport 1,000 tons of the cargo for $30 per ton on condition that the owner could find parcels of other chemicals or cargoes which would fill up his vessel. Thus, the growth in the international trade of chemicals and petrochemicals was brought about by the low-cost transportation of collecting parcels of diverse liquid cargo shipments on a single vessel that was operated with a small profit margin in a depressed market.

Further economies were introduced by combining the chemical, petrochemical, vegetable oil, tallow, and lubricating oil trades between the United States, Europe, and Japan with backhaul cargoes of coconut oil from the Philippines, palm oil from Malaysia, and molasses from sugar-producing nations. A modern 25,000–35,000-dwt parcel tanker has 40–50 independent tank and cargo-handling systems, each constructed of materials such as stainless steel or coated with epoxy, zinc silicate, polyurethane, or rubber to handle a wide variety of cargoes.*

The parcel tanker business is very complex. The shoreside marketing staff must be able to cover the market of a wide variety of shippers and must solicit cargoes that are compatible both in quantity and char-

*A detailed technical discussion on parcel and chemical tankers is contained in "Chemical Tankers," Fairplay International, London.

acteristics with the uncommitted tanks onboard the vessel. A highly qualified and responsible crew inspects the assigned tanks prior to loading the shipment to ensure they have been properly cleaned and are free of residue (including odors) to prevent contamination. They also make the proper valve lineup to ensure that the cargo is pumped into the designated tanks and sample, monitor, and (if necessary) maintain the shipment within the prescribed temperature range. The shoreside engineering staff, cooperating with marketing and shipbuilding personnel, must design highly specialized vessels whose tank configurations (size, coatings, or construction material and location) are most apt to fit the future trading patterns of a wide range of cargoes.

Parcel tanker operators stay in business because of their demonstrated level of service in preserving the commercial value of shipments of chemicals, petrochemicals, and other cargoes. The reluctance of shippers to entrust their cargoes to inexperienced owners and the special nature of the marketing, operating, and design engineering of the vessels are formidable barriers of entry for newcomers in the trade. The pioneering companies (Panocean-Anco, Stolt-Nielsen, and Odfjell) have a virtual monopoly on this business, collectively owning about 80% of the world parcel tanker fleet. With such control, one might expect that the monopolies' excess profits would be the rule rather than the exception. However, 80% control is not enough.

During depressed times in the tanker market, small tankers invade the vegetable oil, molasses, and less-sophisticated chemical trades. High-value chemicals transported in small quantities are subject to market penetration by tanktainers shipped on container vessels. The most vulnerable aspect of this business is the effect of the cost of transportation on the volume of trade. Much of the volume of international trade in chemicals is based on differential pricing between importing and exporting nations. As shipping costs increase, the volume of trade decreases because there is no longer an incentive for trade. Moreover, for areas with a perennial shortage of a certain type of chemical, higher shipping costs may provide the necessary incentive to expand capacity or to alter production schedules to become more self-sufficient.

A characteristic of the chemical trade is its volatility in volume of trade as chemical plants approach full-capacity production. To illustrate this phenomenon, suppose two independent chemical plants, one in the U.S. and the other in Europe, produce 100,000 tons of chemical A and chemical B each at maximum capacity. In Table 8.2, European demand for chemicals A and B remains unchanged, while U.S. demand changes. Both plants import all their feedstock needs.

TABLE 8.2*

Time period	Incremental demand in U.S. for:		U.S. plant production & utilization			European plant production & utilization			Shipping demand parcel tankers	
	Tons A	Tons B	Tons A	Tons B	%	Tons A	Tons B	%	Eastbound Tons A	Westbound Tons B
0	—	—	40	40	80	30	30	60	0	0
1	5	5	45	45	90	30	30	60	0	0
2	5	5	50	50	100	30	30	60	0	0
3	5	5	55	45	100	30	40	70	0	10
4	5	5	60	40	100	30	50	80	0	20
5	5	5	65	35	100	30	60	90	0	30
6	5	0	70	30	100	30	65	95	0	35
7	5	0	75	25	100	30	70	100	0	40
8	0	0	80	20	100	25	75	100	5	45
9	0	0	90	10	100	15	85	100	15	55
10	−5	0	85	10	95	15	85	100	15	55
11	0	0	85	15	100	15	80	95	15	50
12	0	0	80	15	95	20	80	100	10	50
13	0	0	80	20	100	20	75	95	10	45
14	0	0	75	20	95	25	75	100	5	45
15	0	0	75	25	100	25	70	95	5	40
16	0	0	70	25	95	30	70	100	0	40
17	0	0	70	30	100	30	65	95	0	35

Time period	Total shipping demand for feedstock for both plants	Total shipping demand for parcel tankers	Commentary
0	140	0	Both plants are operating at less than full capacity. There is no incentive for international trade because the price differentials of A and B in the U.S. and European markets are less than the transportation costs.
1	150	0	Incremental demand in the United
2	160	0	States is satisfied by increased domestic production.
3	170	10	Suppose the profit potential for
4	180	20	producing A is greater in the U.S. than
5	190	30	producing B. The U.S. chemical

continued

TABLE 8.2* continued

Time period	Total shipping demand for feedstock for both plants	Total shipping demand for parcel tankers	Commentary
6	195	35	company maximizes its profits by
7	200	40	increasing the production of A. Shortages of B are satisfied by imports from Europe.
8	200	50	Both plants are operating at full capacity.
9	200	70	If B is more profitable to produce than A in Europe, both chemical companies maximize profits by concentrating production on the most profitable chemical, importing the other.
10	195	70	The demand for A falls by 5,000 tons in the U.S. The U.S. plant manager initially cuts back on the production of A, lowering his plant utilization to 95%.
11	195	65	The U.S. plant manager can maximize his profits if he brings the plant to full utilization by increasing production of B and reducing imports accordingly. The European plant manager initially reacts to a fall in the exports of B by cutting back on the production of B, which lowers his plant utilization to 95%.
12	195	60	The European plant manager, seeing his plant underutilized, maximizes his profits by increasing the production of A, which reduces imports of A by the same amount. The U.S. plant manager reacts to a fall in exports of A by cutting back on the production of A.
13	195	55	The swapping of excess plant capacity
14	195	50	continues until the European plant
15	195	45	manager can no longer increase
16	195	40	production of A because there are no
17	195	35	more imports to displace.

*All figures in thousands of tons.

In this hypothetical case, the demand for parcel tankers to handle the finished product has fallen by half while the demand for shipping capacity to transport the feedstock has decreased by only 2.5% from peak production levels.

During times of heightened economic activity when chemical plants are nearing full capacity, demand for parcel tankers grows as plant managers begin to maximize their profits by concentrating on the most profitable product line mix. This forces users of the least profitable portion of the product line to start supplementing their needs with imports. This has also been experienced in the clean products tanker trades where interregional trading of refined oil products blossoms when refineries approach full utilization. These trades fade at the first stages of declining refinery runs.

Parcel tankers trade mostly in semiliner service, maintaining a scheduled service between different areas of the world but varying the actual port calls, depending on the circumstances. Some chemicals, such as sulphuric acid, phosphoric acid, caustic soda, liquid ammonia, and liquid chlorine, are traded in sufficient volumes to warrant building single-purpose chemical carriers. Most of the vessels handling these hazardous cargoes are small, expensive, and require experienced crews. Large phosphoric acid carriers of 22,000 dwt have been built for the phosphoric acid production plants in phosrock exporting nations. Large LPG carriers sometimes trade in liquid ammonia.

A nonhazardous liquid cargo transported in bulk parcels is wine. Wine carriers gave European and California wine producers a transportation alternative for selling wine in the eastern U.S. Oceanborne wine movements can be handled as break-bulk cargoes in general-cargo vessels, containerized for shipment on container vessels, shipped in bulk in tanktainers, or shipped in a wine carrier. The California wine companies have the additional options of transporting wine by rail, truck, tank cars, or tanktainers to the eastern market.

The international trade in fertilizers is another example of a trade born from desperation. During one of the periodic shipping depressions, bulk carrier owners, with help from their brokers, approached the fertilizer industry with offers of cheap transportation. This encouraged the building of large-capacity fertilizer plants designed to serve a wide geographic area instead of the usual larger number of small-capacity plants primarily serving local needs. This established the international fertilizer trade and a new demand for bulk carriers. The worldwide trading of fertilizers and chemicals is the beneficial side effects of depressed market conditions.

Refrigerated Vessels

Refrigerated vessels (reefers) may be built to serve a particular market segment such as the year-round banana and frozen foodstuffs trades. Alternatively, they may be built to carry various seasonal fresh fruits and vegetables. The intended trading pattern influences the design of the multideck reefer spaces and the choice of ventilation, air circulation, refrigeration, and cargo-handling systems. On some reefers, conveyor belts link the reefer spaces in the vessel with the shoreside cold storage warehouses, while others use forklifts to move the palletized cartons of fresh and frozen foodstuffs. Crews are responsible for preserving the cargo while onboard the vessel and during its transfer. The commercial value of banana cargoes is in the hands of the crew who controls the ripening process by the temperature in the reefer spaces.

TABLE 8.3
PRINCIPAL REEFER TRADES

Commodity	Major exporting nations	Major importing nations	Year-round or seasonal trade
Bananas	Central and South America, West Africa Taiwan, the Philippines	U.S., Europe, and Japan	Year-round
Frozen meat	Australia, New Zealand, Argentina	U.S., Europe	Year-round
Frozen fish	Scandinavia, Canada	Mediterranean nations, Japan, and U.S.	Year-round
Fresh produce	Australia, New Zealand, North Africa, South Africa	Europe	Seasonal
Citrus fruits	California, Florida, North Africa, South America, Israel	Canada, northern Europe, and Japan	Seasonal

The reefer trades offer little opportunity for combining. Reefers usually return to the exporting nation without any cargoes except for small break-bulk shipments in the reefer spaces or bulky cargoes stowed topside. Reefer chartering is calculated in cents per cubic foot of reefer space. Although the business is dominated by Salen Reefer Services, competition still abounds from operators of reefer vessels not associated with Salen Reefer Services; container, Ro-Ro, and general cargo vessels with large reefer space capacity; and container vessels with refrigerated containers.

Liner service companies can enhance their profitability if they balance the load factors on their vessels in both directions of a trade. The containerized traffic from Europe to Australia was unbalanced on the outbound in relation to the inbound voyage. The containerization of the Australia and New Zealand frozen meat trade to Europe tended to balance load factors and added a new competitive factor in the reefer trades.

Bulk Cement Carriers

Bagged and bulk shipments of cement are usually carried on general-cargo vessels, small-bulk carriers, and Lash barges. Self-unloading bulk cement carriers lower the cost of transportation by reducing shoreside labor costs and port turnaround times. Bulk cement carriers require special terminal facilities, and those serving the U.S. market must meet air particulate (dust) environmental regulations. This has created a double class of bulk cement carriers, similar to a double class of LPG carriers, which can and cannot enter U.S. ports. Bulk cement carriers serving the U.S. market with shipments of cement from Europe, the Philippines, and South Korea return with backhaul cargoes of grain to enhance their profitability.

Liquid Sulphur Carriers

Sulphur and its derivatives, such as sulphuric acid, are key components in the production of fertilizers, rubber, paints, paper, and synthetic fibers and in the processing of ores. A large intraregional European trade in sulphur originates from Poland and France plus oceanborne imports from the United States, Canada, and Mexico. The Caribbean refineries have also become sources of sulphur because they must desulphurize home and industrial heating oils destined for the

U.S. market. South Africa, India, and Australia import their needs largely from Iran and Iraq.

Much of the sulphur in international trade is in a dry, granular state well suited for transport in conventional bulk carriers. However, nearly half of U.S. Gulf Coast exports to Europe are transported in liquid sulphur carriers. Early liquid sulphur carriers were converted tankers fitted with heating coils to keep the sulphur liquefied. Later on, single-purpose liquid sulphur carriers with coiled, self-supporting, insulated tanks were built. They offered short port turnaround time and easy handling shoreside. Since liquid sulphur must fit into a sulphur company's distribution system, most liquid sulphur carriers are built under long-term contractual arrangements (charters) with sulphur companies. One liquid sulphur carrier, the *Marine Sulphur Queen*, achieved some degree of notoriety by disappearing in the Bermuda Triangle in 1963. Some ascribed its demise as the work of extraterrestrial forces; others felt it was the work of hot sulphur from a ruptured tank reacting with sea water.

Cruise Vessels

Some general cargo vessels in liner service earn a little pocket money by carrying a few passengers. For passenger freighters, such as those that operate between Great Britain and South Africa, the revenue from passengers topside is just as important a consideration as the revenue from freight below decks. Since vessels in break-bulk trades spend a considerable amount of time in port and moor close to the heart of the city, passengers have the time and are conveniently located to tour the environs by day, spending the nights onboard the ship. Their major restriction is to be on the vessel at departure time. Some liner service shipping companies offer their passengers the opportunity to stay behind and catch the next scheduled call by a company vessel or travel cross-country to another port to catch a company vessel. Life on these vessels is comfortable, though a bit spartan, with plenty of time for rest, contemplation, and conversation with fellow passengers and crew.

For those who require more stimulation, cruise vessels fitted with gyroscopic stabilizers and offering a wide variety of entertainment carry hundreds of pleasure-seeking passengers from three-day excursions to world cruises. Many cruise vessels are fairly old with a low capital element relative to the costs of operation. The high cost of building new vessels has encouraged investments in modernizing the existing fleet to prolong its useful life rather than building replacements. Cruise vessels are just the opposite of large crude carriers and liquefied gas carriers where capital costs far exceed the cost of manning. Some national flag cruise operators have shifted to flags of convenience/ necessity to avoid union wage scales and restrictive labor regulations, which have made cruise vessel operation under certain national flags uncompetitive. The United States, for the most part, bars national flag transfers, and operators of U.S. flag cruise vessel and passenger liners serving international routes have simply gone out of business because of high manning costs.

The day of the luxurious cross-Atlantic ocean liner, epitomized by the *Queen Mary* (now a floating hotel in California), the *Queen Elizabeth* (a fire-gutted hulk in Hong Kong), the *France*, (presently being refitted) and the *United States* (laid-up) are over, casualties of the airplane and changing tastes. Transatlantic sailings are still made during the summer season on vessels such as the *QE-2* where passengers have the option of flying one way and sailing the other. Many large European shipping companies have a long-standing tradition in passenger liners, passenger freighters, cruise vessels, and ferries. They have maintained a profitable operation in spite of the seasonal aspects of vacation travel, high fixed labor costs, and the dependence on the level of consumer discretionary spending. It is interesting to note that some cruise vessel operators were not hurt during the recession of 1975 and 1976. Some European operators reported more profits than ever from the more luxurious segment of the cruise business as the well-to-do decided to help inflation along in consuming their net worth. Cruise vessel operators sailing out of Miami benefited from Americans giving up their European vacation plans for Caribbean cruises.

The cruise ferry combines the high-speed ferry with the amenities of a cruise vessel. The ship may be employed either as a cruise vessel, as a ferry, or as a combination of both. A luxury cruise ferry liner service, which operated between Great Britain, Spain, and the Canary Islands, allowed passengers to drive their automobiles off the vessel at any port and return when they wished to catch another scheduled call.

Integrated Tug Barges

The integrated tug barge (ITB) looks like any conventional vessel. The only difference is that the propulsion plant, the tug, can be disengaged from the cargo-carrying portion of the vessel, the barge. The tug and the barge are independent of one another and are mechanically linked to form a unit.

The economic advantage of the ITB is its high utilization on high-volume, short-haul trades. Suppose a refinery operator has a large movement of refined oil products to a terminal about 300 miles away, or a day's sail. A tanker requiring two days to load, two days to discharge, and two days at sea can complete a round trip every six days. If the refinery throughput requires a shipment every other day, three tankers would be necessary.

This movement can also be handled by a system of three barges and one tug. At any point in time, one barge is being loaded, another is being discharged, and the third is in transit. Since it takes the same time (two days) for the ITB to make a round trip as it does to load and discharge a barge, the ITB arrives in port just in time to disengage the barge, engage the other, turn around, and proceed back. If the cost of the tug is 50% of the cost of the tanker and the cost of the barge is also 50% of the cost of the tanker, the total cost of the three barges and one tug is the same as two tankers. Thus, the ITB system offers a one-third saving in capital costs and a two-thirds saving in manning costs (only one crew rather than three), smaller maintenance charges (only one propulsion plant rather than three), and smaller marine insurance premiums (less capital value and fewer crew members) than the three tankers. High-volume, short-haul movements are also served by conventional tugs and barges which operate at about half the speed of an ITB and are less costly to build. The decision on which system is preferable is a matter of cost and service.

The U.S. Coast Guard regulates the minimum manning levels of U.S. flag vessels. Older steam turbine, nonautomated U.S. flag tankers have a required manning level of 40–45 men. Modern diesel-driven tankers with automated engine rooms need a crew of about 22 men, while an ocean-going tug is manned with about 15 men. Since an ITB is manned as an ocean-going tug, a few ITBs have been built as replacement vessels for the U.S. handy-sized tanker fleet. A new conventional tanker, performing the same function, would have to be manned with about 50% more crew members.

Offshore Drilling Rigs

The heyday of the large crude carrier reflected a time when a plentiful supply of cheap crude oil was available to fuel an expanding world economy. The factors influencing the demand for crude carriers were a growing world population, greater industrial production, an increasing per capita consumption of oil products (a measure of a rising standard of living), and a greater reliance on remote Middle Eastern sources of crude oil. Whether the oil crisis in 1973 was inevitable or avoidable is irrelevant. It occurred. As a result, every oil-importing nation in the world began or intensified its search for indigenous sources of crude oil. For nations bordering the ocean, the onshore search did not stop at the water's edge. Even crude oil exporting nations such as the Soviet Union, Mexico, and many OPEC countries began exploring in offshore waters to nail down the extent of their oil reserves or to augment onshore production.

There are three basic types of offshore drilling rigs: the jackup rig, the semisubmersible rig, and the drillship. Water depth, the distance from the ocean surface to the ocean bed, is the primary discriminating factor among offshore drilling rigs and not the depth of the well that the rig can drill into the ocean bottom.

The jackup rig is a barge-type structure with three or four legs. When positioned over a drilling site, the legs are jacked down until they rest firmly on the ocean bottom. Then the barge structure jacks itself up 100 feet above the ocean's surface to avoid being struck by waves. The maximum operating depth of 300–350 feet is determined by the length of the legs. This, in turn, is a function of the stability of the rig both in transit when the legs are jacked up and in operation when the legs are jacked down. A jackup rig under tow has a speed of 3–5 knots (about 100 miles a day). It is an ungainly sight with its legs extending 400 feet above the low barge structure. Several have been lost at sea during transits because of their marginal stability, and others have collapsed during drilling operations when the ocean bottom gave way under one of the legs.

Semisubmersible rigs (semis) and drillships are used for oil exploration in water depths in excess of 300–350 feet. Semis consist of a lower set of submersible hulls or pontoons attached by cylindrical columns to an upper structure which holds the drilling equipment. During transit, the lower set of pontoons is empty. Semis are generally towed at 3–5 knots from one site to another, but some are self-propelled with speeds of 9–10 knots. Once over a drilling site, the pontoons are flooded. The rig increases its draft in the water to reduce its exposure to wind and wave action. The upper structure is left clear of the ocean surface in this semisubmerged state. The rig is a very stable platform for drilling in all but the most severe weather.

The first drillships were conversions of 10,000–25,000-dwt tankers, general cargo ships, and bulk and ore carriers. Ore carriers were preferred because of the added strength (scantlings) built into their hulls. Drillships are usually used in calmer waters than semis because they are less stable in rough weather. Drillships have a much greater storage capacity for supplies than semis for independent operation. Whereas jackups and semis require continual shoreside logistic support for drill pipes, mud (the lubricating medium in drilling), stores, and equipment, which are carried to the rig in small supply vessels, a drillship can operate independently in remote areas for months on end. In addition, drillships are self-propelled with speeds of 10–15 knots. This shortens the transit time to arrive on station and avoids towing expense.

Semis and drillships are kept on station by anchors or by a dynamic positioning system. For rigs using anchor systems, the limiting factor in determining the maximum depth of water for drilling operations is the length of the anchor chain. Most semis and drillships equipped with anchors are limited to water depths of 1,000 feet or less, although a few can drill in water depths up to 1,800 feet. Anchor-handling tugs place and retrieve the eight or so anchors holding a semi or drillship on station. For drilling in deeper waters, a drillship or semi must be fitted with a dynamic positioning system, which consists of underwater sounding devices and computer-controlled variable positioning propulsion units to keep the drillship or semi on station. Dynamic positioning adds to the initial cost and to the daily running expenditure for the additional operating technicians and the fuel consumed by the positioning units. A drillship or semi with dynamic positioning may be capable of drilling in waters of a depth of 10,000 feet. If the rig were to operate in waters with a depth of 10,000 feet and drill a well 10,000 feet into the ocean bottom, the rig would be sitting on top of four miles of drill pipe.

Offshore drilling activities create business opportunities for owners of supply vessels for replenishment services, crewboats and helicopters for crew transfers, anchor handling tugs for anchor-equipped semis and drillships, tugs for towing jackups and semis, and salvage, rescue, and firefighting vessels.

Offshore drilling rigs are generally involved with exploratory work. Once an oil field has been discovered, defined, and the decision has been made to bring the field on stream, fixed production platforms—some as high as the Empire State Building—are erected onshore or in shallow waters, towed out to sea, flooded down, and secured upright over the site. Drill packs are installed on the platform to drill a series of production wells, which first extend vertically down from the production platform and, once well into the sea bed, curve out in various directions to tap the field. Production control and oil-gas separating equipment is installed on the platform and connections are made to underwater pipelines. The pipelines, measuring up to 36 inches or more in diameter, are laid by specialized pipelaying barges costing as much as $100 million. The pipelines connect the production platforms in an oil field with onshore tank farms. Tankers are sometimes used to transport crude from a production platform prior to completion of the underwater pipeline. In a few cases, tankers are the sole means of transport from the platform to the refinery.

The cost of a production platform rises geometrically with water depth. As oil field development moves into deeper waters, there is an ever-increasing incentive to switch from a platform to a subsea production system located on the ocean bottom which performs all the functions of a production platform except drilling production wells. This system expands the potential workload for offshore drilling rigs in drilling production wells in addition to exploration wells.

The oil industry has traditionally contracted much of its drilling needs from independent drilling contractors. As offshore exploration increased in the early 1970s, shipowners joined the offshore drilling companies in offering drilling services to the oil companies. Scandinavian owners, flushed with record profits that would have been heavily taxed if not reinvested, ordered rigs (mainly semis) to shield their profits from taxation, to diversify their business interests, and to participate in the development of oil resources located in their backyard. They often formed joint ventures with American drilling interests because of the scarcity of qualified non-American drilling crews. The Scandinavian owners supplied the rigs and the crews willing and able to work in 100-foot seas and 100-knot gales.

Boom times hit the offshore drilling industry after the oil crisis in 1973. Study after study predicted good times for the indefinite future, based on calculations of the number of wells that must be drilled to explore potential oil-bearing geological structures in the millions of square miles of the world's continental shelves. These projections took into account the number of wells drilled per rig per year, the projected number of rigs in the world taking into account rigs lost at sea or made obsolete with time, and rigs under construction or on order at existing and at new rig fabrication yards. Production constraints in the form of available drilling equipment, tubular steel, skilled workers to weld tubular steel, and experienced drilling crews were also taken into consideration. The prosperity that had no end in sight in 1973/74 ended in

1976. After the bubble burst, Scandinavian owners, who had ordered semisubmersible rigs with no contractual arrangements with oil companies, bore the brunt of the suffering. For the owners of 175 jackup rigs, 120 semis, and 90 drillships in existence in 1977, some of which were idle and others operating at low-hire rates, the critical factor for future profitability was not the potential number of exploration wells to be drilled but the amount of exploration funds set aside for offshore work by the oil companies.

TABLE 8.4
COUNTRIES SHARING WATERS OF POSSIBLE DISPUTE

Egypt and Israel
Greece and Turkey (Aegean Sea)
Iraq and Kuwait
Mainland China and Vietnam
Norway and the Soviet Union
Philippines and Malaysia
Spain and Morocco (Strait of Gibraltar)
Taiwan and the Philippines
Taiwan and Mainland China
Taiwan, Mainland China, and Japan near Senkaka Island
Tunisia and Libya
Tunisia and Malta
U.S. and Canada (Georges Bank)
U.S. and Mexico in waters offshore the western boundary line
U.K. and Argentina (Falkland Islands)
U.K. and Denmark (Faeroe Islands)
U.K. and Ireland
U.K. and France (Celtic Sea)
Venezuela and Colombia
Venezuela and Trinidad

(*Offshore*, March 1977)

The level of after-tax profits is an important consideration in the rationing process of capital funds for oil companies. The U.S. Tax Reduction Act of 1975 increased the tax load of U.S. oil companies by taking away the oil depletion allowance. This reduced after-tax profits and, consequently, the size of exploration budgets. Some nations are not willing to underwrite the risks of oil exploration (the cost of sinking a dry hole) in their offshore waters, and yet they leave little in the way of a reward net of fees, royalties, and taxes in case of a successful strike. Other nations have a history of unilaterally abrogating signed contracts without due compensation. Norwegian owners who ordered rigs on speculation were particularly hard-hit by their government's decision to hold back exploration and development activities in the Norwegian sector of the North Sea and prohibit exploration north of the sixty-second parallel. Offshore exploration is discouraged in waters between sovereign states where there is a real or potential dispute on the ownership of potential oil fields.

The softening of the offshore rig market in the mid-1970s was caused by too many rigs for the combined offshore exploration budgets of the world oil companies and state oil agencies. Offshore drilling was restored to financial health in 1979 when the amount of funds set aside for offshore exploration was sufficient to employ the entire world rig fleet. This has very little to do with broad generalizations on the desirability of energy self-sufficiency for oil importing nations and on the number of wells that must be drilled to accomplish this goal.

9

The Vessel Operator

The vessel operator must keep a vessel in a condition of readiness for service at sea. He may be the vessel's owner or a ship manager operating a vessel for a fee, with no ownership interest. Sometimes owners manage vessels for others, in addition to their own, on some form of contractual basis. Large fleet operators, as owners or managers, can obtain volume discounts for stores, equipment, bunkers, insurance, and repairs that are unavailable to an operator of a few vessels. Some small fleet owners have found the cost of using an established, well-experienced owner or ship managing firm less expensive than setting up an operating organization. Most owners, however, prefer to deal directly with operational matters through their own organizations rather than through third parties who may not be motivated or able to give their full attention to their vessels.

The three most important operating expenses are crews, maintenance and repair, and insurance premiums. Though each of these items will be discussed separately, bear in mind that the crew's preformance affects maintenance and repair costs, insurance premiums, and the vessel's capacity to earn its keep. Other operating expense items are stores and equipment, lubricating oils (consumed in greater quantities by diesel than steam-propelled vessels), and general expenses, which are mainly expenditures made by the Master of the vessel plus an allocation to cover the costs of the shoreside staff. Voyage costs (bunkers, canal tolls, port dues, cargo-handling charges) may or may not be the responsibility of the operator, depending on the nature of the employment of the vessel.

Crew Costs

Crew costs include direct wages and indirect costs for training, pension benefits, guaranteed employment obligations, living expenses onboard the vessel, and travel expenses incurred during crew changes. Wages vary considerably, depending on the nationality of the crew. Maritime nations of the industrialized world that have imposed exclusionary manning provisions on vessels flying their flags have given maritime unions the means to win substantial wage and pension benefits. Many national flag operators of developing nations with mandatory citizenship requirements for manning their vessels and flag-of-convenience/necessity operators, who have complete freedom in selecting a crew as long as key positions are filled by licensed personnel, do not have to pay U.S., northern Europe, Australian, and Japanese wage scales. Even if the flag-of-convenience/necessity operators employ European officers paying European rates for their services, the unlicensed seamen may be from Hong Kong, the Philippines, South Korea, Taiwan, India, or Pakistan. Firms in Hong Kong, South Korea, and elsewhere provide officers and seamen for flag-of-convenience/necessity operators.

A national flag operator of an industrialized nation pays union wage scales applicable to that nation. Even company unions not affiliated with national maritime labor organizations do not deviate much from their wage scales. In fact, they may even exceed these levels as an inducement for their members not to join a national labor movement. Wages paid by flag-of-convenience/necessity operators are negotiated between an operator and a crew. The level of wages may be higher (on an after-tax basis) or lower than wages paid by national flag operators, depending on the circumstances. Although a flag-of-convenience/ necessity vessel operator can shift from one nationality to another if wages or performance fall out of line, many operators and crews have developed a bond of loyalty after years of association. Billets in an operator's shoreside organization may be filled by experienced seagoing personnel from his vessels. Family ties may be another bond cementing an operator to the crews manning his vessels.

National flag operators of developing nations and flag-of-convenience/necessity operators of conventional vessels have small indirect costs for training, pensions, and inefficient utilization of personnel mandated by union work rules. In contrast, Japanese flag operators must provide a liberal paid vacation plan, maintain a crew 50% above actual manning levels, provide for lifetime security including not being permitted to disband a crew of a laid-up vessel, and pay three times the wages received by other Far Eastern crews. The United States had the world's record for the highest direct and indirect crew costs for most of the post-war period, but the gaps between the U.S. and North European, Australian, and Japanese costs have narrowed considerably. In recent years, Scandinavian and Japanese manning costs equaled or exceeded American costs.

The standard of living onboard a vessel varies widely with the nationality of the crew. American, northern European, and Australian crews demand air-conditioned private rooms and baths, top-quality high-protein meals, adequate clothing allowances, and amenities such as libraries, swimming pools, movies, and often a gymnasium. At the other end of the spectrum, some Asian crews have bunk beds, fish and rice meals, and a hole in the deck for toilet facilities. Travel expenses can be minimized if the vessel occasionally calls on the home port of the crew. Likewise, a European manned crude carrier has much lower travel expenses if it is trading from the Persian Gulf to Europe rather than to Japan.

Flag-of-convenience/necessity operators have a formidable economic advantage over national flag operators of the industrialized world. They can employ cheaper crews, both in terms of direct and indirect costs, change crew nationalities if necessary, pay low vessel registration fees, limit their liability by means of one-ship holding companies (also available to many national flag operators), and not pay taxes on profits. Some national flag operators—forced to pay high union wages, conform to labor and government regulations, and be liable for payment of taxes on profits—would barely survive the competitive onslaught of national flags of developing nations and flags-of-convenience/necessity were it not for government maritime aid programs. These take the shape of guaranteed employment schemes (cargo and flag preference programs) and financial aids (government guaranteed financings, shipyard grants, and operating subsidies). Some national flag shipping companies depend on government maritime aid programs for their very existence.

Maintenance and Repair

Maintenance and repair (M & R) expenses are quite small when a vessel is first delivered because the equipment is new and under manufacturers' warranties and the performance of the vessel is under a shipyard guarantee. M & R expenses increase as a vessel ages, depending on initial quality standards, the types of cargoes, the areas of employment, and the operating and maintenance performance of the crew.

Drydocking for hull preservation work is a routine maintenance item. The underwater portion of the hull is sandblasted to remove marine growths, rust, and old paint, and the hull is repainted with several coats of different types of marine paints which protect it from the corrosive properties of sea water and inhibit marine growth by the slow release of toxic chemicals. Marine growth is a generic term covering a wide range of plant and animal life (including barnacles) which impedes the passage of a vessel. Barnacles are made up of a thousand different species of marine crustaceans which make their home on rocks, pilings, driftwood, seawood, clams, oysters, whales, and vessel hulls. Ships waiting nearly a year to offload their cargoes in the tropical waters of Nigeria in 1975/76 were barely able to get underway after being encrusted with several feet of marine growth.

Marine paint companies compete vigorously on the basis of price, service, and the real or perceived attributes of their products. They have improved the adhesion properties of the paint, its leeching rate, and the effectiveness of chemical additives to curb marine growths. They have enhanced the slipperiness factor, which reduces the resistance of water to the forward motion of the vessel and generates savings in fuel consumption. The upshot of all this is that drydockings for hull preservation are now every 18–24 months rather than every year. Vessel operators have also resorted to "shave and haircut" drydockings, where only specific affected areas of the hull are sandblasted and painted, and to listing the vessel and treating the portion of the hull above the waterline. The adoption of these cost-saving techniques and lengthening the normal drydocking interval because of improvements in marine paints have reduced hull preservation costs. The market mechanism of owners competing for the available business eventually passes these hull preservation cost savings to the users. The free market rewards the innovator who improves the quality or efficiency of his product with enhanced profits and forces the industry to follow suit. Then, through competitive pressures, the free market takes the profits away and passes them on as savings to the consumer.

One firm kills marine growths by vibrations set off by detonating very small explosives on a net placed under a vessel in port. A more convenient means to kill marine growths is to take advantage of the environment. Salt water marine growths die and fall off a vessel's hull in fresh water ports or rivers. Tropical marine growths have difficulty surviving the rigors of calls to cold-water ports. The latest variation in environmental hull cleaning is a visit to Tokyo Bay where pollution has reached a level sufficient to purge a hull of what must be some of the world's hardiest rascals.

Classification societies were first organized as a means for marine insurance underwriters to keep tabs on the physical condition of their assets. All vessels, including tugs, barges, dredges, and offshore drilling rigs, are built and inspected at set intervals by a classification society. Lloyd's Register, American Bureau of Shipping, Norske Veritas, and Bureau Veritas are nongovernment, nonprofit, independent organizations supported by fees charged to operators and shipbuilders for services rendered. They certify the soundness and seaworthiness of merchant vessels from design to retirement. The rules by which vessels are built and inspected are established by naval architects, marine engineers, and other speciality engineers. Each vessel has a number of certificates which must be kept updated for it to "remain in class." Detailed computerized records are kept on every vessel registered with a classification society listing all vessel particulars, a history of changes or modifications made to the vessel, and a status on all material deficiencies.

Some operators participate in a continuous survey program. Much of the equipment and machinery is inspected by a local representative of a classification society when a vessel is in port. A continuous survey program spreads out the cost of keeping a vessel in class and gives an operator a greater sense of confidence on the eventual findings and costs of the obligatory four-year special surveys. However, a continuous survey program does not lend itself to a large chartered crude carrier shuttling between oil terminals with only 24 hours of port time and with each hour delay costing $2,000.

All vessels are drydocked every four years for a special survey.* The rudder, shaft, and propeller are pulled for inspection, cargo spaces are opened up, and the main engines, auxiliary electrical equipment and machinery, ship control, communication, navigation, anchor and cargo-handling gear, and all other equipment (not already taken care of in a continuous survey program) are readied for inspection by classification society surveyors. Even the thickness of the steel in the hull is measured. In short, everything that can be inspected is inspected. Special surveys become more costly as a vessel ages, particularly if steel

*Some operators with a good operating history qualify for an additional year of grace, or a total of five years, between delivery of a vessel and its first survey and between the first and second surveys. After that, special surveys occur every four years.

must be replaced in the hull. Many vessels are scrapped during a weak market environment, not so much as a result of a special survey as in anticipation of one.

Some classification societies are authorized by nations of registry to inspect a vessel and issue SOLAS (Safety of Life at Sea) and Load Line (deadweight markings on the hull) certificates in accordance with the requirements of the United Nations SOLAS and Load Line Conventions. Major classification societies survey containers in addition to container vessels. They also provide inspection services for constructing pipelines, conventional and nuclear-powered electric generating plants, and oil refining and chemical processing plants.

Remaining in class is not just a condition imposed by insurance underwriters. A nation of registry requires a vessel to remain in class as a condition for flying its flag. Charterers and financial institutions insist that an operator warrants his vessel is in class before entering into a charter or loan arrangement. They also insist the owner keep his vessel in class throughout the charter period or tenure of the loan. A vessel out of class cannot fly the flag of any nation and cannot obtain insurance, charters, or capital.

Marine Insurance

The two principal types of marine insurance are hull and machinery, which insures against loss from the traditional perils of a vessel at sea, and protection and indemnity (P & I), which insures against claims arising from injury or death of crew members, passengers and third parties, loss or damage of cargo, and other matters. Hull insurance is offered by syndicates of professional marine insurance underwriters, while P & I insurance is provided by associations of shipowners.

Today's marine insurance goes back to the 1600s. An individual who had assumed a shipping risk for his own account would go to Lloyd's Coffee House in London to reduce the extent of his exposure to loss by laying off, or syndicating, a portion of the venture among his acquaintances. From this evolved Lloyd's of London. Lloyd's does not underwrite policies per se but sets the rules, approves the applications, monitors the solvency of its members, and owns the building where the underwriting is conducted. Its role is similar to the New York Stock Exchange. The London Hull Institute underwrites much of the world's hull insurance and has traditionally set industry standards. The predominance of the London Hull Institute has been eroded by the emergence of hull underwriting syndicates outside the London market, such as the American Hull Insurance Syndicate headquartered in New York. An underwriter limits the magnitude of any one shipping loss and reduces his overall exposure to risk by taking a small share of a diversified portfolio of policies. The actual settlement of a marine casualty claim is made by each member of an underwriting syndicate contributing his proportionate share.

Hull insurance covers the traditional perils of a vessel at sea including sinking, stranding, fire, collision and other matters as set forth in the London Hull Form:

> Touching the Adventures and Perils which the Underwriters are contented to bear and take upon themselves, they are the Seas, Men-of-War, Fire, Lightning, Earthquake, Enemies, Pirates, Rovers, Assailing Thieves, Jettisons, Letters of Mart and Counter-Mart, Surprisals, Takings at Sea, Arrests, Restraints and Detainments of all Kings, Princes and Peoples of what nation, condition or quality soever, Barratry of the Master and Mariners and of all other like Perils, Losses and Misfortunes that have or shall come to the Hurt, Detriment or Damage of the Vessel, or any part thereof . . . .

The *Inchmaree* was one of the early steam-propelled vessels built during the nineteenth century's transition from wood and sail to iron and steam. It suffered machinery damage which the owner claimed to be within the scope of the traditional perils at sea. The hull underwriters protested this claim in court and won. Subsequently, however, shipowners were able to prevail on the underwriters to expand the traditional perils at sea to include the machinery of steam-propelled vessels by adding the first *Inchmaree* clause. These clauses now provide coverage for accidents while the vessel is loading, discharging or handling cargo, bunkering, and for damage caused by explosions, accidental electrical machinery or generator breakdown, bursting boilers, shaft breakage, contact with aircraft, rockets, or vehicles, and negligence of charterers, repairers, crews, or pilots.

Hull underwriters can declare a vessel a total loss when the expense of recovering and repairing it exceeds the agreed or insured value of the vessel. A total loss may be actual (a vessel sinking in deep waters) or constructive (a vessel stranded on a rocky reef or sunk in shallow waters). When a vessel is declared a total loss, whether actual or constructive, the owner must tender his abandonment of claim of ownership. This must be accepted by the underwriting syndicate before the owner receives the agreed amount of the policy. Any proceeds from salvage efforts belong to the underwriters. Those contemplating raising or searching the sunken hulk of the *Andrea Doria* negotiate with the appropriate underwriting syndicate—the present owners—not with the original shipowning company.

Collision liability in hull policies limits the exposure of the underwriters to the agreed or insured value of the vessel regardless of the outcome of resulting lawsuits. Other conditions imposed by the underwriter limit their maximum exposure or liability when the vessel is under tow or pilotage. Major exclusions in hull policies which provide no compensation include damage as a consequence of capture, seizure, or arrest (lawful or otherwise), civil war, revolution, rebellion, insurrection, labor disturbances, and detonation of a mine, torpedo, or conventional or nuclear bomb. All these exclusions are covered by a separate policy called the Hull War Risks and Strikes Policy. The war risks policy is written by a different syndicate than hull insurance. It compensates an owner for damage incurred from a mine, bomb, or torpedo not carried as cargo, detonation of a nuclear weapon as long as the detonation was not hostile in intent(!), civil war, revolution, and political or labor disturbances except seizure by the Government of the United States or the country of registry. When the U.S. and Britain seized foreign flag vessels in their ports at the outbreak of both World Wars, owners received full compensation for their vested interest, including provisions for debt repayment and full insurance for damage or loss while their vessels were in wartime service. Other nations have not been so sympathetic to the interests of owners of seized vessels.

The premium for war risk insurance is quite small compared to the hull and machinery insurance premium because of the automatic termination and cancellation provisions which, clearly stated, automatically terminate and cancel the policy on any hostile detonation of nuclear weapons, requisitioning or seizing of the vessel by legal authorities, or an outbreak of war involving (directly or indirectly) two or more major powers (U.S., Great Britain, France, Soviet Union, and Mainland China). War risk insurance can be cancelled altogether within a stipulated period solely at the discretion of the underwriters. It may be eliminated from a particular area (Angola, Cambodia, Lebanon in 1975/76) or be kept in force only by a surcharge for a war risks addendum when breaching the trading warranty area, such as calls to some Middle East nations or Suez Canal transits in 1975/76. Hull insurance also has a trading warranty area that can be breached in certain waters around Alaska and Greenland. Hull insurance is void if the trading warranty area is breached without an addendum from the underwriters.

A vessel insured for $10 million with a $10,000 deductible has a higher premium than one with a $100,000 deductible because the operator in the latter case is willing to pay the first $100,000 on each and every claim—his portion, so to speak, of the underwriters' risk. Lower premiums also result from savings in reducing the number of minor claims that must be processed. The size of the deductible is a subjective decision on the part of the operator, depending on his loss record, his liquid reserves to foot the deductible, and the amount in savings on premiums on policies with large deductibles. Adjusting the deductible is consistent with the whole purpose of marine insurance, which is to protect the owner from catastrophic losses that may threaten his viability.

A financial institution making a loan on a vessel usually insists on minimum marine insurance to cover the outstanding amount of the loan. Suppose the loan amount is $10 million and the underwriters maintain that the vessel should be insured for $30 million based on original cost, replacement cost, market or book values, or some other criterion. Further suppose that the owner elects to minimize his insurance costs by insuring the vessel for $10 million. If the vessel is declared a total loss, the loss payee of the policy, the financial institution, receives $10 million, which amortizes the loan, leaving the owner with no compensation for his vested interest. Suppose, instead of a total loss, that the vessel sustains $9 million in damages. The underwriters may retort, when presented with a claim for $9 million, that the owner had essentially self-insured himself for two-thirds of any loss. They may attempt to settle the claim for $3 million, leaving the owner with a nonrecoverable loss of $6 million and the financial institution with second thoughts on having a vessel insured only on the basis of the amount of the loan.

Marine insurance brokers receive commissions from the underwriters for their services. These include handling insurance matters for operators and offering advice on the amount of coverage, the size of the deductible, and the selection of the best underwriting syndicate in terms of premium rates, quality of service, and degree of reliability. Premium rates for hull insurance depend on the size and type of the operator's fleet, his loss or claims record, the loss record of the world fleet, fluctuations in repair costs from inflation and market forces, shifts in exchange rates between currencies used to pay premiums and to settle claims, and competitive pressures among underwriting syndicates.

The world fleet loss record varies from year to year, sometimes in

inverse relation to the state of the market. In theory, underwriting profits from years of low casualty rates build up the reserves of the underwriters to meet their obligations during times of high rates of marine
casualties. The record-breaking marine loss year of 1978 should have
drawn down the reserves of the underwriters. These reserves can only
be replenished by an eventual rise in premium rates. As premium
quotes begin to rise, operators attempt to control hull insurance costs by
seeking quotes from competing syndicates, by adjusting the amount of
the insurance or the size of the deductible, or possibly by self-insuring
singly or jointly with other operators.

Protection and indemnity insurance provides coverage for claims
rising from loss of life, injury, and illness including hospitalization and
medical expenses for members of the crew and third parties (passengers, longshoremen, and visitors) and damage to the cargo, piers, and
harbor works. Additional coverage for claims rising from a collision in
excess of the agreed amount of hull insurance can be provided through
P & I insurance. Shipowners organized their own associations, called
P & I Clubs, in the nineteenth century when hull insurance underwriters refused to respond to owners' requests for this type of insurance.
The hull underwriters did not wish to participate in a form of insurance
where there were no set limitations on their exposure to loss. In hull
policies, their maximum exposure to loss is the agreed amount for the
vessel. Nearly all P & I insurance is still written by P & I Clubs whose
memberships are largely owners.

P & I Clubs establish annual calls or premium payments from their
members based on the respective claims record of each club. Adjustments or additional calls are made if settlements exceed expectations
during the year. P & I Clubs are very sensitive to a prospective member's
operating history to avoid penalizing existing members by admitting a
new member who may have a high claims record.

P & I Clubs also offer P & I addendums to their tanker-owning members that certify minimum standards of financial strength and provide
coverage for cleaning up oil spills, as required by the U.S. Water Quality
Act of 1970 and similar laws of other maritime nations. Coverage for
cleaning up oil spills is also provided by TOVALOP (Tanker Owners
Voluntary Agreement concerning Liability for Oil Pollution).

In insurance parlance, average means loss. A particular average is a
loss whose settlement is made by one underwriting group; a general
average is a claim whose settlement is made by more than one underwriting group. The classic example of general average is a vessel saved
from floundering in a storm by throwing the cargo overboard. It is only

fair and equitable that the hull insurance underwriters share in the loss sustained by the cargo insurance underwriters because the sacrifice of the cargo saved the hull underwriters from a far worse loss. The York-Antwerp Rules were established to guide the apportionment of general average claims among the various underwriting groups.

A third type of insurance, not commonly used by operators, is loss of hire insurance. This insures the flow of revenue from a charter if hire is interrupted because of a vessel breakdown and other stipulated causes. The premium depends on the amount of charter revenue being insured, the deductible days of off-hire before the insurance takes effect, the maximum number of off-hire days per year, the operating history, and the condition of the vessel. The loss of hire claim at an insured rate of $10,000 per day with a ten-day deductible for an off-hire period of 12 consecutive days is $20,000 (12 days less the ten-day deductible multiplied by $10,000 per day). The loss of hire underwriters limit their exposure to loss by the maximum number of off-hire days per year and, like other underwriters, in taking advantage of the opportunity to back out of further commitments on the annual renewal date. The most common application of loss of hire insurance is the case of a single vessel owner whose charter income is largely dedicated to meeting operating and financing charges. Without other meaningful sources of cash income or cash reserves to meet debt obligations, loss of hire insurance protects the owner and the financial institution against loss of revenue from an extended interruption of charter hire caused by a vessel breakdown.

The First-Class Operator

The most critical function of an operator is the selection, or recruitment, of a competent and well-motivated crew. The crew's adherence to good seamanship practices is of utmost importance in preserving the owner's vested interest in a vessel and in his capacity to enter into commercial transactions. Good seamanship practices are sailing a vessel in accordance with the Rules of the Road, using all aids to navigation, showing appropriate lights at night and visual signals by day, slow steaming and sounding appropriate signals in restricted waters and at times of reduced visibility, and posting alert lookouts and manning stations with qualified personnel who are upgraded in proficiency by an effective training program. Good seamanship includes avoiding storms and, if caught in one, reducing speed, changing course, and taking on additional ballast if necessary. Good seamanship cannot eliminate vessel mishaps and casualties, but it can minimize the chance and the extent of the damage. The smallest benefit of good seamanship to an operator is a savings in marine insurance premiums from his low claims record.

The magnitude of maintenance and repair expenses, along with the number of off-hire days, is linked to the vessel's initial quality standards, its age and operating history, and the competence and willingness of the crew to follow good engineering practices. These include operating equipment in accordance with manufacturers' instructions, carrying out preventive maintenance programs on a regular basis, spotting problems at an early stage of development, nursing equipment and machinery with minor problems until a convenient time for repairs, and taking prompt, effective, remedial action for nondeferrable equipment and machinery breakdowns. The details of running a vessel go far beyond adherence to good seamanship and engineering practices. For example, a simple matter of not ensuring an adequate supply of potable (drinking) water can have very serious consequences.

The shore-based staff is responsible for marketing services to shippers or charterers, either directly or through the efforts of freight forwarders and brokers. It is also responsible for handling marine insurance, cash disbursements, financial controls, and accounting. The staff schedules the fleet to meet its contractual obligations and arranges for tug and pilot assistance, stores, equipment, water, bunkers, spare parts, and repairs. The staff also handles crew transfers and settles matters with customs, public health, and port authorities. The engineering staff is involved in evaluating various shipyard proposals, suggesting changes or modifications to plans, selecting vendors for various pieces of equipment, monitoring yard progress when constructing or repairing a vessel, and inspecting second-hand tonnage prior to its acquisition. These engineering activities establish the initial quality standards of a fleet and the foundation of future performance.

The shoreside staff may be quite small in relation to the number or the value of the vessels in an owner's fleet. One or two individuals may handle all these functions in one- to three-vessel fleets. The degree of effort in marketing the services of the fleet depends on the type of vessels and the nature of their contractual arrangements. While liner service companies require large shore-based marketing and accounting staffs who deal routinely with hundreds or thousands of shippers to keep their vessels continually employed, a tanker owner can fix the employment of his vessel for five years over a morning cup of coffee.

The reputation of an operator is based on the demonstrated performance of his seagoing crews and shoreside staff. The reputation of being a first-class operator is of inestimable value in an economic system that rewards performance. It is an intangible asset that does not show up on a balance sheet. Established shippers and first-class charterers do not wittingly entrust their goods nor bind themselves through charters to a poor vessel operator.

A first-class operator is cost conscious and attempts to minimize the total cost of operation over the long haul. He may be willing to pay his crew a little above the market rate. This is done not out of charity, but in recognition of potential savings in maintenance and repair costs, insurance premiums, and enhanced revenues from fewer off-hire days of having a first-class crew. A poor operator can greatly enhance his cash flow in the short term by selecting the cheapest crew available without regard to their competence or motivation, by maximum deferment of maintenance and repair items, and underinsuring a vessel with an underwriting group whose low rates reflect their lack of willingness to honor claims. Such a short-sighted policy eventually ends in disaster as the poor operating and maintenance standards of the crew and the past deferring of repair items erupt in a spiraling number of off-hire days. Revenues fall from the lengthening periods of inoperability and from shippers and charterers becoming increasingly reluctant to become entangled in a deteriorating situation. The soaring repair costs are compounded by nonrecoverable losses from the settlement of insurance claims. The falling revenue and rising costs squeeze the cash flow, finally snuffing out the operator and his investment in the vessel.

The market is not the only mechanism culling out the poor operator. The four-year special survey may cut short his days when the estimated bill to restore the soundness and seaworthiness of his vessel is presented to him. Another formidable weapon is the exercise of the rights of sovereign states to force operators to adhere to international conventions and domestic laws as conditions for granting permission, or clearance, to enter their ports. When all is said and done, a vessel unable to enter port is of dubious economic value to anyone.

International Conventions

An international convention is a gathering of representatives of nations which agrees on matters of common interest. The International Rules of the Road is the result of an international convention that codified the unwritten obligations and privileges guiding the conduct of vessels meeting, crossing, and overtaking each other on the high seas.

Admiralty (maritime) courts establish fault in collisions on the high seas by determining which party failed to abide by the Rules of the Road. In 1958, the United Nations Law of the Sea Conference codified the long-standing tradition of the right to innocent passage of a merchant vessel through the territorial waters of a maritime nation.

International conventions do more than codify existing customs and traditions. The *Titanic* led to the first SOLAS Convention which established minimum safety standards for seagoing vessels. This disaster also gave birth to the International Ice Patrol and the requirement that radios be monitored twenty-fours hours a day for distress messages. Another example of a precedent-setting convention is the Hague Rules that established, in the 1920s, the liability, and the extent of that liability, for carriers of goods at sea. An international convention, even though ratified by the requisite number of nations, is not binding on any nation unless incorporated in its statutory law. A shipper or cargo insurance underwriter seeking compensation from an ocean carrier for a loss under a bill of lading signed in the U.S. does not pursue matters in an international court under the Hague Rules but in the U.S. judicial system under provisions of the Carriage of Goods at Sea Act.

In 1954, the maritime nations of the world ratified the International Convention for the Prevention of the Pollution of the Sea by Oil, which makes discharging oil and oily substances within 50 miles of land punishable by a fine of $500–2,500, one year in jail, suspending licenses of personnel involved, and withholding clearance to enter port. It also requires keeping an oil record book for all potentially contaminating discharges from slop tanks, ballast tanks, and water used for tank cleaning. Each page of this record must be signed by the Master of the ship. As with other conventions, it has no force in any maritime nation unless enabling legislation has been passed. In the case of the U.S., the Prevention of the Pollution of the Sea by Oil Act, which drew its entire substance from the international convention, is the enabling legislation that gives the Coast Guard the right to board any vessel, regardless of its flag, and inspect its oil record books. This Act also gives the U.S. judicial system the authority to prosecute and punish offenders.

An international convention may become law for a maritime nation even though it has not been ratified. The updated SOLAS convention, now under the auspices of the Inter-Governmental Maritime Consultative Organization (IMCO) of the United Nations, has not been ratified by the requisite number of nations, but Norway and Liberia require valid SOLAS certificates issued after authorized classification society inspections on all their registered vessels. Many nations will not grant clearance for a vessel of any flag to enter their ports unless it carries a valid SOLAS certificate.

Maritime nations occasionally establish laws concerning granting clearance for vessels entering their ports without reference to an international convention. The U.S. passed the Federal Water Quality Improvement Act in 1970 which prohibits discharge of oil within 12 miles of land, for any reason, and establishes fines and jail sentences for failure to report a spill or oily discharge to the U.S. Coast Guard. The act also requires that all tanker owners entering U.S waters demonstrate minimum standards of financial strength to pay for any potential clean-up but not the consequential costs of an oil spill. This provision was fulfilled by P & I Clubs writing addendums for their tanker-owning members and by the formation of TOVALOP.

Another example of unilateral action taken by a sovereign nation is that all LPG carriers must have valid U.S. Coast Guard certificates of compliance onboard as a condition for entering U.S. ports. This has brought about the double class of LPG vessels. Similarly, U.S. environmental laws have created a double class of bulk cement carriers, those which can and cannot enter U.S. ports. The point here is not whether U.S. standards are too stringent or other nations' standards are too lax but how a sovereign state can control the standards of vessels entering its ports by the exercise of its right to grant or deny clearance.

A vessel operator must also deal with the rights of sovereign states to quarantine a vessel because of the health of the crew, passengers, or animal and plant cargoes, to forbid loading or discharging edible food cargoes because of the state of cleanliness of the cargo spaces or the cargo itself, to search for contraband, to arrest or detain members of a crew for breaking the law, and to control imports and exports.

Other matters which concern operators are IMCO's proposals for uniform safety standards for vessels carrying hazardous cargoes, a single code of compliance for LPG carriers, segregated ballast tanks, crude oil washing and inert gas systems for crude carriers, and international licensing of crews. In addition, U.N. Law of the Sea Conferences are being held on the rights of innocent passage through straits, the ownership of mineral wealth on the ocean bottom, and the extent of fishing rights and territorial waters off maritime nations.

10

Vessel Charters

A charter is a contractual arrangement based on the mutual commercial interests of a charterer, who requires a vessel to meet his transportation needs, and an owner, who places his vessel at the disposal of the charterer. Although most major oil, steel, aluminum, and grain companies have large fleets, a portion of their base and all their marginal needs are satisfied by a variety of charters with shipowners and shipping companies. Much of the world business in commodities is conducted by companies and trading houses who profitably dedicate their scarce capital and managerial resources to their area of specialty rather than to shipping. Consequently, these firms own few vessels and charter-in most or all of their transportation requirements on an as-needed basis. Some feel that even their long-term transportation needs are more competently and economically satisfied by charters with shipping companies than by ownership.

All companies involved in international bulk commodity trade deal with volatile shipping rates. Rates soar if 99 vessels are chasing after 100 cargoes and collapse if there are 101 vessels. The volatility of the single-voyage, or spot, market for bulk carriers is seen in Table 10.1.

Eighteen months separate the low point (June 1972) from the high point (January 1974). During this time, the cost of transporting some rather dull commodities on a spot basis increased sixfold. If iron ore, coal, and grain were highly valued commodities transported over short distances, then a sixfold change in the transportation component of the delivered cost would not be particularly significant. Most bulk commodities are relatively low valued and are transported over long distances.

TABLE 10.1
INDEX OF SINGLE-VOYAGE FIXTURES

	Rate index
January 1971	170
June 1971	80
January 1972	80
June 1972	70
January 1973	180
June 1973	260
January 1974	470
June 1974	370
January 1975	190
June 1975	110
January 1976	120
June 1976	165
January 1977	140

Compiled by Drewry Shipping Statistics, London, for iron ore from Australia to Japan, coal from eastern U.S. to Japan, and grain from U.S. Gulf to Europe. Base of 100 for rates of January 1967.

During the mid-1970s, the magnitude of the transportation component in the delivered cost of commodities was diminished by a sharp markup in the price of raw materials and a fall-off in shipping charges. Lower shipping charges resulted from developing more efficient vessels that could transport commodities cheaper and from a general surplus of vessel capacity in relation to demand that depressed shipowners' profit margins.

Medium- and long-term charters emerged from a desire by charterers to fix their transportation costs at a set rate over a period of time independent of spot market fluctuations and a desire by owners to fix their revenue stream over the same period of time. Suppose two competitors, Company C and Company D, import a bulk commodity from a single source paying the same price on an FOB (Free on Board) basis. Each arranges for its transportation on a single-voyage basis, which is $20 per ton. An owner approaches Company C with a proposal to transport a portion of its needs for $20 per ton for the following five years. Company C accepts the proposal and enters into a five-year charter. At the start of the charter, both companies are in the same competitive position and remain that way as long as the spot market rates are $20

TABLE 10.2
COMPARISON OF TRANSPORTING IN DELIVERED PRICE

	Approximate cost of a ton of crude oil at a Persian Gulf port	Approximate cost per ton for trans- portation from the Persian Gulf to Europe*	Total delivered cost at the European port	Oceanborne transportation cost as percentage of delivered cost
Jan. '71	$17	$14	$31	45
Jan. '72	17	5	22	23
Jan. '73	17	7	24	29
Oct. '73	17	24	41	59
After the oil crisis:				
1974	75	10	85	12
1975	80	6	86	7
1976	80	9	89	10

*As compiled by Drewry Shipping Statistics, London, for a medium-sized tanker.

per ton. If, two years into the charter period, spot market rates increase by 50% to $30 per ton, Company D is at a competitive disadvantage to the tune of $10 per ton (which may be its entire profit margin) on that portion of the commodity movement covered by Company C at $20 per ton. If, by chance, Company C had chartered-in more tonnage than required at $20 per ton, the company could relet its excess capacity at $30 per ton and pocket the $10 per ton as incremental profits on a zero capital investment in fixed assets. However, if rates fall by 50% to $10 per ton, Company D's competitive disadvantage becomes an advantage, and any excess chartered-in tonnage generates incremental losses, rather than incremental profits, for Company C.

Major users of transportation set up wholly owned shipping subsidiaries to fix the cost of shipping through owning and chartering-in vessels. The subsidiary may have to serve the parent's needs exclusively, or it may have to compete for the parent's business on an arm's-length basis posting its own profit and loss statement. Of course, if the going gets a bit rough, a few less-than-arm's-length transactions may take place to prevent an embarrassing situation from developing in the shipping subsidiary. Burmah Oil is a classic example of a parent encouraging its subsidiary to expand far beyond the parent's transportation needs. It was eventually forced to liquidate much of its profitable oil properties because of its floundering shipping interests.

A charterer enters into a multiyear charter hoping that the expenditures for transportation under the charter will be less than being exposed to the vagaries of the spot market during the charter period. An owner has the opposite opinion, feeling that he will profit more by entering into the charter than remaining in the spot market. An owner may have other motivations besides profit maximization in entering a multiyear charter arrangement. Bearing in mind that a vessel free and clear of debt can be laid up at little expense during depressed market conditions while a mortgaged vessel is still expected to meet its debt obligations, an owner may not be psychologically prepared to gamble on spot market rates as a means to repay a loan and provide a return on his equity investment. Similarly, a financial institution may not be prepared to lend on an asset that operates in a volatile market environment without the assurance of a stream of hire payments from a first-class charterer. From this point of view, a long-term charter reduces the overall cost of transportation; a financial institution, looking through the charter to the creditworthiness of the charterer, is willing to back a shipping venture with long-term and relatively inexpensive funds. Without the charter, a financial institution may provide only short-term funds at a higher rate of interest to compensate for the greater degree of risk or may decline to provide any funds at all.

There are about as many business philosophies toward shipping as there are owners. The mainstay behind each owner's approach to shipping is that it maximizes his worth in the long run. An owner may not order a vessel unless he has a full payout charter in hand that generates the necessary funds to meet all debt obligations and provides a minimum rate of return on his equity investment. He is just as confident of his approach to shipping as the owner who shuns all but the short-term and spot markets to be in a position to recoup his entire investment in a few months' employment at peak market rates. Most owners compromise between these two philosophies by operating their fleets under a portfolio of charters which expire in a regular fashion so that a portion of the fleet can profit in a strong spot market. The desired degree of coverage of period charters to fixed operating and financing costs varies greatly from owner to owner.

Some owners work closely with charterers to order vessels specifically tailored to the charterers' needs. Others believe the way to maximize their worth is to anticipate the future needs of charterers and order vessels that are not in current demand, gambling that demand will materialize by the time of the vessel's delivery. If the owner is correct in his assessment, he has the opportunity to negotiate a scarce asset. If the demand for the vessel does not materialize, the owner must suffer. An owner cannot indefinitely maintain a business philosophy that is out of step with the marketplace. He may act like an autocrat, but he must serve the needs of the marketplace.

It is impossible to assess at the start of a charter period whether the charterer has minimized his transportation costs or the owner has max-imized his worth by entering into the charter. During the course of the charter period, the economic advantage of a charter is unequally shared, with the charterer benefiting when single-voyage rates are high com-pared to the charter rate and the owner benefiting when they are low. Only time will determine which party benefited more by the charter. All that can be said is that a charter is fixed because it is in the best commercial interests of the charterer and owner.

Rates for medium- and long-term charters of five or more years are influenced more by the acquisition or building costs of ships than any other factor. Spot market rates are important in setting the tone of the negotiations between charterers and owners for medium- and long-term charters. In a strong market, spot rates, which fluctuate in response to the immediate and near-term relationship between the supply and demand for vessel capacity, far exceed medium- and long-term charter rates. Therefore, all medium- and long-term charters are fundamentally sound in a strong spot market because the charters provide low-cost transportation in relation to the spot market. Any excess chartered-in tonnage is generating windfall profits for the charterer. During a depressed spot market when rates may not even compensate for voyage and operating costs, first-class charterers stand out by their willingness and ability to honor their charter obligations. Less than first-class char-terers have been known to break a charter at the first opportunity. In one instance, a charterer assembled the owners of chartered-in vessels into a room and threatened to bankrupt his shipping subsidiary unless all those present renegotiated the charter rates and terms to his satisfac-tion. So, too, a first-class owner stands out by his level of performance and willingness to honor his obligations when the charterer is profiting enormously. A few less-than-first-class owners have used a delayed clearing of a charter hire payment by a bank as an excuse to break a charter because the payment, though received in time, had not been credited to their account by the time stipulated in the charter party. In shipping, memories of precipitous actions taken by charterers and own-ers in pursuit of their short-term interests last a long time. Remaining an ongoing business has much to do with keeping the system honest.

In the past, the Master commonly owned a vessel. While off-loading a cargo, he would wander around the waterfront, looking for more business. To make matters more efficient, a local tavern would become a common meeting place for owners and shippers. Eventually, the owner found that his business interests could be better pursued if he relied on an intermediary and paid him a commission for remaining in contact with shippers during his absence. In the 1600s, the common meeting ground for owners, shippers, and brokers in London, the world center of international commerce, was the Virginia Wine House. Over the years, the meeting place moved to the Virginia and Baltic Coffee House, then the Antwerp Tavern, and finally to the Baltic Exchange, where brokers representing charterers and brokers representing owners now congregate to transact business. Although charters can be and are concluded directly between a charterer and an owner, most charters, from a few weeks' single voyage to 20-year bareboat and time charters, are arranged through the intervention of brokers. Independent brokers are catalysts in fixing charters because their remuneration is a commission generated on consummated transactions. Near hits don't count in the brokerage business. House brokers differ; they receive compensation for representing the interests of a particular charterer or owner in addition to receiving commissions on actual fixtures.

A charterer may work through one broker on an exclusive basis, through a few preferred brokers who have demonstrated their capacity to cover the market, or through the entire brokerage community by making a public announcement of his transportation requirements. Brokers representing charterers generally work through brokers representing owners. They may contact owners directly who have suitable and available tonnage and who may be interested in committing a vessel near the rate the charterer is willing to pay. Charterers rely on brokers to stir up the marketplace to ensure they obtain the lowest transportation rates, and owners rely on brokers to obtain the highest rates for their vessels. Brokers make their living by successfully straddling these two diametrically opposed objectives. Depending on the services rendered, a charter party may direct a fixed commission, which is paid throughout the entire charter period, to one or more brokers.

Centers of brokerage activity are London, New York, Tokyo, Hong Kong, Piraeus (Athens), Oslo, and Hamburg. A London broker practices his trade after serving an apprenticeship, passing an examination, and being formally admitted to the Baltic Exchange. In New York, a broker conducts business with a telex and telephone from his office and is considered a broker solely by virtue of transacting business as a broker.

The role of charterer and owner is interchangeable. An end user of transportation is called the chartered or disponent owner (sometimes despondent owner in a depressed market) by virtue of the charterer's right to direct the employment of the vessel and to relet the vessel consistent with the provisions of the underlying charter party. Similarly, an owner who invests his capital in ships as a service for others becomes a charterer when he charters-in a vessel for any reason such as meeting a transportation obligation or taking a speculative position in anticipation of higher rates during the charter period. For the sake of clarity, a charterer is assumed to be an end user of transportation (oil, steel, aluminum, grain, forest products, automobile, chemical, sulphur, cement, fertilizer and nonferrous metal companies, and trading houses) and the owner is an individual or company that invests capital funds in vessels to meet the shipping needs of end users.

The written contract binding a charterer and an owner is known as a charter party. Charter parties assign the costs and risks of transporting cargoes between the charterer and the owner. Usually, the party responsible for paying the costs bears the business risks involved with the costs. For instance, the business risk of Panama Canal tolls doubling resides with the party responsible for paying the canal tolls. Special provisions in a charter party may, for instance, make the charterer responsible for reimbursing an owner for escalations of specified costs above a predetermined level. Charter parties assign the risks of the consequences of a vessel breakdown and the inability to load or discharge a cargo because of port congestion or harbor and terminal labor disruptions to either the charterer or the owner.

The cost of moving a cargo between two terminals in different ports can be broken down into the following components:

Cargo handling charges:	The cost of transferring a bulk commodity from the loading terminal to the vessel and from the vessel to the receiving terminal.
Vessel voyage costs consisting of:	
Port charges:	The costs associated with making a call at the loading and discharging ports including pilotage and tug charges, wharfage and port dues, shore services, and other charges not related to the actual transfer of cargo.

Bunker costs:	The cost of fuel consumed at sea and in port.
Canal dues:	Fees paid to transit the Suez and Panama Canals, the St. Lawrence Seaway, and possibly charges which may someday be levied on vessels passing through narrow waters such as the Malacca Strait.
Vessel operating costs:	The cost of keeping a vessel in a state of readiness for service at sea including crew, maintenance and repair, insurance, lubes, stores and equipment, and general expenses.
Vessel capital costs:	A vessel is a capital asset that is expected to generate funds to provide the return of, and on, the investment for its construction or acquisition.

Single-Voyage Charters

The most common contractual arrangement between a charterer and an owner is the single-voyage charter. The owner receives a freight payment for the movement of a cargo between two or more ports, from which he must pay all voyage and operating costs. Cargo-handling charges are paid by the owner if gross terms apply and by the charterer if free in and out (FIO) terms apply.

Voyage charters provide for demurrage and dispatch payments if the time in port exceeds, or is less than, lay time. Lay time is the total eligible time counted from tendering of the notice of readiness after the arrival of the vessel at the loading terminal until the completion of loading and from tendering of notice of readiness after the vessel's arrival at the receiving terminal until the completion of unloading or discharging the cargo. An owner cannot tender his notice of readiness until all matters are settled with customs and public health and port authorities and the vessel is ready in all respects for loading or unloading. A notice of readiness can be submitted only during the times of the day and days of the week set forth in the charter party.

Time computations for demurrage and dispatch claims are done by brokers or port agents. In the tanker trades, time is counted on the basis of 24-hour days and 7-day weeks (SHINC terms). In some dry-bulk trades, Sundays–holidays excluded–weather working days (SHEX WWD) terms apply. If lay time is 12 days and time counted in port is 15 days, the owner submits a claim for three days' demurrage to the charterer; if time counted is ten days, the charterer submits a claim for two days' dispatch to the owner. Demurrage and dispatch rates are quoted in dollars/day and are set at a rate which encourages an owner to minimize port time. Since an owner's scope of action is limited to his vessel and not to terminal operations, he will attempt to negotiate a demurrage rate close to his earnings rate under the charter. For instance, if an owner can earn $5,000 per day under a charter as written, he will attempt to negotiate a demurrage rate of $5,000 per day. In the dry-bulk trades, the demurrage rate finally negotiated frequently does not fully compensate an owner for port delays beyond lay time. In this example, the demurrage rate may be $3,000 per day. Dispatch rates are customarily set at half the demurrage rate.

Demurrage may not protect an owner's interest if a shoreside labor disruption starts before he has tendered his notice of readiness. If the disruption starts before the tendering of the notice, the owner may bear the cost of a vessel lockout unless the charterer is able to redirect the vessel to another terminal. Demurrage and dispatch claims should be easily computed and settled. Unfortunately, this is not the case. The lack of demurrage has bankrupted more than one shipping company. In early 1974, one firm agreed to transport goods to the Persian Gulf on simple liner terms, meaning the goods are shipped at a fixed charge regardless of any difficulties which may arise. The firm calculated its shipping rates on a basis of a six-week waiting period for a berth in the Persian Gulf, triple the normal time experienced prior to the oil crisis. A vessel was chartered-in and loaded and arrived in the Persian Gulf six weeks later. By this time, congestion was much worse than anticipated. After remaining anchored for six months, paying charter hire payments to the owner with no offsetting compensation in the form of demurrage from the shippers, the firm was forced to close its doors. The owner of the vessel and the shippers of the goods were left to sort things out among themselves.

Not all demurrage stories have sad endings. Consider the Nigerian civil servant who discovered the way to riches by kickbacks in ordering cement for the government. In 1975, he could stroll along the Lagos waterfront and gaze upon five hundred or so vessels laden with enough cement to meet their nation's needs for years on end. The vessels were receiving demurrage from the Nigerian government at rates reflecting the market at the time the cement contracts were awarded. As time went on and market conditions deteriorated along with the cement cargoes, it became more profitable for an owner to remain part of the cement blockade than to trade in the open market. The major problem facing the owners was the low morale of the crews. Some were on the verge of mutiny after being stuck onboard a vessel anchored for months in the sweltering heat of West Africa. A government coup brought the demurrage holiday to an end for all, including owners who were submitting demurrage claims to the Nigerian authorities for nonexistent vessels. Owners became upset when demurrage ceased, but the Nigerian Navy prevented any unauthorized departures. Some owners were persuaded at gunpoint to off-load their cargoes without any further ado over demurrage claims.

Consecutive-Voyage Charters and Contracts of Affreightment
In a consecutive-voyage charter, the charterer contracts with the owner to make a number of round-trip voyages for a designated vessel between two ports (or a range of ports) at a stated rate of dollars/ton of cargo. Both consecutive-voyage charters and contracts of affreightment apportion the costs and risks of transporting cargoes similar to single-voyage charters. The two major differences between consecutive-voyage charters and contracts of affreightment are that the latter do not designate a specific vessel and the shipments, or liftings, are not necessarily spaced in relation to the round-trip voyage time. An example of a contract of affreightment is shipping 50,000 tons of coal, 10% more or less, between a U.S. East Coast port and ports in Japan once per quarter for 20 consecutive quarters. Since no vessel is designated, an owner can nominate a vessel that may be owned, already chartered-in, or available for charter. Contracts of affreightment call for close cooperation between the charterer and the owner because one lifting per quarter leaves a fair amount of discretion on the owner's behalf as to when the lifting actually takes place. The charterer's desired time for a lifting is influenced by the state of raw material inventories, the anticipated level of production, other shipments in progress, and contractual obligations with coal exporters. An owner's desired time of a lifting is influenced by the deployment schedule of his fleet and market rates. In other words, the owner's and charterer's ideas of a lifting date may not coincide, and a compromise must be worked out.

Contracts of affreightment enable owners of combination carriers to combine the crude oil and dry-bulk trades without committing the vessel to the exclusive service of any one charterer. A portfolio of contracts of affreightment can act as a hedge to ensure a minimum level of revenue income to support fixed operating and financing charges while exposing the fleet to the profit potential of the spot market. An example of hedging is to fix a fleet of combination carriers on contracts of affreightment transporting dry-bulk commodities from the Atlantic basin to Japan, returning with spot cargoes of crude oil. The contracts of affreightment may cover the fixed operating and financing charges, leaving the profitability of the fleet dependent on the level of spot tanker rates. If rates for tankers and bulk carriers diverge sufficiently, the incremental profits of the combination fleet trading exclusively in crude oil may well exceed the possible incremental losses of chartering-in bulk carriers to fulfill the contracts of affreightment.

Contracts of affreightment and consecutive voyage charters may be written with so many safeguards for the owner that all risks are essentially borne by the charterer. At the other end of the spectrum, these charters may be no more than letters of intent where the charterer gives the owner the right to transport the quantities stated in the charter party at the stipulated rates without any obligation on the charterer's part if actual shipments are less than those stated in the charter. In other words, the charter parties do not have any meaningful "take or pay" provisions.

Many flat-rate, long-term contracts of affreightment fixed in the early and mid-1960s lost all their economic value to owners by the mid-1970s. These contracts originally provided sufficient revenue to pay all vessel operating and voyage costs and left an allowance for capital hire, but by the mid-1970s the entire revenue barely compensated for bunker costs alone. Japanese charterers voluntarily revised the rates to cut the losses being sustained by the owners—not out of charity, but in recognition of their long-term interests as users, and owners as sup-

TABLE 10.3

ASSIGNMENT OF COSTS UNDER A SINGLE OR CONSECUTIVE VOYAGE CHARTER
AND A CONTRACT OF AFFREIGHTMENT

	Charterer	Shipowner
Cargo handling costs	As set forth in the charter party	
Vessel voyage expenses Bunkers Port charges Canal dues		X
Vessel operating costs Crew Maintenance and repair (M & R) Insurance & others		X

pliers, of a vital service. Naturally, the charterers took advantage of this opportunity to revise terms of the charter parties and resolve matters in dispute in their favor. The charterers' attitudes toward owners varied considerably. Certain owners who cooperated with the charterers on selecting lifting dates to the charterers' satisfaction fared better than those who didn't. There is a considerable amount of give and take in shipping, and the degree of this depends on the charterer's and owner's relationship established over the years.

Consecutive voyage charters and contracts of affreightment in crude oil afforded no protection for owners against the fourfold rise in bunker costs in 1973 if the freight rate were in dollars/ton. If the rate were in Worldscale points, owners were compensated for the higher bunker costs when Worldscale rates were revised about a year later. The World-scale rate base is now adjusted every six months for changes in bunker costs and port charges.

The total cost of transportation for the charterer is his share of the cargo handling costs and the consecutive voyage charter payments. An owner's capital hire element under a consecutive voyage charter is the charter hire less any cargo handling costs and all voyage and vessel operating expenses.

Time Charters

In a time charter, the owner bears all the costs and risks of vessel operation and the charterer is responsible for all cargo handling charges and voyage costs. Time charter hire ceases the moment a vessel is not in a condition of readiness for service at sea and resumes when the vessel has been restored to an operable condition.* Off-hire time strongly influences profitability because operating costs continue to accrue regardless of the state of readiness of the vessel. If an owner is receiving $5,000 per day for a vessel on time charter and his operating costs are $3,000 per day, his capital hire is $655,000 for an annual off-hire period of 15 days of planned maintenance:

Revenue	
(350 days × $5,000 per day)	$1,750,000
Operating costs	
(365 days × $3,000 per day)	1,095,000
Anticipated capital hire	$ 655,000

*Some time charters have a 24-hour clause which gives an owner 24 hours to correct an operational problem before the vessel is considered off-hire, or not in a condition of readiness for service at sea.

If actual off-hire is 35 days, revenue declines by 6% to $1.65 million while capital hire, which is the difference between revenue and operating costs, decreases 15% to $555,000. The clock starts ticking on off-hire time as soon as the owner deviates from the charterer's intended track for any reason such as scheduled planned maintenance, transfer of a sick crew member, or emergency repairs. It ceases when the vessel is back on the charterer's intended track. All port charges and bunker costs associated with the deviation are for the owner's, not the charterer's, account. The charterer deducts off-hire time and any advances made for an owner's account from the monthly or semimonthly time charter payments. Time charter hire may be adjusted to account for the vessel's actual speed and fuel consumption compared with the owner's warranties in the charter party.

The charterer must continue time charter payments as long as the vessel is operable, even though there may be no cargoes available or the vessel cannot load or discharge its cargo because of port congestion or shoreside labor disputes. If the charter permits the charterer to lay-up the vessel, the owner passes all savings from reduced manning, maintenance, insurance, and other operating expenses to the charterer, which should not, in theory, affect the owner's capital hire. An owner may not sell the vessel with the charter nor always be able to assign the charter payments to a financial institution without the consent of the charterer, which cannot be unreasonably withheld. A time charter is for a set period of time. The charterer may extend the charter period to complete the last voyage and redeliver the vessel to the specified geographic area or location if the last voyage commenced with the expectation there would be enough time left to complete it. A charterer may break a time charter for "force majeure" or "Acts of God" that thwart or frustrate the intent of the charter to provide a transportation service, such as a vessel seizure by a government. A time charter can also be broken if an owner fails to perform his function as operator. A charterer's sympathy to an owner's troubles as operator is somewhat in tune with the state of the market.

The most common time charter parties for dry-cargo ships are the Baltime and the New York Produce Exchange Form. Although conceptually the same, both differ in details, with the Baltime slightly more biased in the owner's favor. Major oil companies have their own standardized time charter and bareboat charter forms. Major commodity trades use standardized charter party forms. Standardized charter forms make it easier for charterers and owners to conduct business because they negotiate exceptions and additions to a well-known and accepted document. Charters employing tens of billions of dollars in capital assets are routinely arranged between charterers and owners without any involvement by lawyers.

Charters stipulate the city (usually London, New York, or Tokyo) where arbitrations are to be held and whose laws govern any dispute on the interpretation of the charter party regardless of the vessel's location when the dispute arose. If a charterer and owner cannot settle a dispute between themselves, both agree on the issues at stake and on the selection of one or three arbitrators. If one arbitrator is appropriate, he must be mutually acceptable to both parties; if three, then the charterer and owner each choose one and the two arbitrators select the third. Arbitrators may belong to a society whose members are primarily businessmen well versed in shipping. Retired judges and maritime lawyers also serve as arbitrators.

An arbitration ruling may be final or may be a recommendation to a maritime court. Even if the ruling is final, a court decree may be necessary to enforce the award. Awards are based solely on the commercial issues at stake without any consideration for punitive damages. If a charterer or an owner took precipitous action and profited $500,000 by so doing and the arbitration rules in favor of the injured party, the award is $500,000 and possibly compensation for court costs.

Many, though not all, long-term time charters were once fixed at constant rates throughout the charter period. Suppose an owner in 1965 fixed his 80,000-dwt vessel at a rate of $3/dwt/month for ten years. At the time, the owner estimated his first year's operating cost at $600,000 (1966) escalating at 5% throughout the charter period. The owner borrowed $12 million to be repaid over ten years at a spread over a floating rate of interest. Based on his experience in the early 1960s, he estimated that the interest rate would average about 8%. The owner felt that the estimated 5% inflation in operating costs and 8% interest charge on borrowed funds were conservative estimates (Table 10.4).

The thin cash flow in the early years of the charter period was when the owner had the most confidence in his inflation and interest rate estimates. Since the fall-off in interest charges as the loan is amortized was expected to be greater than the build-up in operating costs from inflation, the owner hoped to accumulate a comfortable cash cushion to cover potential difficulties during the course of the charter period. This type of full payout charter was supposed to prevent sleepless nights. However, the high interest and inflation rates during the first half of the

TABLE 10.4
PROJECTED 10-YEAR CASH FLOW

	Revenue[1]	Operating cost[2]	Capital hire[3]	Amortization of debt[4]	Interest[5]	Projected net cash flow	Year-end cumulative cash position
1966	$2,760,000	$600,000	$2,160,000	$1,200,000	$960,000	$ 0	$ 0
1967	2,760,000	630,000	2,130,000	1,200,000	864,000	66,000	66,000
1968	2,760,000	662,000	2,098,000	1,200,000	768,000	130,000	196,000
1969	2,760,000	695,000	2,065,000	1,200,000	672,000	193,000	389,000
1970	2,760,000	729,000	2,031,000	1,200,000	576,000	255,000	644,000
1971	2,760,000	766,000	1,994,000	1,200,000	480,000	314,000	958,000
1972	2,760,000	804,000	1,956,000	1,200,000	384,000	372,000	1,330,000
1973	2,760,000	844,000	1,916,000	1,200,000	288,000	428,000	1,758,000
1974	2,760,000	886,000	1,874,000	1,200,000	192,000	482,000	2,240,000
1975	2,760,000	930,000	1,830,000	1,200,000	96,000	534,000	2,774,000

(1) The monthly hire paid in advance at the first of the month is $3/dwt × 80,000 dwt or $240,000. The owner figured that the vessel would be off-hire for one half month per year resulting in an annual revenue of 11.5 months × $240,000 per month or $2,760,000.

(2) An inflation rate of 5% is assumed.

(3) The difference between the revenue and operating costs is the capital hire. This serves debt obligations (if any) and provides a return of and on the equity investment.

(4) Ten year amortization of a $12 million loan.

(5) Interest is figured on annual amortization payments at 8%. Most shipping loans are repaid on a quarterly or semiannual basis.

TABLE 10.5
ACTUAL COSTS, 1966–1975

	Inflation rate	Operating costs	Interest rate	Interest costs
1966		$ 600,000	5%	$600,000
1967	4%	624,000	6%	648,000
1968	6%	661,000	6%	576,000
1969	10%	728,000	8%	672,000
1970	12%	815,000	9%	648,000
1971	15%	937,000	9%	540,000
1972	17%	1,096,000	10%	480,000
1973	15%	1,261,000	12%	432,000
1974	10%	1,387,000	15%	360,000
1975	8%	1,498,000	8%	96,000

1970s did not help owners with long-term fixed rate charters (Table 10.5). If the owner experienced no major operating difficulties so that his revenue projections were accurate, the actual cash flow compared to his projected cash flow was as in Table 10.6.

TABLE 10.6
PROJECTED VS. ACTUAL CASH FLOW

	Projected		Actual	
	Net cash flow	Year-end cumulative cash position	Net cash flow	Year-end cumulative cash position
1966	$ 0	$ 0	$360,000	$ 360,000
1967	66,000	66,000	288,000	648,000
1968	130,000	196,000	323,000	971,000
1969	193,000	389,000	160,000	1,131,000
1970	255,000	644,000	97,000	1,228,000
1971	314,000	958,000	83,000	1,311,000
1972	372,000	1,330,000	−16,000	1,295,000
1973	428,000	1,758,000	−133,000	1,162,000
1974	482,000	2,240,000	−187,000	975,000
1975	534,000	2,774,000	−34,000	941,000

The owner was ahead of his projections in the early part of the charter period until the record inflation and interest rates during the first half of the 1970s made a shambles of this and all other long-term time charters, without provisions for escalation of costs. It was not unusual for charterers in need of the services of their chartered-in fleet in the strong market of the early 1970s to make ex-gratia payments to cut the extent of the losses being sustained by owners. After this experience, owners were reluctant to enter into charters of more than three years' duration without rate increases. This was achieved by fixed step-ups or by escalation provisions for reimbursement above a certain level. Some charters had their rates linked to a published index of inflationary activity such as the Consumer or Wholesale Price Index.

TABLE 10.7
ASSIGNMENT OF COSTS UNDER A TIME CHARTER

	Charterer	Shipowner
Cargo handling costs	X	

Vessel voyage expenses
   Bunkers
   Port charges
   Canal dues
	X	

Vessel operating costs
   Crew
   Maintenance and repair (M & R)
   Insurance & others
		X

The total cost of transportation for the charterer is the time charter hire, cargo handling, and voyage costs. The time charter hire income less the cost of operating a vessel is the owner's capital hire to support any financing charges and provide a return of and on his investment.

A trip time charter lasts from the time the vessel is chartered-in to the time the cargo is discharged. Since cargo handling and voyage expenses are for the charterer's account, some owners prefer to bid on a trip time charter rather than on a single-voyage basis to avoid estimating cargo handling and port charges in unfamiliar parts of the world. A trip time charter precludes demurrage and dispatch claims since the charterer pays for the service of the vessel until the cargo is discharged, regardless of the cause of any delays beyond an owner's control. If a charterer wants to transport a cargo of grain from the U.S. Gulf to any of a half dozen ports in Southeast Asia (actual destination unknown when fixing the vessel), an owner bidding on a voyage charter basis would have to quote a rate for each port whereas an owner bidding on a trip time charter would quote a single rate. Although trip time charters have become more popular in recent years, most business is still done under voyage charters.

Bareboat Charter

In a bareboat charter, also called a time charter by demise, the owner delivers the vessel bare to the charterer who carries out all the functions of a vessel operator. Once the charterer accepts the vessel and starts to pay the monthly payments to the owner, the stream of payments continue without interruption for the duration of the charter period. Bareboat charters can be broken if the vessel is declared a total loss by the underwriters (the amount of hull insurance which the charterer must keep in force is stated in the charter party), is seized by a sovereign

TABLE 10.8
ASSIGNMENT OF COSTS UNDER A BAREBOAT CHARTER

	Charterer	Shipowner
Cargo handling costs	X	

Voyage expenses
  Bunkers
  Port charges
  Canal dues
	X	

Vessel operating costs
  Crew
  Maintenance and repair (M & R)
  Insurance & others
	X	

state, or its ability to deliver cargoes is thwarted or frustrated by an Act of God. At the end of the charter period, the charterer redelivers the vessel, free of all liens, to a place and in a condition set forth in the charter party. The charter party might require the charterer to complete a special survey at his expense or might permit the charterer to defer repair items near the end of the charter period. Usually, the vessel is redelivered to the owner with a certification from a marine surveyor that the vessel is in a normal state of wear and tear for its age.

The charterer may operate the vessel with his own crew or contract the operation to a ship managing firm, another shipping company, including the owner himself, on a cost plus fixed fee basis with the charterer bearing all risks of operation. The charterer is free to relet, or charter out, the vessel as disponent owner as long as none of the provisions of the underlying bareboat charter restricting the types of cargoes and ports of call are violated and as long as the relet charter period does not extend beyond the bareboat charter period. Reletting does not relieve the charterer of any of his obligations to the owner.

The cost of transportation as seen by the charterer is the bareboat charter hire payments, cargo handling, vessel voyage and operating costs. From the owner's perspective, bareboat hire income less any brokerage commissions is a pure cash contribution to his operations, representing the owner's return of and on the capital investment in the vessel. The owner's major concern in a bareboat charter is to monitor the physical condition of the vessel.

Bareboat charters may have a purchase option built into the charter party, giving the charterer the option of purchasing the vessel for a stated amount at the end of the charter period. A hire purchase charter gives the charterer the option to purchase the vessel for a very nominal sum, say $1. For a given situation, the hire purchase charter rate is greater than the comparable bareboat charter rate to compensate the owner for surrendering the residual value of the vessel to the charterer at the expiration of the charter. Owners sometimes sell vessels to others through hire purchase charters with ownership reverting on the receipt of the last charter payment. Pertamina, the state-owned oil company of Indonesia, would have become a sizable tanker fleet owner at the expiration of a number of hire purchase charters entered into in the early 1970s. However, some of these charters were cancelled a few years later.

Bareboat charters lie at the heart of Japanese shikumisen or tie-in shipping deals where an owner with access to low-cost, non-Japanese crews sets up a one-ship holding company under a flag of convenience/ necessity. The company may be owned entirely by the shipowner or jointly with the charterer. The charterer (the Japanese shipping company) enters into a bareboat charter with the owner and into a cost plus fixed fee operating agreement for a 10–15-year period. The Hong Kong owner relies on the creditworthiness of the bareboat charterer to obtain financing on the best possible terms to purchase the vessel from a Japanese shipyard, usually associated with the same industrial group or combine as the shipping company. The tie-in arrangement provides low-cost transportation for Japanese exports and imports by virtue of the favorable financing supported by the bareboat charter and by virtue of employing a crew which performs the same function of a Japanese crew at a third of the cost. Nothing has spurred the growth of the Hong Kong shipping interests more than the success of the All-Japanese Seamen's Union in winning higher wages and more costly benefits for its members.

All multiyear medium- and long-term charters place the risk of economic utility squarely on the shoulders of the charterer as long as the owner fulfills his responsibilities under the charter party. A charter insures an owner against a falling rate structure throughout the charter period. The charterer's compensation for taking on this obligation is the economic benefits accruing whenever spot rates exceed the charter rate. With the exception of hire purchase charters, which are not commonly utilized, the risk of economic utility reverts to the owner at the expiration of a charter. The owner bears the possible onus of employing a vessel in a depressed market caused either by an oversupply of vessel capacity or by the development of a technologically superior, or more efficient, vessel during the charter period. He also enjoys all the benefits of ownership if there is a booming market for his type vessel when the charter expires.

11

The Need for Capital

Shipping as a capital intensive industry is a fairly recent phenomenon. Immediately following WWII, surplus 14,000-dwt Liberty and Victory general cargo carriers and surplus 16,500-dwt T-2 (there were also T-1 and T-3) tankers were purchased for as little as a few hundred thousand dollars. The key people in a shipping firm were the operating personnel. Owners concentrated their attention on the marketing and operating problems within their organizations and considered the garnering of outside sources of capital of secondary importance in the general scheme of things. It is ironic that today's well-publicized shipping fortunes of hundreds of millions of dollars rose pyramid style out of small capital investments in a business where financial acumen was not considered a particularly valuable talent. The opportunity for entrepreneurial-minded shipowners to expand the scope of their business activities was linked to several post-war developments, including the rise of Japan as a major economic power, a growing world population enjoying a higher per capita standard of living, the exhaustion or lack of domestic supplies of raw materials, diversification of raw material sources, and specialization of industrial output by major trading nations.

Japan is an island nation almost devoid of mineral and energy resources. The need for secure sources of raw materials to support its growing industries and secure markets for its manufactured products became more imperative as the twentieth century progressed. The goals of the Southeast Asia Co-Prosperity Sphere were achieved in the post-World War II era by a concerted effort on the part of Japanese trading houses to capture an impressive share of the world market of a wide range of goods. By becoming a major trading nation, Japan earned the foreign exchange to purchase the raw materials and energy required to sustain its industrial output. Some of its industrial output is exported and the rest consumed domestically to provide the Japanese people with the highest standard of living in Asia.

Japan's first major export industry following the war was steel products (structural and plate steel, rolls of steel sheet, coils of steel wire, steel pipe, billets, rods, ingots, slabs, and bars). At the same time, it embarked on a major shipbuilding program to replace its war-ravaged merchant fleet to handle its semifinished and finished goods exports and raw material imports (every ton of steel produced requires 2.5 tons of imported iron ore and metallurgical coal). Japanese shipbuilders introduced mass-production techniques in fabricating and assembling ships. They were able to capture half the world's order book for new-buildings because of the high productivity of their yards, their access to low-priced steel, their marketing skills, and the availability of shipyard credit for prospective buyers.

Building vessels of advanced ship design and cargo-handling technology lowered the cost of exporting goods and importing raw materials. Since 10–15% of total Japanese steel production was consumed in constructing vessels to serve the domestic economy and to be sold in the international marketplace, ships (and subsequently automobiles) became other forms of steel exports.

Besides being an important consumer of steel and earner of foreign exchange, the shipbuilding industry is a large employer. It is also an effective means of transforming an untrained labor force into a source of skilled and disciplined workers for other industrial firms. The shipbuilding projects in Brazil, South Korea, and Taiwan are intended to hasten their transition from agrarian to industrialized societies. They were conceived with the Japanese experience very much in mind. Developing nations are not the only ones who view shipbuilding as an instrument of social change. The United States government has financially supported a shipyard in Brooklyn whose goal, besides building ships, is to train unemployable welfare recipients as welders and semi-skilled laborers for potential entry into industry.

Japan is the largest single factor influencing demand for shipping capacity. About one-quarter of the world's tanker fleet, one-half of the world's bulk carrier fleet, and much of the world's large-capacity container vessel, LPG, LNG, automobile, and forest products carrier fleets are dedicated to satisfying the shipping requirements of this one nation. However, the emergence of Japan as a major world economic power is not the only factor influencing shipping demand. Despite all the commentary on poverty, the world's population, which has grown considerably since WWII, enjoys a higher standard of living in the 1980s than ever before. Even so, shipping demand has exceeded the growth in the consumption of energy and raw materials measured in terms of an increasing world population with a higher per capita standard of living. While the average annual growth of tons of bulk commodities in ocean-borne trade was 6.5% from 1965 to 1975, the corresponding growth in ton-miles of shipping demand was 10% (Fearnley and Eger Chartering, Oslo). As more remote sources of raw materials were tapped and as major users of raw materials, such as steel and aluminum companies, diversified their sources of supply, the average voyage distance lengthened, adding to the demand for shipping capacity.

The U.S. is a prime example of a nation becoming increasingly dependent on foreign sources of raw materials. In the early 1960s, it was essentially self-sufficient in crude oil and iron ore but now imports nearly half its crude oil and one-third of its iron ore needs. It is also exhausting nearby sources of raw materials and must import from more remote areas. Where Venezuela, about 2,000 miles away, was once the main source of foreign crude oil imports, much of the incremental growth in demand for crude oil is now satisfied from sources halfway around the world in the Persian Gulf.

The U.S. is both a major world raw material importer (crude oil, iron ore, bauxite) and exporter (grain, coal, phosrock). Nearly half of total U.S. grain production is exported. The United States is an important exporter of finished goods. It is also the principal market for European and Far Eastern exports.

The general agreement among major trading nations to reduce tariffs and other barriers to trade has encouraged the specialization of industrial output. The U.S. has a major share of the world market in computers, aircraft, and earth-moving and construction equipment. Foreign nations pay for these imports by selling consumer goods (shoes and clothing from Spain, Brazil, Italy, Korea, and Taiwan and electronic gadgetry from Japan) in the U.S. marketplace. Prior to the 1960s, the imported automobile was a rarity in the U.S. By the late 1970s, foreign automobiles had captured about 20% of the market. Once, Volkswagen (shipping distance, 3,500 miles) dominated the market; in the 1970s, Toyota and Datsun (shipping distance, 5,000 miles to U.S. West Coast ports and 10,000 miles to U.S. East Coast ports) took over the lead. The growing Japanese motorcycle and automobile exports to Europe are shipped 11,000 miles via the Suez Canal or nearly 15,000 miles via the Cape of Good Hope.

The major contribution of the world's shipowners to this unprecedented growth in demand for shipping capacity was their ability to satisfy this demand without increasing the cost of transportation. In fact, the cost of transportation has fallen considerably, expressed in constant dollars or as a percentage of the value of goods transported. Forty-five men were required to move 15,000 tons of crude oil in a T-2 tanker. Now 30 men can move quantities as large as 550,000 tons. Gangs of longshoremen and stevedores were required to transfer a few hundred tons of breakbulk cargo between ship and shore per day. Now a container-handling crane operator can take a 40-foot container filled with 30 tons of goods off a container vessel and put another one on in less than two minutes.

Maritime labor unions call this process the "increased productivity of labor," while owners are more apt to use the phrase "substitution of capital for labor." Both are correct because labor is more productive when capital is plowed into shipbuilding facilities that can more efficiently build vessels which, in turn, can more efficiently transport commodities and goods. Everyone's standard of living rises as the transportation component in the final cost of goods falls. The point to remember is that the public benefits every time a shipbuilder/shipowner introduces a better-designed vessel or an owner increases his vessel's utilization by combining trades or adopting modern cargo-handling technology.

This is nothing more than the workings of entrepreneurs in a free market developing new technologies and methods for accomplishing tasks more economically for their own advantage. Being a hard taskmaster, capitalism is also at work during depressed market conditions. The use of tankers in the grain trade was brought about by owners and brokers desperately seeking employment for unwanted tankers. The international trade in chemicals came into being under the same circumstances, leading to the development of the sophisticated parcel tanker. The international trade in fertilizers is not something that existed from time immemorial but is a post-war development resulting from owners and brokers frantically seeking employment for surplus bulk carriers.

It takes more than imagination, foresight, and business acumen for owners to change the face of shipping by the development of new vessel types and commodity trades; stubbornness of purpose is also a necessary ingredient. Although building larger tankers may have been an evolutionary process or developing the chemical and fertilizer trades were beneficial aspects of bad times in shipping, abandoning the tradi-

tional method of handling break-bulk cargoes in favor of containerization on the principal liner routes was a revolutionary development
which faced tremendous opposition from vested interests in every
port.

About two-thirds of the world tonnage has been built since 1965. In
1965, there was one tanker over 160,000 dwt, while over 800 existed in
the late 1970s. Since containerization began in earnest around 1965,
most of the world's large container vessels are of recent vintage, as are
combination carriers, large-sized LPG and LNG carriers, Lash, Ro-Ro,
car and forest products carriers, and parcel and chemical tankers. And
so, too, the need for large amounts of capital.

Inflation has amplified the need for capital far beyond that expected
from just the sheer physical growth of the world fleet. A general cargo
vessel of standard size and performance characteristics doubled in construction cost between 1967 and 1972 and doubled again by 1976. The
shipyard price for a 250,000-dwt crude carrier rose from $20–25 mil-
lion in the late 1960s to $50 million by 1973. Much of the profit antic-
ipated by ship builders during the 1973 ordering spree was eaten away
by the ravages of inflation between the time of ordering and delivering
the vessel. A 125,000-cubic meter LNG carrier ordered in 1976 carried a
price tag of $130–150 million, while those delivered that same year
were originally contracted for $60–90 million. In 1975, the world's
shipowners took delivery of a record-breaking 60 million dwt of all
types of vessels for which they paid about $20 billion. About 15–20% of
this amount was spent on fitting out, supervision, design and other
predelivery expenses, interest charges on construction financing, and
shipyard profits. The remainder was spent by the world's shipyards on
the labor, steel, and propulsion machinery and other associated systems
(roughly in the proportion of 40%, 40%, 20%). The capital requirements
of shipping have taken quite a jump since the days of a $300,000 T-2
tanker.

12

Sources of Capital

Equity and debt are the primary sources of capital required to pay for the $20 billion of vessels delivered in 1975. Other sources are a variety of government grants, tax incentives, and subsidies available as maritime aids to certain national flag fleet owners. Equity is the cash investment in a vessel drawn from an owner's reserves accumulated from fleet operation and vessel sales and, to a lesser extent, from the sale of stock.

There is no commitment on the part of any shipping venture to repay an owner for his equity investment. Nor, for that matter, does the owner know what return, if any, he will earn. It is impossible to predict accurately what is going to be left over after all future operating and financing charges are deducted from future revenues and what proceeds will be received from the eventual disposal of the vessel. The return of, and on, an equity investment is unknown until the vessel has been liquidated (sold, scrapped, or lost at sea). If the actual return on a vessel's investment were calculated by an owner after its disposal, the return would probably be quite different from his original expectations. An investment in a vessel reflects, more than anything else, the best business judgment on the part of the owner at the time of making the decision.

Debt is capital acquired by a shipowner from outside sources where the owner morally and legally obligates himself to make a prearranged series of repayments of principal (amortization of debt) and to pay a charge for the use of the funds (interest). From the point of view of the financing institution supplying the capital funds in the form of debt, amortization is the return of capital and interest is the return on capital.

The interest rate reflects the cost of money for the financial institution. It may either be fixed or spread above a floating rate such as the prime rate for loans funded in the domestic U.S. dollar market, the London Interbank Offering Rate (LIBO) in the Eurodollar market, or the Singapore Interbank Offering Rate (SIBO) in the Asiandollar market. Financing charges, or debt servicing obligations in the form of amortization and interest payments, are theoretically made irrespective of the success of the shipping venture.

The Element of Risk

Every business venture has an element of risk. The mixture of equity and debt in the capital structure of a firm must reflect the degree of that risk. Shipping and real estate are unusual in that an entrepreneur can obtain a charter (lease) from a first-class charterer (tenant) of impeccable creditworthiness that fixes the revenue stream for a period of time independent of interim market conditions. A building or a ship may be purchased on the basis of the present value of its future income stream from a lease/charter with little relation to its current value as an asset without a lease/charter. Charters and leases lessen the role of equity in financing because the obligations of the charterer or tenant reduce the scope of the risk of the venture.

TABLE 12.1
PROJECTED CASH FLOW (1970)

	Revenue, U.S. $	Anticipated exchange rate $/DM	Revenue, DM	Total operating costs and financing charges, DM	Cash generation: DM	$
1970	10 MM	0.27	37 MM	29.6 MM	7.4 MM	2 MM
1971	10	0.27	37	29.6	7.4	2
1972	10	0.27	37	29.6	7.4	2
1973	10	0.27	37	29.6	7.4	2
1974	10	0.27	37	29.6	7.4	2
1975	10	0.27	37	29.6	7.4	2

Although an owner charters a vessel to protect its revenue-generating potential and obtains marine insurance to protect his investment from the traditional perils of the sea, he must still face the perils of doing business: poor performance by a crew or shoreside staff, operat-

ing difficulties, collecting receivables from reluctant shippers and charterers, arbitrary reductions in charter rates or cancellation of charters by
a less than first-class charterer, and involuntary cancellation of charters
resulting from the bankruptcy of a charterer. During the 1970s, owners
had to contend with the highest rates of inflation and interest and the
greatest instability of currency exchange rates for any peacetime period
in this century.

Consider the plight of a West German shipowner who fixed his vessel on a six-year U.S. dollar time charter starting in 1970 and whose
operating and financing charges were in Deutsche marks (DM). The
owner financed his vessel with debt that called for equal principal
repayments at a fixed rate of interest. He calculated that the declining
interest payments as the loan was amortized would compensate for
escalating operating costs. In other words, the sum of operating costs
and financing charges would remain unchanged throughout the charter
period. At the end of 1975, the shipowner reviewed his performance
and found that he was correct in all aspects of his assessments except
for a stable exchange rate between the Deutsche mark and the dollar.
His cash flow, based on actual rather than anticipated currency
exchange rates, was not quite up to his earlier expectations.

TABLE 12.2
ACTUAL CASH FLOW

	Revenue, U.S. $	Anticipated exchange rate $/DM	Revenue, DM	Total operating costs and financing charges	Cash generation: DM	$
1970	10 MM	0.27	37.0 MM	29.6 MM	7.4 MM	2.0 MM
1971	10	0.28	35.7	29.6	6.1	1.7
1972	10	0.31	32.3	29.6	2.7	0.9
1973	10	0.31	32.3	29.6	2.7	0.9
1974	10	0.38	26.3	29.6	−3.3	−1.3
1975	10	0.40	25.0	29.6	−4.6	−1.8

An owner may benefit from favorable currency exchange rate fluctuations. Any portion of operating costs in British pounds or Italian lira
for U.S. dollar charters during 1970–1977 provided short-term windfall
profits as these currencies depreciated over 40% in value against the
dollar. These profits tend to be short-lived because crews paid in
pounds or lira pressed for wage increases to counteract the loss of pur-

chasing power of the currency. For fixed-rate interest loans in pounds or lira, an owner accrued real profits from currency depreciation because the same financing charges required far fewer dollars in 1976/ 77 than they did in 1970. A few owners have speculated in foreign currencies by ordering vessels financed with long-term, fixed-rate ship- yard credits denominated in currencies which they expected to depre- ciate against the U.S. dollar. Most shipowners consider shipping enough of a challenge and avoid the added risk of adverse currency exchange rate fluctuations.

The most effective method of avoiding the risk of adverse currency exchange rate fluctuations is to deal in one currency (most commonly the U.S. dollar) or match the outflows and inflows of each individual currency. If an owner has only U.S. dollar charter income and a sub- stantial outflow of Japanese yen to service yen-denominated debt ob- ligations, he can reduce his risk to adverse dollar/yen exchange rate fluctuations if he can enter into Japanese yen charters. By matching the inflow and outflow of yen, the owner is no longer directly concerned about changes in the relationship between the yen and the dollar.

The greatest risk facing an owner is the marketplace, the final judge of all business decisions. Small changes in the overall level of world trade and patterns of trade significantly affect the supply/demand situ- ation for various types and classes of vessels. The marginal changes in demand for vessel capacity in relation to the supply of vessel capacity have pronounced effects on spot market rates which, in turn, influence the thinking of charterers and the value of the ships in the sale and purchase market. If an owner had chartered his tanker in 1967 for six years, the vessel would have come off charter during the greatest tanker boom in market history. The owner could have cared less for any prob- lems that he may have had to endure throughout the charter period because of the opportunities afforded him in the sale and purchase or short-, medium-, or long-term charter markets. Yet if the owner had entered into an eight-year charter, the tanker would have come off charter in one of the worst tanker market depressions in history with the vessel worth a slight premium over scrap value. There was no way for an owner to know whether it would have been better for him to enter into a six- or an eight-year charter or any charter at all, for that matter.

Entrepreneurs will not invest their capital unless they feel the potential reward exceeds the perceived risks. Shipowners face all the hazards of shipping and risk their capital, hoping to enrich themselves. A fleet built up by an individual on an initial investment of a few tens of thousands of dollars just after World War II was sold in 1968 for $50 million and sold again in 1973 for $200 million. It is this possibility that attracts individuals to shipping. The romantic aspects of being a ship-owner tend to fade if all one has for his efforts is a string of losses.

The Role of Debt

Although a shipowner's equity, the cash generated from fleet oper-ation and vessel sales, is an important source of capital to finance the acquisition of newbuildings, it would be misleading to suggest that an initial investment in one $100,000 tanker would throw off all the cash required to purchase two $1 million tankers which, in turn, would pay for four $10 million tankers. To appreciate the role of debt in building up shipping fortunes, one must go back to the early post-war period.

Purchasing a lowly 16,500-dwt T-2 tanker for a few hundred thou-sand dollars, an owner employs the vessel to haul 15,000 tons of crude oil between port A and port B for $7 per ton with nearly all the revenue of $105,000 ($7 per ton × 15,000 tons of cargo) dedicated to meeting operating and voyage costs. Some years later, the world crude oil trade has expanded; the world tanker fleet is no longer large enough to handle the volume of trade, and oil companies are forced to seek more tonnage. Some of this incremental demand for tanker capacity is satisfied by ordering vessels from shipyards for the oil companies' accounts and chartering arrangements with owners. To heat up the competition, the chartering managers, directly and through brokers, contact as many entrepreneurial-minded owners as possible. By playing one against another, the chartering managers squeeze the last possible penny out of owners proposing to build more T-2 tankers and offering long-term charter rates equivalent to $7 per ton to cover operating and voyage costs in hauling crude between ports A and B plus X dollars per ton to cover financing charges.

In a free market, an owner's motivation in originating, or copying, a new concept such as a 36,500-dwt supertanker is to gain a competitive edge by offering a rate that results in lower transportation costs for a charterer than that proposed by other owners. Since the operating costs of a 36,500-dwt supertanker remain about the same as a T-2 tanker (lower maintenance charges of a new vessel and savings on crew costs from introducing automation compensating for higher insurance premi-ums), the $105,000 in operating and voyage costs between ports A and B are now spread over 35,000 tons of cargo rather than 15,000 tons. An owner is not about to offer a chartering manager in need of tanker capacity a rate of $3 per ton ($105,000 divided by 35,000 tons of cargo) when the market rate for T-2 tankers is $7 or more. The owner proposes a rate that is slightly below the lowest possible rate that his competitors can offer for new T-2 tonnage. However, the chartering manager, being a fleet operator himself, realizes full well the economy of scale of larger-sized vessels. He counters with a rate that reflects the potential savings of a supertanker. Counteroffer follows counteroffer as the shipowner strives to maximize his profit and the charterer strives to minimize his transportation cost. Finally, both parties agree on rate and terms and "confirm a clean fixture" where the charterer agrees to pay $6 per ton for crude shipped between the two ports over a period of time.

The owner does not have the cash necessary to purchase the vessel. All he has is a scrap of paper that locks in a cash surplus of $3 per ton ($6 per ton in revenue less $3 per ton in operating and voyage charges) for oil transported between two ports for the duration of the charter period. Payment is made on condition that the operator performs, i.e., fulfills his obligations under the charter party. The owner must find an outside source of capital, a financial institution willing to lend against or discount the potential cash surplus (earnings) thrown off by the charter. The owner can then combine the loan with his equity funds to acquire the vessel.

This story has a very happy ending if everyone's expectations are realized over the course of the charter period. The charterer has been able to satisfy an incremental demand in tanker capacity at a savings from the going rate without having to commit any of his capital resources for the acquisition of another tanker. The lender is happy because the loan will be fully paid out from the proceeds of the charter from a very substantial corporation where the risks (the willingness and ability of the charterer to pay and the ability of the owner to perform) are commensurate with his reward (the spread between the cost of buying and selling money). The owner is happy because he will own a vessel free and clear of debt at the end of the charter period with half its useful life remaining on an initial cash outlay representing a small fraction of its original cost.

A successful shipowner has access to charterers because of his reputation to perform and his willingness to originate, or copy, new concepts in shipping to enhance his competitiveness. He has access to shipyards to reserve berths, or acquire berth options, during the negotiations with the charterer because of his previous newbuilding orders, and he has access to outside sources of capital to finance his fleet acquisitions because of his previous borrowings. A successful shipowner must have the resourcefulness, patience, and tenacity to translate these channels of communication into a physical vessel that is properly constructed, financed, and operated to perform its intended function.

One of the determinants of the eventual size of an owner's fleet in an environment of expanding world trade is his capacity to corral outside sources of capital. If the incremental expansion of world trade requires 20 more vessels, each costing $10 million, an owner with $10 million in cash and no outside sources of capital can buy one vessel. If he can obtain 50% financing from an outside source of capital, his $10 million can support the acquisition of two vessels; if 80% financing is available, then five vessels; if 90%, then ten; if 100%, then all 20 and more, for there is no theoretical limit to the expansion process except the availability of credit.

However, leveraging or gearing is a double-edged sword. While a greater reliance on debt at the expense of equity permits a more aggressive vessel acquisition program, the increased cash outflow to service debt obligations reduces the margin for error. Suppose that the market rate for the $10 million vessel is $4 million per year in revenue and the vessel has an operating cost of $1 million per year. If an owner purchases the vessel with equity funds alone, the cash surplus to meet all unforeseen contingencies is $3 million per year ($4 million income less $1 million in operating costs). This cash surplus is reduced by the amount, tenure, and interest rate of any underlying debt.

TABLE 12.3

Revenue	Operating costs	Debt	Amortization	First-year interest	Cash surplus
$4 MM	$1 MM	None	—	—	$3.0 MM
4 MM	1 MM	50% ($5 MM) 5-yr tenure at 8%	$1 MM	$0.4 MM	1.6 MM
4 MM	1 MM	100% ($10 MM) 5-yr tenure at 8%	2 MM	0.8 MM	0.2 MM
4 MM	1 MM	100% ($10 MM) 10-yr tenure at 8%	1 MM	0.8 MM	1.2 MM

Table 12.3 illustrates that the ability to accumulate adequate cash reserves to meet unforeseen contingencies varies considerably with the amount and the tenure of the underlying debt. The search by owners for

the longest possible tenure on debt is an effort to improve current cash flow at the price of extending the debt servicing period.

Market rates for vessel capacity move independently of vessel operating and financing costs. Unless there is sufficient charter coverage to maintain a flow of cash to service debt obligations, the first companies squeezed in an economic downturn are those that are more leveraged than their competitors. The flow of cash is the only thing that matters. Stockholders and accountants may be excited over book profits and markups or markdowns in net worth, but cash is needed to pay the operating, financing, and overhead expenses and to build up a cushion of reserves to meet unforeseen contingencies and satisfy equity requirements in new investments. It is sometimes difficult to pay a cash dividend out of a book profit.

Sources of Debt

The principal sources of debt in shipping are shipyard credit facilities, commercial banks, specialized ship lending institutions, and pension and insurance funds. Shipyard credits are the most important source of capital in shipping, far outweighing all other forms of debt. In fact, shipyard credits may well equal the total of all other sources of debt, plus equity, in the capital structure of the world's shipping companies.

Shipyard Credits to Foreign Shipowners

Shipyard credits are funds provided directly or guaranteed by government agencies to induce owners to place orders for newbuildings in public or privately owned shipyards of that nation. Regardless of the institution offering shipyard credits, the actual source of credit is the public purse. In an attempt to prevent destructive competition among national powers, the Organization for Economic Cooperation and Development (OECD) establishes the maximum extent of shipyard credit terms that can be offered by member nations to finance vessels built for export. The member nations of the OECD account for a large share of the world shipbuilding capacity, including Japan with half of the world order book, and other major European shipbuilding nations. Non-OECD shipbuilding nations whose export financing terms are not restricted by OECD regulations are Brazil, East Germany, Poland, South Korea, Taiwan, and Yugoslavia.

In the early 1970s, the maximum OECD shipyard credit terms for vessels built for export (i.e., to be registered in a nation other than the shipbuilding nation) were 70% financing, 7-year tenure, at 7% interest. That is, if an owner had 30% of the cost of the vessel (cash reserves or borrowing against other assets), he could acquire a vessel with an obligation to pay 10% of the cost of the vessel every year for the following seven years with an interest charge of 7% on the outstanding balance. Not all owners end up with the same shipyard credit terms because the OECD only sets the maximum terms that can be offered. The actual shipyard credit terms granted to an owner are a matter of negotiation between a shipowner and a government administrator, who is influenced in his dealings by the state of the nation's order books.

Shipyards are built with the idea of constructing ships on a continuing basis, providing a steady source of employment for shipyard workers and workers in marine-related industries regardless of the state of the world economy. Shipyard credits keep a nation's shipyards busy. When the shipping market is depressed and commercially oriented financial institutions withdraw from the marketplace, shipyard credits ensure that qualified owners have the financial clout to order vessels.

The varying credit policies of the Export Import (Exim) Bank of Japan illustrate the role of shipyard credits in the industrial life of a nation. In the 1960s and early 1970s, the Exim Bank required that shipyard credits offered to non-Japanese flag owners buying Japanese-built vessels be guaranteed by an acceptable non-Japanese commercial bank for the first 2–3 years. Considering the owner's equity contribution and the portion of the shipyard credit financing covered by a bank guarantee, the Exim Bank's maximum exposure to risk was about 40–50% of the original cost of a two or three-year-old vessel. Sometimes the Exim Bank would drop the requirement for a bank guarantee if there were recourse to other forms of security, such as a charter or guarantees from a substantial owner. In other words, its lending policies were commercially prudent.

In 1975, however, the dearth of new orders was threatening to close down Japanese yards. The shipyards had already reduced their output by eliminating overtime and reassigning workers to other industrial undertakings. They had sapped the market dry of new orders by slashing newbuilding prices 30% or more below European quotes for comparable vessels. For the Japanese yards, the losses incurred in building these vessels were less costly than paying full wage benefits to an idle shipyard work force. The maximum OECD permissible credit terms could not be violated by government institutions like the Exim Bank of Japan. These restrictions, however, were neatly sidestepped by top-up financing packages arranged through the Japanese trading houses. Owners were given the opportunity to purchase vessels for less than actual building costs with 90–95% nonrecourse financing with repayment stretched over 10–15 years at a fixed rate of interest between 8 and 9%. The maximum loss an owner sustains under nonrecourse financing is the loss of equity because the creditor cannot look beyond the vessel itself as security for his loan. Many owners placed orders for ships because it was difficult to ignore this bargain-basement sale with little down and E-Z payment credit terms. Some of these orders were hardly more than bets on an upswing in economic activity by the time the vessels were delivered because of the owners' limited exposure to loss. This whole episode, which was repeated in nearly all other shipbuilding nations, was a classic example of the use of shipyard credit facilities to ensure continuity of shipyard work.

Shipyard Credits to Domestic Shipowners

The OECD's maximum shipyard credit terms apply only for vessels built for export, that is, vessels that will fly the flag of a nation other than the shipbuilding nation. Other forms of shipyard (i.e., government) credit are available for domestic owners operating national flag vessels. These maritime financial aid programs promote the growth of national flag fleets for defense, prestige, or economic reasons. Maritime aid programs are very common throughout the world.

In Japan, a tax-paying national flag shipping company is eligible to apply for interest-subsidized loans of 13-year tenure for vessels built and registered in Japan and manned by Japanese crews. The Japanese shipping company obtains financing from a commercial Japanese source (banks or insurance companies) and the financing institution holding the debt at an 8% coupon may receive 3% from the government and the remaining 5% from the shipping company. A qualified loan under this program is usually covered by a full payout charter from a Japanese end user.

The Japanese interest subsidy program with longer tenure debt is designed to make Japanese flag vessels, with their high manning costs, more competitive. The interest rate subsidy program works best for large, highly capitalized vessels in compensating Japanese owners for the extra costs of employing Japanese crews. The program is less successful for smaller-sized vessels where the interest subsidy does not fully offset the extra cost of manning with a Japanese crew. The Japanese shipping companies have resorted to the long-term tie-in arrangements with Hong Kong owners to ensure the competitiveness of their less capital-intensive vessels in the international marketplace.

In the United States, an active U.S. flag merchant marine manned by experienced seagoing crews and an ongoing shipbuilding program employing a force of trained and experienced yard workers is considered vital to national defense. An active fleet is an adjunct to the nation's naval forces and an active shipbuilding program can be readily converted to building warships in times of national emergency. However, U.S. flag owners could not possibly compete in the world marketplace with conventional tankers, bulk carriers, and container ships costing twice as much as their foreign flag competitors' vessels and manned with the world's costliest crews. Comprehensive maritime assistance programs are necessary if it is in the defense interests of the nation to have a U.S. merchant fleet and a cadre of experienced merchant seamen and yard workers.

The heart of U.S. maritime financial aids is the Title XI insurance program where the owner pays a fee of about 0.5% to the government on the outstanding amount of merchant marine bonds in return for a guarantee from the government on the timely payment of the bonds' principal and interest. Title XI insured merchant marine bonds are issued up to 87.5% of the cost of a vessel built without a construction subsidy and 75% of the net cost of a vessel built with a construction subsidy. The bonds have a maturity of 20–25 years, carry a fixed rate of interest equivalent to direct government obligations of the same tenure, and are purchased primarily by U.S. pension and insurance funds.

A U.S. flag operator in international trade or foreign commerce receiving both construction and operating subsidies is placed on the same footing, cost-wise, as his foreign flag competitors. Technically, a fully subsidized U.S. flag operator has an economic advantage over his non-U.S. flag competitors because of the longer maturities of the Title XI insured merchant marine bonds and the ability to sell the substantial tax loss benefits of ownership to a third party through a tax-leveraged leasing arrangement. The resulting lease payments are about half the annual capital charges that a non-U.S. flag operator must pay for a comparable vessel. The cost of a leasing arrangement to a U.S. flag operator is that he pays financing charges over the vessel's entire useful life and does not retain its residual value. His foreign flag competitor has completed making financing charges in half the time and has the full use of the vessel, free and clear of debt, for the remainder of its life.

Not all U.S. flag shipping companies in foreign commerce are subsidized. Those that do receive construction and operating subsidies are still exposed to the rigors of competition because only parity of costs, not profitability, is guaranteed. Some U.S. flag shipping companies have sustained heavy losses without any hope of further government assistance. Some have been forced to drastically revamp their shipping activities in response to market conditions, and a few have actually been declared bankrupt. The need to remain competitive has been a driving force for U.S. liner service operators to pursue the development of more efficient vessels such as container, Lash, and Ro-Ro vessels. These vessel types are primarily American contributions to the world shipping industry. The U.S. method of subsidizing its privately owned national flag fleet is superior to the subsidy program of Italy and France, where public funds reimburse the losses sustained by nationalized shipping companies without much in the way of incentives for the companies to stem the extent of the losses.

The Belgian government offers 80% Belgian franc financing with a 15-year tenure at a usurious 3% rate for national flag owners. The Brazilian government offers 80% cruzeiro financing over a 15-year period at 8% interest for vessels built, owned, and manned by Brazilians. In both cases, the lower interest rates and longer tenure of debt than that available in the private or commercial sector are subsidies for owners participating in these programs. Brazil also levies a 20% surtax on freight charges of all goods imported in non-Brazilian flag vessels and earmarks these funds for the development of its shipbuilding industry and merchant marine.

Britain had an interesting program to ensure a sufficiently sized British flag merchant fleet for national defense purposes. At one time, the British government would pay an investment grant of 20% of the cost of a vessel direct to a shipyard, which did not have to be in Britain, if the owner, who did not have to be a British citizen, would register the vessel under the British flag. The vessel had to be manned by British officers, but not necessarily British seamen, and would be under the control of British authorities in case of national emergency. Of course, the owner would be subject to British taxes on profits once the reserves for depreciation were exhausted. However, little was actually paid in taxes because the owner was free to emigrate (change the country of registry) about the time the vessel was fully depreciated. This program, which allowed owners to build up their fleets with little in the way of equity between the investment grant and shipyard credits, is no longer available in its original form.

The argument that subsidized national flag shipowners will eventually repay the subsidies through taxes on their profits is misleading because governments receive far less in tax revenue than they spend in maritime subsidies. National flag shipowners in the industrialized world have convinced government policymakers that their ability to compete against nontaxpaying vessels registered under flags of convenience/necessity would be severely impaired if they were as heavily taxed, on a current basis, as domestic corporations. The tax laws of many maritime nations have special provisions for shipping companies to defer the payment of taxes by rapid depreciation of the vessel for tax purposes, sometimes in excess of 100% of its cost, and the establishment of tax-deferring special reserve accounts for pretax profits that are set aside for eventual investment in ships. These programs do not eliminate tax liabilities; they defer their payment, indefinitely, if the shipping company keeps expanding its asset base. Taxes are due and payable if depreciation reserves are exhausted or if withdrawals are made from the special reserve accounts for working capital, dividends, or other nonqualifying purposes.

Taxation can distort the investment decision process. Norwegian owners, flush with record profits during the 1973 tanker boom, ordered large crude carriers and semisubmersible drilling rigs. They started depreciating these assets immediately, even before they were built, as permitted by Norwegian tax law rather than pay most of the profits to the tax authorities. If an owner orders a $50 million large crude carrier and, by doing so, reduces his tax bill to the government by $30 million, the owner's net investment in the newbuilding is $20 million. If the vessel earns $20 million over its lifetime (neglecting interest for the moment), someone has taken a $30 million loss. In this case, it is the government which bears the loss through lower tax revenues. Confiscatory tax rates motivate investors to accept a larger degree of risk in their investment decisions because they are gambling with the government's money, not their own.

The Norwegian tax code forces an owner to reinvest his profits immediately if he wishes to defer the payment of taxes. This is quite unlike the U.S. tax deferment program which permits postponement of reinvestment of pretax profits deposited in a capital construction fund. Timing fleet expansion programs to the provisions of a tax code rather than to the conditions of the marketplace led to an excessive ordering of large crude carriers and semisubmersible drilling rigs by some Norwegian owners in 1973. These owners were in a severe cash bind by 1975/76, which prompted the establishment of the Norwegian Guaranty Institute to prevent their wholesale liquidation and to preserve the nation's borrowing capacity to fund the development of the North Sea. It is ironic that confiscatory tax laws intended as a source of funds for the Norwegian government should be the root cause of another government support program. It is also ironic that the largest single source of capital to finance the expansion of the world fleet, which is largely owned by capitalistic-minded entrepreneurs, is public funds in the form of shipyard credits.

Pension and Insurance Companies

Another source of debt is U.S. pension and insurance companies which, in addition to investing heavily in the nearly $6 billion of Title XI insured merchant marine bonds outstanding in 1978/79, finance vessels owned by or under long-term full payout charters to first-class charterers. European insurance companies invest directly in shipping. Unlike their American counterparts, they may issue guarantees on debt placed with other financial institutions. An example is a European insurance company guaranteeing the balloon payment of a commercial bank loan to a shipping company. While a straight five-year equal principal repayment debt of $1 million amortizes at $200,000 per year, the same loan with a 50% balloon would amortize at $100,000 per year. The $500,000 balloon payment would be due at the end of the fifth year. If the balloon payment is guaranteed by an insurance company, the commercial bank making the loan looks to the shipping company for the $100,000 in annual amortization payments plus interest charges and looks to the insurance company if the shipping company cannot pay it off. If the guarantee is exercised, the insurance company looks to the shipping company to recoup its money. The insurance company receives an annual fee from the shipping company for taking on the risk of guarantor. It is not at all unusual for European and Japanese banks and insurance companies to be involved as guarantors in ship financings.

Ship Financing Institutions

Specialized ship financing institutions concentrate their efforts in shipping loans much in the same way as savings banks and building loan societies are involved with home mortgages. Some ship financing institutions are a consortia of commercial banks, each owning a share of the equity stock. This arrangement conveniently syndicates shipping loans among the participating banks. A few ship financing institutions have shipowners and commercial banks as shareholders. Although the bankers may feel that this arrangement provides them with captive customers, it really provides the shipowners with a captive source of funds to finance their expansion plans. This marriage of borrower and lender may work well in good times, but the principles of commercial lending are exceedingly difficult to practice when the prospective borrower, as shareholder, is also the lending officer's employer.

Commercial Banks

Commercial banks are important sources of capital in the form of debt for financing newbuildings both before and after delivery and for financing the acquisition of second-hand tonnage. Although shipyard credits are a less costly way to finance newbuildings after delivery, they are not always available or their terms may not be attractive from an owner's perspective. Granted that owners, as entrepreneurs, are optimistic, the major constraints on their aggregate expansion plans are the level of market rates and the availability of credit. Unlike shipyard credit, commercial loans are attuned to the state of the market. Commercial banks have been criticized for withdrawing from the shipping scene when shipping rates plummet. This is exactly what they are supposed to do. A falling market is a signal to the world's shipowners and commercial lenders that further expansion of the world fleet is not a desirable allocation of capital resources. The bankers' general retreat from considering new proposals, though not from supporting their established clientele, is to be expected in a market-oriented or commercial environment.

A prospective borrower does not always appreciate that a banker does not lend his personal funds. He lends the funds of his depositors, who expect to be repaid in full on demand. The banker pays a depositor a rate of interest of X percent for leaving his funds with the bank and lends the money out to others at X + Y percent. Y is the interest spread between buying and selling money. The greatest annual loss rate that can be tolerated in a portfolio of loans is equal to the interest spread less the cost of doing business. If a bank is earning a net spread of 1% on a portfolio of shipping loans, a loss rate in one year of 1% on the outstanding amount of booked loans would wipe out the entire profit margin. With a net spread of 1%, a bank must be 99% sure of being repaid in making a shipping loan just to break even.

In 1975, an owner had a chance to acquire a five-year-old 100,000-dwt tanker for just above its scrap value. In presenting his proposal to a banker, the owner pointed out the historic profit potential of buying and selling ships at the appropriate time in the market cycle, the $30 million replacement cost of the vessel, the asset coverage provided by the scrap value, the low valuation of the vessel fully reflecting the dismal state of the market, and the dim prospects of improvement in the near future. The borrower proposed leaving the vessel in lay-up at an

annual cost of $200,000 per year for the following three years and con-
servatively estimated break-even operation in the fourth year, followed
by surplus cash generation of $1 million in the fifth and $2 million in
the sixth year combined with the sale of the vessel for $6 million at the
end of the sixth year.

TABLE 10.4
CASH FLOW PROJECTION

	Cash to acquire vessel	Lay-up costs	Cash surplus from operation	Sale of vessel	Net cash flow
1975	$-3 MM	$-0.2 MM			$-3.2 MM
1976		-0.2 MM			-0.2 MM
1977		-0.2 MM			-0.2 MM
1978			$0 MM		0.0 MM
1979			1 MM		1.0 MM
1980			2 MM	$6 MM	8.0 MM

TABLE 10.5
INTERNAL RATE OF RETURN

Year	Net cash flow	20% discount factor	Discounted cash flow
0	$-3.2 MM	1.00	$-3.20 MM
1	-0.2 MM	1.20	-0.17 MM
2	-0.2 MM	1.44	-0.14 MM
3	0.0 MM	1.73	0.00 MM
4	1.0 MM	2.07	0.48 MM
5	8.0 MM	2.49	3.21 MM
		Net present value of the cash flow stream discounted at 20%:	$ 0.18 MM

A discount factor of 21.36% would reduce the net present value of
the cash flow stream to zero. This means that the internal rate of return
of this investment, which is the purchase price plus lay-up costs, is
21.36%.

The bewilderment expressed by the prospective borrower over the
banker's reluctance to become involved is symptomatic of a basic con-
fusion over the meaning of equity and debt. The $3 million purchase of

a laid-up tanker may be an excellent equity investment, but it lacks the essential elements to support debt financing. The projected cash flow is not amenable to an orderly retirement of debt, nor is the risk of loss of capital in this venture, which is fully reflected in the rate of return expectation of the equity owner, commensurate with the banker's rate of return. From a banker's perspective, there is a mismatch between cash generation and debt retirement and between risk and reward. Yet this transaction can be partly or wholly financed with debt if other cash-generating assets can be pledged as the primary means of repayment rather than the hopes of an eventual revival of the tanker market.

Commercial bank lending practices can be broadly divided into asset and cash flow financing. The basic premise of asset financing is that the asset, or vessel, always has a market value in excess of the amount of the outstanding debt. Exim Bank of Japan's exposure to risk (40–50% of the original cost of a 2–3-year-old ship) is an example of asset financing. Another example is a banker willing to lend against half the cost of a vessel if an owner puts up the other half in equity. In this case, the lender feels that the risk of a vessel losing more than half of its value in the early years of its life is sufficiently remote to be commensurate with his reward (the spread on the loan). If an owner cannot meet his debt obligations, the vessel is simply sold and the proceeds liquidate the bank's debt. The owner bears the entire loss if the proceeds fall somewhere above the amount of outstanding debt and the original cost of the vessel. The owner is compensated for taking this risk by being the sole beneficiary of any increase in the value of the vessel above his vested interest. Asset financing dispenses with the need of projecting cash flows and conducting in-depth credit reviews until the vessel is unable to earn its keep and is worth far less than the principal amount of the loan.

Charters provide a source of revenue for a timely and orderly repayment of debt in a business marked with volatile rates for the employment of vessels. A charter from a creditworthy charterer is an insurance policy that preserves the cash-generating capacity of the vessel to meet debt obligations in times of depressed market conditions. Although cash flow financing is built around a charter, the charter is in no way responsible for the repayment of debt. The owner, not the charterer, signs the loan documents. The lender generally constructs a fall-back position, or a back-up credit structure, of security interests in other vessels, personal or corporate guarantees, and triggering mechanisms in the loan covenants designed to give the lender leverage in negotiating with the borrower should the charter fail to support the repayment of debt. All these measures reduce the scope of the lender's risk to make it commensurate with his reward.

Although tankers, bulk, ore, combination, LNG, and LPG carriers, and offshore drilling rigs are charterable, the vast fleet of container ships, general cargo vessels, small bulk carriers, parcel tankers, refrigerated vessels, and other types in liner, semiliner, and tramp service are not. The task of financing vessels for which no substantial end user exists to bear the economic risk of depressed market conditions is possible. Most money is lent to firms that supply goods and services for which there is no guaranteed market. The major difference between financing a tanker under charter and a container vessel in liner service is the mixture of equity and debt in the vessel's capital structure.

Commercial banks exhibit a wide diversity of lending philosophies toward shipping. Some have a firm commitment to the industry, while others treat potential shipping transactions on a case-by-case basis as just another source of lending. Lending practices also vary over a wide spectrum. Some banks play a passive role in ship financing by participating in syndicates and relying on the lead bank to appraise the risks involved and to protect the interests of the participating banks. The collapse of the Colocotronis shipping empire in 1976 brought to light the existence of participating banks in syndicates with no real knowledge of the shipping industry. Their trust in the lead bank pursuing their best interests was shattered by events, and some of the participating banks felt obliged to sue the lead bank, not the owner, to protect their investments.

Another banking practice is to lend on an island-of-assets basis where a loan is made on a package of vessels that provides adequate support for the repayment of the loan. The lenders may not be fully aware of the remaining interests of the owner. The failure of Maritime Fruit Carriers in 1976 may have been a shock for the lenders involved with the profitable reefer vessels whose profits fell short of the cash deficits generated in the tanker side of the business.

Some owners maintain that the island-of-assets approach in lending is appropriate because each vessel is its own corporate universe by virtue of the one-ship holding company. An owner does not hold the stock of one company that owns ten vessels. He holds the stock of ten companies, each of which owns one ship. Thus, a self-liquidating loan on Vessels A, B, and C should not be affected by the bankruptcy of the company owning Vessel D. Although this may be true in a strict legal sense, it does not seem to hold up in practice. Few, if any, lenders involved in the collapse of Colocotronis and Maritime Fruit Carriers felt confident of their ability to escape unscathed, even though their particular loan seemed secure on an island-of-assets basis.

Most commercial banks strive to develop what is called a sound banking relationship where both the lender and borrower understand and respect each other's position and where neither party can dictate his will to the other. A sound banking relationship is not a guarantee against bad loans because every shipping failure had a sound banking relationship with some bank. Just as all charters are good in a strong market environment, so, too, are all lending practices sound. Depressed market conditions reveal weak charters and unsound lending practices. Many owners in trouble in 1975/76 complained bitterly about the eagerness of bankers to lend funds in 1973 to finance speculative orders of large crude carriers, semisubmersible drilling rigs, and other vessel types. Having committed themselves to speculative expansion programs with freely available credit, the owners watched the once ebullient optimism of their banking friends melt to concern, then caution, and finally legal action to protect their vested interests. No doubt these owners must have commented at one time or another on the availability of easy credit as a bane and a curse as they stood aside and witnessed the carnage of liquidation of the efforts of several generations of their families. Perhaps a sequestered nest egg escaped the creditors' eyes. If so, these owners may be able to reestablish themselves at some point in the future.

Bankers and owners exhibit a wide range of business philosophies toward shipping. No single philosophy on shipping or lending can be deemed correct for all time. By definition, any philosophy on shipping or lending that has survived hard times has some merit. Perhaps all that can be said is that the free communication process of conducting business in a market environment leads to a mass sorting out of owners and bankers with compatible philosophies. Time is the final judge of these arrangements.

13

Return of Capital

On the surface, it appears that each party involved with vessel financing has a different goal. The owner sees his equity investment as a way to maximize his wealth by adding another vessel to his fleet. A commercial lender considers a shipping loan as another opportunity to buy money at one price and sell it at another, profiting from the spread between the two. A government-sponsored shipyard credit administrator is concerned about bolstering his nation's exports by providing credit to qualified foreign purchasers of domestically built vessels. Alternatively, he may be motivated in promoting the nation's merchant marine fleet for a variety of economic, social, political, or national defense reasons.

In any shipping venture, the owner's equity investment is capital. The commercial lender's loan to the owner is capital. The civil servant's shipyard credit provided to an owner is capital. Regardless of their diverse motivations, all parties involved in a vessel financing are united in one common objective of recouping their capital investment.

They are also united in desiring a return on capital in addition to a return of capital. Owners, commercial lenders, and shipyard credit administrators would not be satisfied if the 60 million dwt of vessels delivered in 1975, which cost about $20 billion to build, returned $20 billion in surplus cash net of operating costs over the life of the fleet. Just to return the capital vested plus provide a modest return of 10%, the fleet will have to generate over $40 billion in surplus cash net of operating costs over its lifetime. A return of 10% does not begin to compensate for the risk of loss of capital that is inherent in any shipping venture.

If this fleet does not generate this amount of surplus cash, the equity owners would be the first to suffer from diminution of their return on capital, followed by a possible loss of capital. If this fleet's cash shortfalls increase, commercial lenders of private sources of capital and shipyard credit administrators of public sources of capital will join the plight of the equity owners. Equity owners are compensated for being first in line to suffer a loss of capital by being the sole beneficiaries of all cash generation above that required to meet debt obligations.

Throughout most of history, investors in shipping, as owners or lenders, looked exclusively to the commercial value of the vessel to recoup their investment and make a return on it. The commercial value of a vessel is determined by the market rates obtained in performing a useful service of transporting goods and commodities. Market rates, in turn, are dictated by the relationship between the supply and demand for vessel capacity and anticipated changes to that relationship. For the world fleet to be a commercial success, the demand for each segment of the fleet must occasionally be very close to the supply of vessels to create a strong market environment where owners can liquidate overhanging debt, enter into profitable charters, and build up cash reserves for the subsequent bust that is sure to follow.

The depressed market rates in tankers and bulk carriers and certain other type vessels in 1975 was a direct consequence of a 25% oversupply of vessel capacity in relation to demand. In 1976, the rate structure improved marginally at best, even though an upturn in world trade cut the surplus in half. Rates will not improve dramatically until demand for vessel capacity in active service is about evenly matched with the supply of vessel capacity. An owner, commercial lender, and shipyard credit administrator cannot recoup their capital investment in a market environment unless there is an occasional boom. A boom cannot occur until there is a balance between the supply and demand for vessel capacity. The central question facing owners and lenders alike during the latter half of the 1970s was timing the next boom. The next boom, however, was being postponed because of the difficulty in reducing the world production of ships.

There would be no question of curtailing yard output if equity from owners and debt from commercial lenders were the only sources of capital available to purchase vessels. Since the return of capital for these sources depends on market rates, the depressed rate structure prevailing for most, though not all, areas of shipping during the 1970s would have effectively dampened the delivery rate of newbuildings. However, too many governments expect shipyards to fulfill social and political goals in addition to building ships. For example, Brazil looks upon shipbuilding as a means to transform itself into an industrialized society. Shipbuilding is expected to be a training ground for unskilled labor, an employer of a large number of workers, and a heavy consumer of steel produced by Brazil's budding steel industry. Vessel exports bolster foreign exchange inflows for Brazil, and building up the Brazilian flag fleet reduces foreign exchange outflows by substituting cruzeiro for dollar shipping costs. Brazilians are very proud of their shipbuilding industry and in having their growing merchant fleet call on ports all around the world. How then, one may ask, can the Brazilian government avoid having its fleet valued at some abysmally low figure in times of a general worldwide surplus of vessel capacity? Is it possible for the Brazilians to bypass the requirement that revenues less operating costs must provide a return of and on capital, be it cruzeiros or dollars, for the labor and material dedicated to the construction of the Brazilian flag fleet?

Brazil does avoid the market's low valuation of its shipping activities, and assures a return of, and on, vested capital by awarding exclusive trading rights to its national flag fleet. It has entered into a number of bilateral agreements with its major trading partners where 40% of all cargoes are reserved for Brazilian flag vessels, 40% for the national flag vessels of the trading partner, and the remaining 20% for all other flag vessels of the world. Having ensured its fleet guaranteed cargoes, the rates are administratively determined without reference to and independent of market rates to cover operating costs and to assure a return of and on vested capital. The 40-40-20 division of trade between maritime nations has been embodied in the ratified but unenacted UNCTAD (United Nations Conference on Trade and Development) Code of Conduct for Liner Services. This code would allot flags on vessels in the world's conference systems on the basis of 40-40-20 of the volume of trade between nations in a fashion similar to the Brazilian bilateral agreements.

Opposition to this code is spearheaded by spokesmen of organizations representing the cross traders who stand to lose 80% of all trading opportunities in the liner service trades if the code is enacted. The cross traders have invested in ships that are primarily dedicated to meeting the shipping needs of other nations. Their main argument is that enactment would generate an artificial demand for vessel capacity. This would raise the cost of transportation, thus undoing the principal contribution of shipowners over the past three decades.

This can be demonstrated by considering the hypothetical situation of three nations (Alpha, Beta, and Gamma) having the following volume of trade in a given year:

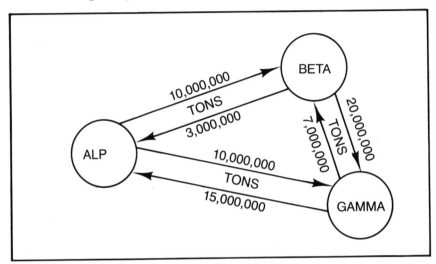

The trade is served by one type of general cargo vessel capable of carrying 10,000 tons of cargo. Each stay in port is four days long, and the one-way voyage times at sea between each country are Beta/Gamma, 5 days; Gamma/Alpha, 17 days; Alpha/Beta, 15 days.

In a free market environment with no fiat restrictions on trading privileges, the efficient allocation of capital assets would be for some vessels to ply back and forth between each pair of nations with full cargo loads in both directions (no ballast voyages).

The remaining volume of trade is Beta/Gamma, 13 million tons; Gamma/Alpha, 5 million tons; Alpha/Beta, 7 million tons.

An efficient use of vessel capacity is to ply around the circle from Alpha to Beta to Gamma and back to Alpha with full cargoes. The time at sea per round trip is 37 days, time in port 24 days, for a total voyage time of 61 days. Each vessel can make 5.7 trips per 350-day year (allowing 15 days for maintenance) transporting 57,000 tons of cargo per year between each of the three countries. Five million tons of cargo would require 88 vessels. Adding in the previous tally of 235 vessels, the resulting fleet size is 323 vessels. The remaining trade to be accounted for is Alpha/Beta, 2 million tons; Beta/Gamma, 8 million tons.

TABLE 13.1

Country pair	Volume of trade, tons	Days at sea per round trip	Days in port per round trip	Total days per round trip	Trips per 350-day year	Total tons cargo per vessel per year	Total vessels for volume of trade	Rounding up
Alpha-Beta	3,000,000	30	16*	46	7.6	76,000	39.5	40
Alpha-Gamma	10,000,000	34	16	50	7.0	70,000	142.9	143
Beta-Gamma	7,000,000	10	16	26	13.5	135,000	51.9	52
						Total vessels:		235

*For each round trip, a vessel will load in Alpha (4 days), discharge in Beta (4 days), load again in Beta (4 days), and discharge in Alpha (4 days) for a total of 16 days. Total sea time is twice the one-way voyage time at sea.

This trade can be served by vessels transporting goods between Alpha and Beta, then Beta and Gamma returning to Alpha in a ballast condition. Sea time is still 37 days per round trip plus 16 days in port for a total voyage time of 53 days, or 6.6 trips per year. Sixty-six thousand tons of cargo per vessel per year can be carried between Alpha and Beta and between Beta and Gamma. Two million tons of cargo moving in this trade would require another 31 vessels. When added to the previous tally of 323 vessels, the required fleet is 354 ships. The remaining trade of 6 million tons of cargo between Beta and Gamma is handled by vessels moving between these two nations carrying cargo from Beta to Gamma, returning in a ballast condition. Sea time is 10 days; port time is 8 days; round-trip time is 18 days. Each vessel makes 19.4 trips per year transporting a total of 194,000 tons of cargo annually. Another 31 vessels are required for the 6 million-ton movement. Adding this to the previous tally yields a fleet of 385 vessels. This fleet can efficiently handle all the trade among the three nations.

If Alpha, Beta, and Gamma ascribed to the provisions of the UNCTAD Code of Conduct for Liner Conferences, 80% of the trade would be divided between national flag fleets of each of the three countries. Twenty percent of the trade could be handled without fiat restriction as already described. Seventy-seven vessels (20% of 385 vessels) would be employed in this manner. The remaining trade, net of the 20% handled by the fleet of 77 ships, would be:

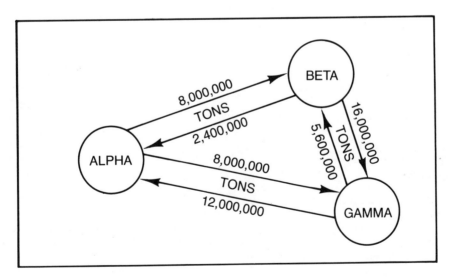

This volume of trade is reserved strictly for Alpha, Beta, and Gamma flag vessels. They have exclusive trading rights to 50% of their respective nation's exports and imports.

Alpha Vessels

Alpha vessels are guaranteed the following cargoes:

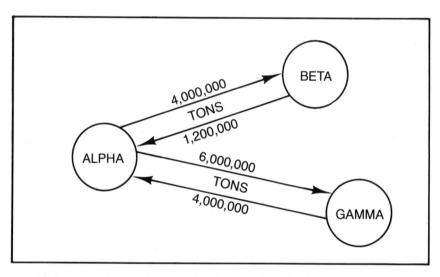

Alpha vessels can be efficiently employed plying back and forth between Alpha-Beta carrying 1.2 million tons of cargo and between Alpha-Gamma carrying 4 million tons of cargo:

TABLE 13.2

Countries	Cargo, tons	Total cargo per vessel per year, tons	Total vessels for tons of cargo
Alpha-Beta	1,200,000	76,000	15.8
Alpha-Gamma	4,000,000	70,000	57.1

The remaining cargoes reserved for Alpha vessels are 2.8 million tons from Alpha to Beta and 2 million tons from Gamma to Alpha.

This movement can be efficiently handled by Alpha flag vessels transporting cargoes from Alpha to Beta, then proceeding in ballast to Gamma for a return cargo to Alpha. Voyage time is 37 days at sea, 16 days in port, for a total of 53 days. One vessel can make 6.6 trips per year transporting a total of 66,000 tons. Two million tons will require 30.3 ships. The remaining 800,000 tons from Alpha to Beta will need another 8.7 vessels. These will return to Alpha in a ballast condition. Total Alpha vessels will equal 112.

Beta Vessels

Cargoes reserved for Beta vessels are:

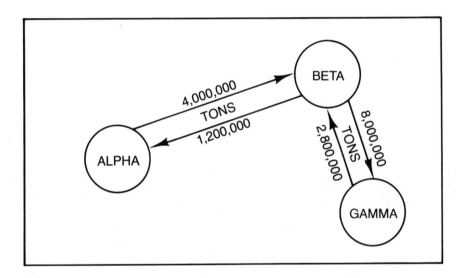

TABLE 13.3
BETA VESSELS EMPLOYED WITH FULL CARGOES IN BOTH DIRECTIONS

Countries	Cargo, tons	Total cargo per vessel per year, tons	Total vessels for tons of cargo
Beta-Alpha	1,200,000	76,000	15.8
Beta-Gamma	2,800,000	135,000	20.7

TABLE 13.4
BETA VESSELS EMPLOYED ON BALLAST-BACK BASIS

Countries	Cargo, tons	Total cargo per vessel per year, tons	Total vessels for tons of cargo
Beta-Alpha	2,800,000	92,000	30.4
Beta-Gamma	5,200,000	194,000	26.8
Total Beta vessels: 94			

Gamma Vessels
Cargoes reserved for Gamma vessels are:

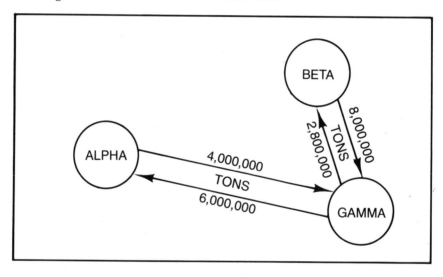

TABLE 13.5
GAMMA VESSELS EMPLOYED WITH FULL CARGOES IN BOTH DIRECTIONS

Countries	Cargo, tons	Total cargo per vessel per year, tons	Total vessels for tons of cargo
Gamma-Alpha	4,000,000	70,000	57.1
Gamma-Beta	2,800,000	135,000	20.7

TABLE 13.6
GAMA VESSELS EMPLOYED ON BALLAST-BACK BASIS

Countries	Cargo, tons	Total cargo per vessel per year, tons	Total vessels for tons of cargo
Gamma-Alpha	2,000,000	83,000	24.1
Gamma-Beta	5,200,000	194,000	26.8
Total Gamma vessels: 129			

The total number of vessels required under the proposed UNCTAD Code would be:

20% portion of trade free of all restrictions	77
Alpha vessels	112
Beta vessels	94
Gamma vessels	<u>129</u>
Total fleet requirement under proposed UNCTAD Code	412
Total fleet requirement in a free market environment	385

By establishing a fiat restriction on trading patterns, an additional 27 vessels are required to handle the same volume of world trade than in a free market environment. This example is both hypothetical and static. In reality, the inefficiency is compounded by the loss of flexibility to adjust to changing patterns of trade. If trade between Alpha and Beta were to fall off markedly and, simultaneously, increase sharply between Beta and Gamma, only Beta flag vessels would be able to shift employment in response to market forces. Alpha flag vessels, being excluded from 80% of the growing Beta-Gamma trade, would be left without employment opportunities at the same time that a shortage of Gamma flag ships is developing on the Beta-Gamma trade route. While a construction spree for more Gamma flag vessels is getting underway, Alpha flag vessels are being laid up for lack of employment.

In a market environment, wage demands by North European, North American, and Japanese merchant seamen are tempered: the more their wages are out of line with the rest of the world, the greater will be the loss of competitive position by their respective national flag shipowning companies in the international marketplace. The ever-growing share of the world fleet registered under national flags of developing nations and flags of convenience/necessity checks the demands for ever-higher compensation. However, the bargaining power of maritime unions would be immeasurably improved if a guaranteed 40% share of a nation's international commerce could be cut off by a strike by its members. Moreover, management would have no real incentive to oppose maritime labor demands because shipping rates would be administered rather than be subject to the laws of the marketplace. Relieving management of the disciplining aspects of competition would also remove the incentive to provide a high level of service to shippers and to originate and implement technological improvements. Errors in judgment would no longer be punished by the shipping firm being forced out of business. They would be perpetuated in the pricing mechanism of the freight rate.

The volume of world trade is affected, in part, by the cost of shipping. Increasing the cost of transportation would adversely shift the comparative price advantage of Alpha's products in the far-removed Beta and Gamma markets. The most likely consequence of rising rates because of fiat trading restrictions is a fall-off in trade between Alpha and its trading partners.

The cross traders have no real objection to sovereign states subsidizing national flag fleets on a parity-of-cost basis as long as they can compete on an equal footing for the available cargoes. The cross traders' objection to the UNCTAD Liner Service Code is their arbitrary exclusion from 80% of the liner service trade.

The proponents of the UNCTAD Code view the manner in an entirely different light. Some developing nations feel the code is an answer for having their own national flag fleets. In fact, they agree with the cross traders on one key point. Both feel that the 40-40-20 apportioning of world trade is capricious and arbitrary, having no other virtue than being nice round numbers. However, they disagree on what the ideal apportionment of world trade should be; the cross traders prefer 0-0-100, while some supporters of the code prefer 50-50-0. Shipyard interests in some nations support the code because they see more orders for newbuildings. Maritime labor unions see more jobs for their members (neglecting those who lose their jobs through the substitution aspects of the code) and view the code as a potent weapon in their bargaining arsenal. Managers of some shipping companies see more business opportunities for themselves and view the code as a way to rid themselves of the burden of competing for the shippers' business. Many politicians and economists support the adoption of shipping policies and programs that create an artifical shortage of vessel capacity.

Building more ships provides employment opportunities for tens of thousands of workers in shipyards, steel mills, and related marine industries. In their minds, every dollar spent on vessel construction has an amplified effect on economic activity as the successive spending for goods and services ripples through the economy. In a world awash with excess vessel capacity, the arguments in favor of the UNCTAD Code and other cargo and flag preference programs must sound similar to those the Pharaoh heard on the economic benefits of building a larger tomb.

Sanctioning exclusive rights in maritime affairs is nothing new in the world of shipping. Nearly every maritime nation forbids foreign flag vessels from participating in domestic trades. In the United States, the Jones Act, passed in the 1920s with legislative precedence dating back nearly to the founding of the country, excludes non-U.S. flag vessels from trading between any two U.S ports of the continental United States, Hawaii, Alaska, Puerto Rico, and Guam. The establishment of an exclusive preserve for U.S. flag vessels does not void the principle of return of capital nor its effects on shipping rates. In 1975, over 40 U.S. flag tankers were laid up for lack of employment and a few vessels were on the verge of defaulting on their merchant marine bonds. This would have triggered the infusion of government funds, guaranteed by the Title XI insurance program. That year, the U.S. Maritime Administration negotiated a cargo preference requirement for one-third of all grain shipped between the U.S. and the Soviet Union. U.S. flag tankers employed in this program received $16 per ton of grain, which paid the operating and debt servicing obligations of these vessels, while market rates for performing the same function were $10 per ton.

The proponents of flag and cargo preference programs cannot dismiss or avoid the principle of return of capital vested in the labor and material consumed in the building of a fleet. Somehow and somewhere, this capital must be returned to the investor even if the investor is the government itself. In the case of the Soviet grain deal, the 60% premium in rates to ensure the return of capital of U.S. flag vessels was borne by the Soviet people.

Flag and cargo preference programs are already in effect in many South American nations, France, Spain, Morocco, Egypt, South Africa, Israel, Turkey, Pakistan, India, Thailand, Indonesia, the Philippines, and South Korea. The OPEC nations are considering flag preference programs to ensure cargoes for their newly acquired tanker fleets; many other nations, some who have long advocated freedom of the seas, are doing the same in one form or another.

Excess shipbuilding capacity, estimated to be twice that needed based on the long-term growth trends in international trade, is plaguing all shipbuilding nations. Some yards were built as government show-pieces or financed with government funds. Other yards built with private capital have already become wards of the state, as in Britain and Sweden. Taking into account the full employment promises of most elected governments, there can be little doubt that ships will be built simply for the sake of keeping shipyards busy.

The U.S is in a position to carve out a part of its burgeoning tanker needs and make it the exclusive preserve for future tankers where rates can be administratively set to cover operating and capital charges. Only 4% of oil imports from foreign sources are in U.S. flag tankers. Britain, on the other hand, cannot carve out a portion of its exports or imports and make it the exclusive preserve of British flag vessels in order to create more work for its yards because the British flag fleet is already twice the size necessary to serve British needs. British owners are major cross traders in their own right, and actions taken by any nation to aid its shipyards by awarding exclusive trading rights will hurt British owners as well as the other cross traders.

Government support programs to order vessels just for the sake of keeping the shipyards busy are ultimately self-defeating in a market environment. The continued, unwanted production of ships postpones the day when the supply and the demand for vessel capacity are restored, allowing rates to rise for investors, as owners and lenders, to recoup their investments. If market rates do not improve because the size of the world fleet from continued shipyard production is always one step ahead of the growth in the level of world trade, governments stand to lose the most because government funds, through shipyard credits, are the largest single source of capital. The consequence of continued government support of shipyards in the form of newbuilding orders on a noncommercial basis is the establishment of cargo and flag preference programs where rates can be administered to ensure a return of capital. Transportation costs, as a consequence, must rise. The free market cannot, by definition, reward the misallocation of capital.

14

A Commercial Transaction

The time is 1979. Charles has been the chartering manager for a medium-sized oil company since 1975. As an aspiring executive, he hopes to be reassigned to another position in the firm in another year or so. The high-ranking oil execs in the marine division have seen many chartering managers come and go during their careers. Like his predecessors, Charles had little experience in marine matters when he was first assigned chartering manager and depended on the old-timers for advice and counsel. Once he became familiar with his new function, he began to exert his authority. He now ensures a smooth flow of crude oil to the refineries as a first order of priority and makes decisions that minimize the company's cost of transportation.

The marine department works closely with the corporate planning group to assess the future shipping needs of the company. Future crude production including new contractual arrangements under consideration are analyzed to project the demand for shipping capacity. By comparing this to the projected supply of shipping capacity, consisting of the company-owned fleet plus newbuilding deliveries less vessel disposals and vessels coming on and going off charter, it has been concluded that another 80,000-dwt tanker is required by 1983. However, the long-range plans of the company include the construction of a new oil terminal designed to handle vessels of 120,000–150,000 dwt. Although this project is still in an early stage of investigation, the feeling within the company is that the project will be approved by the

Board of Directors. The terminal, if approved, will be completed in the 1990 time frame and, when completed, 120,000–150,000-dwt tankers will be more desirable than 80,000-dwt vessels. Until that time, 120,000–150,000-dwt tankers are useless in satisfying the company's needs because the existing terminal can only handle vessels up to 80,000 dwt.

Charles has already contacted three ship brokers concerning a potential need for an 80,000-dwt tanker built to his specifications for carrying oil. Although he has occasionally negotiated long-term charters direct with owners without a broker, experience has shown him that he can obtain lower rates and better terms on short- and medium-term charters using brokers. Since a broker's remuneration is a commission on a fixture, Charles feels they stir up the marketplace far more effectively than he can do on his own. The three brokers contacted by Charles are his principal brokers. They attained this position by their demonstrated ability to cover the market, that is, by establishing contacts with first-class operators of suitable tonnage. Except for certain long-term charters, Charles is hesitant to bypass the brokers, for he does not want to lose their good will. In fact, there have been times when he directed a commission be split with one of his principal brokers even though the broker was not directly involved with a fixture. The brokers, in turn, work hard to maintain their good will with Charles, for if they don't produce, they would be unable to maintain their position. Owners keep careful score as to which brokers have Charles' confidence.

Charles has just finished laying out all the offers. The one he likes best is from Hans, who offers an 80,000-dwt vessel built to the charterer's specifications for delivery in the beginning of 1983 with the following time charter rates:

1983	$5.00
1984	5.20
1985	5.40
1986	5.60
1987	5.80

plus an option on the part of the charterer to extend the charter for another two years at a rate of $6.00. Two other owners offer lower rates. One, with a lower rate for 1983, has terms in the charter party that pass on many of the risks of vessel operation, traditionally borne by an owner, to the charterer. The other owner with lower rates has a reputation of being a poor operator. Even though Hans is not the cheapest, his rates, in conjunction with his reputation as a good operator and his willingness to accept the traditional risks of vessel ownership, make his offer the most attractive.

Charles is also considering the alternative of owning the vessel and has been in touch with several shipyards. In the competitive process of sorting out yards in terms of price, berth availability, delivery dates, vessel characteristics, performance specifications, and reputation for service and quality of work, Charles has selected Yama Shipyard, which has one berth dedicated to the series production of 80,000-dwt tankers. By coincidence, this is the same yard selected by Hans to build the vessel if he obtains a charter from Charles. Although Hans already has a 60-day berth option, Charles feels that he can take over the option if Hans fails to exercise his option, which would be likely, though not certain, if Hans does not fix the vessel with Charles. The manager of Yama Shipyard offers Charles an 80,000-dwt tanker built to his specifications for $25 million. The Exim Bank will provide 70% financing of the cost of the vessel ($17.5 million) to be amortized over seven years in equal semiannual principal repayments at a fixed rate of 7% interest. Yama Shipyard expects to receive 10% of the equity on placing the order, 25% on keel laying, 25% on launching, 25% on fitting out of the vessel, and 15% on delivery (final acceptance of the vessel by the owner).

Charles cannot commit the company as charterer to a five-year obligation or order a vessel for the company's account without the approval of the Board of Directors. Nor can Charles present a charter to the Board without a comparison with the costs of owning a vessel outright. Charles knows from previous experience that two members of the Board will be at odds with one another over the company's chartering policy.

Charles takes the sequence of yard payments during construction and calculates the predelivery interest charges, which are 10% of the yard price. Predelivery expenses, including owner's items for fitting-out the vessel, engineering and supervision expenses, and legal and administrative charges, amount to another $500,000 for a total capitalized cost of $28 million:

Yard price	$25,000,000
Predelivery interest	2,500,000
Predelivery expenses	500,000
Capitalized cost	$28,000,000

TABLE 14.1

Year	Operating costs	Amortization of shipyard credit	Interest on shipyard credit	Internal capital charge on equity investments (15% × $10,500,000)	Total costs	Equivalent time charter rate	Shipowner's proposed rate
1983	$1,300,000	$2,500,000	$1,138,000	$1,575,000	$ 6,513,000	$ 7.08	$5.00
1984	1,430,000	2,500,000	963,000	1,575,000	6,468,000	7.03	5.20
1985	1,573,000	2,500,000	788,000	1,575,000	6,436,000	7.00	5.40
1986	1,730,000	2,500,000	613,000	1,575,000	6,418,000	6.98	5.60
1987	1,903,000	2,500,000	438,000	1,575,000	6,416,000	6.97	5.80
1988	2,094,000	2,500,000	263,000	1,575,000	6,432,000	6.99	6.00*
1989	2,303,000	2,500,000	88,000	1,575,000	6,466,000	7.03	6.00*
1990	2,533,000			1,575,000	4,108,000	4.47	
1991	2,787,000			1,575,000	4,362,000	4.74	
1992	3,065,000			1,575,000	4,640,000	5.04	
1993	3,372,000			1,575,000	4,947,000	5.38	
1994	3,709,000			1,575,000	5,284,000	5.74	
1995	4,080,000			1,575,000	5,655,000	6.15	
1996	4,488,000			1,575,000	6,063,000	6.59	
1997	4,937,000			1,575,000	6,512,000	7.08	
1998	5,430,000			1,575,000	7,005,000	7.61	
1999	5,973,000			1,575,000	7,548,000	8.20	
2000	6,571,000			1,575,000	8,146,000	8.85	
2001	7,228,000			1,575,000	8,803,000	9.57	
2002	7,951,000			1,575,000	9,526,000	10.35	
2003	8,746,000			1,575,000	10,321,000	11.22	

*Charterer's Option

The capitalized cost of $28 million will be financed by shipyard credit ($17.5 million) and the oil company's equity as owner ($10.5 million). The marine department is charged 15% per year for the use of company funds for as long as the company owns the vessel. Charles plans to register the vessel under a flag of convenience. There are several reasons for not registering the vessel under a national flag, even though the subsidy programs available would equate the cost of transportation between the two flags. Among them is the loss of flexibility in operating and disposing of the vessel because of legal restrictions in the maritime subsidy program. Another is the time-consuming dealing with the government maritime subsidy administrators, which Charles wishes to avoid. Charles also figures that he will have to add four full-time employees to handle the mountain of paperwork entailed in receiving subsides. There is also the lingering doubt of the wisdom of an oil company, already criticized about the "meager" amount of taxes paid to the government, being a direct beneficiary of monies from the public purse through maritime subsidies.

Charles estimates that his 1983 operating costs under a flag of convenience will be $1.3 million, escalating at a rate of 10% thereafter. He prepares Table 14.1 to be presented at the upcoming Board meeting.

Charles notes the pernicious effects of inflation where the operating costs increase sixfold during the course of the vessel's useful life. He wonders if the Board will question the continued use of a 15% charge for capital at a time when inflation is anticipated to continue at 10%. As Charles views Hans' rates, he wonders how Hans can offer a rate substantially less than his own when Hans' acquisition and operating costs are about the same as his. However, there is no doubt in Charles' mind that if a charter is fixed with Hans, Hans will be forced to live with his rates.

Hans has been in shipping all his life, inheriting a small fleet from his father. He aggressively seeks opportunities to expand his fleet whenever possible and prefers to have a charter in the early years of a vessel's life to meet its debt-servicing obligations. After that, he believes that the spot- and short-term charter markets afford the best opportunity to maximize his profits. Like many other owners, Hans is a one-man show. Although there are competent and responsible people working for him in operations, engineering, chartering, and accounting, there is no doubt in anyone's mind where the center of power lies. Hans has spent his life cultivating his contacts with shipyard managers, charterers, brokers, and bankers. His efforts pay off once again when one of the brokers firmly entrenched with the charterer contacts him about the potential five-year charter with the steel company.

"What's the market for this business?" Hans is asking for the general range of indications other owners are quoting to the charterer.

"About $5–6, Hans."

"What do I need to get the business?"

The broker is being asked the nearly impossible question: What is the highest possible rate I can offer without losing the business? This is a neat tightrope trick for the broker, for he is trying to make a fixture, which is his source of income, between an owner who is attempting to maximize his profits and a charterer who is attempting to minimize his costs.

"At least $5–5.50, maybe with an option thrown in."

Hans has concentrated his vessel orders among four yards. One of these is Yama Shipyard, which is building a series of 80,000-dwt tankers. He calls the manager of the shipyard for a quote.

"About $25–27 million depending on the extras and charterer's specifications. For Exim credit, you'll need a charter or a commercial bank guarantee."

Hans does some preliminary figuring and concludes that the market rate can support the acquisition of a vessel if he can obtain favorable financing. He looks at the ingredients of the shipping deal: the cost of the vessel, a charter for five years from a first-class charterer, and the availability of 70% shipyard financing. Uppermost in Hans' mind is whether or not he wants to own an 80,000-dwt tanker. He realizes that most, if not all, of the cash generated by the charter in excess of operating costs will be dedicated to retiring debt. At the end of a five-year charter period, Hans will have a vessel with some debt still outstanding and little or no recoupment on his equity investment of over $10 million. The value of the vessel in the sale and purchase market, or in the charter market, both intimately entwined with the supply/demand situation for this type vessel when it comes off charter, will determine whether or not Hans has recouped his equity investment and what rate of return he has earned. He mulls over the current trends in shipping and the economic forces at work and notes the following points:

- Medium-sized tankers have not been built in large numbers since the advent of the VLCC in the late 1960s. Two-thirds of the existing fleet is over ten years old.
- Some of these vessels are in poor physical condition as a result of the depressed market during the 1970s. Owners were tempted to

defer maintenance as a cost-saving measure. Large capital investments are now necessary for these vessels to pass their third and
fourth surveys. Moreover, further investments may be necessary
to have the vessel comply with the U.S. Port and Tanker Safety
Act and the proposed IMCO regulations.

- Many of these tankers are not efficient in their fuel consumption
because they were built when bunker prices were cheap. Today,
they are inefficient. A newbuilding with a slow-speed diesel capable of burning the worst grades of bunkers is highly desired in
comparison to these tankers.

- An owner satisfying the charterer's need for an 80,000-dwt tanker
is in a good position to bid on the 120,000–150,000-dwt vessels
that the charterer will need in the 1990s.

- Continued deterioration of the purchasing power of paper currencies keeps pushing up the cost of building ships year after year.
The only thing "gained" in delaying an order for a new vessel is a
higher price. Besides, it is supposed to be financially sophisticated to acquire real assets with low-interest debt such as shipyard
credits and to pay off the debt with depreciated dollars while profiting from the inflationary increase in the value of the asset.

- Many owners seem to be ordering medium-sized tankers. This
could lead to another overtonnaging situation as occurred in large
crude carriers during the 1970s. However, some noted economist
said that world crude oil production will increase over the next
ten years. As long as supply and demand are occasionally in balance, rates must reflect current building costs in the long run. In
the 1990s the capital charge on a 1983-built vessel will be peanuts
compared to what an owner will have to pay for a newbuilding—
conceivably double the current $25 million cost. Even if acquiring
an 80,000-dwt tanker turns out to be a wrong decision at this time,
inflation and the growth in world trade will eventually salvage the
situation just as they have over the last 30 years.

This thought process, which was 99% complete when the broker
first called, moves Hans to action. He knows from experience that relatively few attempts to develop new business actually succeed. There
are many competitors to reckon with and circumstances concerning a
transaction can change overnight.

The manager of Yama Shipyard is happy to receive a call from Hans
about setting up an appointment in the shortest possible time. At the
meeting, the manager tells Hans that the vessel built to the charterer's

specifications will cost $25 million if he wants to use the shipyard credit facilities of the Exim Bank. The manager warns Hans that he will need either a charter or a commercial bank guarantee for the first 2–4 years to qualify for the shipyard credit. Hans and the manager negotiate for some time, and the manager finally agrees to a price of $24 million if Hans pays cash for the vessel. Hans tells the manager that he wants a 60-day berth option as a selling point to the charterer. During the 60-day period, Hans has the right to purchase Hull Number 1010, which is scheduled to be built in Building Berth 2 and completed by the beginning of 1983.

"Give me about ten days' time so I can negotiate with the charterer and decide if I want the option."

"You want an option on an option for the next ten days?"

"Yes, a berth option will give my offer more credibility and I need about ten days to sort out things first."

This shipyard manager agrees to the arrangement at no cost to Hans. His reasons include recognizing Hans' ability to put a shipping deal together. This has resulted in several previous newbuilding orders for Yama Shipyard. The shipyard manager also realizes that the yard will probably obtain the charterer's order for the vessel if the oil company decides to own the vessel rather than charter it. Moreover, the manager is negotiating Hull 1010 with another owner for another charterer. Hans' possession of the berth option may be just the incentive necessary for this owner to enter into a firm order on the condition that Hans fails to exercise his option. Both the shipyard manager and Hans are satisfied with this arrangement. On his return to the office, Hans calls the broker.

"If I come in at a rate of $5–5.50 plus possession of a berth option, what else do I need to do to clinch this deal?"

"I'm glad you called. I was just talking to Charles and I mentioned your name. He has a high regard for you, Hans. He remembers that contract of affreightment he had with you a few years ago and how you let him skip a couple of shipments because he had no storage space available. I didn't bother to tell him that you made more money by skipping those cargoes and employing the vessel elsewhere than by moving his cargoes.

"Thanks for the favor."

"Anything for a friend."

"Let's cut the comedy. Look, I want this deal."

"Hans, I think a three- or five-year option for the charterer's account after the initial five-year charter will do the trick."

"Look, I'm not going to give my ship away; maybe two years."

"Try it. Keep your rates around $5–5.50. Remember a Board meeting is not too far away and we want to give Charles a little time to think things over. Want me to call Charles and let him know you're making an offer?"

"No, let me lay some more groundwork and I'll get back to you."

Hans turns his thoughts to financing, which has not been much of a consideration up to this point, because the yard is offering 70% shipyard credit. The worst thing that can happen is that he will be forced to rely on shipyard credit. This would immobilize $10 million of his cash reserves. Although this would close out other investment opportunities, there is still plenty of time to seek out a more advantageous financing package before he must commit himself to Exim financing.

Hans does his commercial borrowing from three principal banks, usually playing one against the other to obtain the best pricing and terms. He calls two of the three account officers for their opinion on the state of the credit market and their appetite for ship financing. Hans is unable to reach Frank, the account officer at bank 2, who has always given him good advice on financial matters. After talking with the two other bankers and hearing about one other bank (bank 4) that has completed a ten-year transaction with an acquaintance, Hans concludes that he has a slim chance for 90% financing with a twelve-year tenure. He prefers to borrow as much he can for as long as possible. This conserves his cash resources by reducing his equity infusions and enhances his near-term cash flow by the slower rate of maturity on outstanding debt. Cash reserves and cash flow are critical in determining Hans' capacity to undertake new business deals.

Having the charter rate dictated by market forces, a shipyard price determined primarily by the cost of labor and steel, the availability of outside sources of capital influenced by the state of the credit market, and the appetite of bankers for shipping loans, Hans calls in Ace, his number pusher, to evaluate the return on a $3 million equity investment. He hands Ace the figures in Table 14.2.

"For both the optimistic and the pessimistic cases, assume residual values of $15 million and $20 million at the end of 1989. Pay off all remaining debt at that time as though the vessel were sold to another party."

"Let's see, there will still be $10 million in outstanding debts in 1989. That means the $15 million or $20 million from the sale of the vessel will net out to $5 million or $10 million after paying off the $10 million in outstanding debt."

Ace runs off to bury himself in reams of paper. Hans, who has already made up his mind about this investment opportunity, goes through this exercise as a backup for his mental calculations.

TABLE 14.2

Shipyard price (no Exim financing)	$24,000,000
Predelivery interest (10% of yard price)	2,400,000
Predelivery expenses	600,000
Capitalized cost	$27,000,000
Equity	3,000,000
Amount to be borrowed from commercial bank	24,000,000
Tenure of debt (Semiannual equal principal repayment)	12 years

Proposed charter terms (assuming exercise of option by charterer in 1988 and 1989):	1983	$5.00
	1984	5.20
	1985	5.40
	1986	5.60
	1987	5.80
	1988	6.00
	1989	6.00

	Optimistic case	Pessimistic case
Interest rate on debt	7%	10%
1983 projected operating costs	$1,000,000	$1,200,000
Escalation rate on operating costs	6%	10%

TABLE 14.3
ACE'S CASH FLOW PROJECTION—OPTIMISTIC CASE

Year	Time charter rate ($/dwt/month)	Annual revenue (11.5 months/year)	Operating costs (6% inflation)
1983	$5.00	$4,600,000	$1,000,000
1984	5.20	4,784,000	1,060,000
1985	5.40	4,968,000	1,124,000
1986	5.60	5,152,000	1,191,000
1987	5.80	5,336,000	1,262,000
1988	6.00	5,520,000	1,338,000
1989	6.00	5,520,000	1,419,000

continued

TABLE 14.3 CONTINUED
ACE'S CASH FLOW PROJECTION—OPTIMISTIC CASE

	Amortization of debt	Interest on debt (7%)	Cash flow
1983	$2,000,000	$1,610,000	$ −10,000
1984	2,000,000	1,470,000	254,000
1985	2,000,000	1,330,000	514,000
1986	2,000,000	1,190,000	771,000
1987	2,000,000	1,050,000	1,024,000
1988	2,000,000	910,000	1,272,000
1989	2,000,000	770,000	1,331,000

ACE'S CASH FLOW PROJECTION—PESSIMISTIC CASE

Year	Time charter rate	Annual revenue	Operating costs (10% inflation)
1983	$5.00	$4,600,000	$1,200,000
1984	5.20	4,784,000	1,320,000
1985	5.40	4,968,000	1,452,000
1986	5.60	5,152,000	1,597,000
1987	5.80	5,336,000	1,757,000
1988	6.00	5,520,000	1,933,000
1989	6.00	5,520,000	2,126,000

	Amortization of debt	Interest on debt (10%)	Cash flow
1983	$2,000,000	$2,300,000	$−900,000
1984	2,000,000	2,100,000	−636,000
1985	2,000,000	1,900,000	−384,000
1986	2,000,000	1,700,000	−145,000
1987	2,000,000	1,500,000	79,000
1988	2,000,000	1,300,000	287,000
1989	2,000,000	1,100,000	294,000

To obtain the net cash flow, Ace must make two more adjustments. He adds an outflow of $3 million in 1982, representing the equity investment, and for 1989 an inflow of $5 and $10 million representing the sale (residual value) of the vessel for $15 and $20 million less the retirement of $10 million in outstanding debt (Table 14.4).

TABLE 14.4
NET CASH FLOW

Residual value	Optimistic case		Pessimistic case	
	$10 MM	$15 MM	$10 MM	$15 MM
1982	$−3,000,000	$−3,000,000	$−3,000,000	$−3,000,000
1983	−10,000	−10,000	−900,000	−900,000
1984	254,000	254,000	−636,000	−636,000
1985	514,000	514,000	−384,000	−384,000
1986	771,000	771,000	−145,000	−145,000
1987	1,024,000	1,024,000	79,000	79,000
1988	1,272,000	1,272,000	287,000	287,000
1989	6,331,000	11,331,000	5,294,000	10,294,000
Internal rate of return of cash flow stream:	23%	30%	2%	13%

Hans reviews Ace's work. The internal rate of return for the optimistic projections exceeds his objective of 20%. On the pessimistic projections, Hans' thoughts center on the ability of the rest of his fleet to fund the negative cash flows during the first four years. In his mind, Hans does not believe the residual value assumptions of $15 million and $20 million. Based on recent experience in both world trade and inflation, he feels that $25–30 million would be a more appropriate assessment. Hans calls the broker to sound him out on his rate assumptions, including the two-year option.

"Well, what do you think of these rates—low enough to get the business without giving away the family jewels?"

"Looks good to me. Quite frankly, Hans, they aren't the lowest rates, but Charles thinks highly of you as an operator. Make this a firm offer and I'll do my part."

"No address commission back to the charterer?"

"No, just my usual 1¼%."

"If the charterer decides to negotiate further with me, I want to do it directly with him from here on out."

"Just as long as I'm in the charter party to receive my commission, you can do whatever you like. I suggest that you use the charter party for the vessel *Abex* of 2 June 1977 as a basis for negotiation. Charles likes it; owners don't seem to complain. I'll send a copy over for you to look at right away."

Hans, with the assistance of one of his vice presidents, makes a firm offer with some stipulated changes on the *Abex* charter. Over the next few days, Charles and Hans meet and negotiate over the terms of the charter party. Charles does not negotiate on rates, although he usually does, because he feels that they are fair. He concentrates his efforts on the terms of the charter party. Hans is furious over this. To him, Charles' bland acceptance of the rates does not mean that they are fair, but that they are too low.

Hans thinks that the lack of bargaining is the fault of the broker. If the price is low—perhaps too low—Hans will be assured of the charter and the broker will get $60,000 or so in commissions per year for the duration of the charter party. However, Hans continues with the negotiations even though he feels he might have bid too low; his priority is to obtain that ship.

Finally, Hans and Charles come to terms on all matters. Hans has a fixture in hand as soon as the Board approves the transaction. Hans has also been keeping the shipyard manager apprised of the situation. The shipyard manager has been taking advantage of the situation to pressure the other owner in committing himself to the vessel if Hans should fail to exercise his option.

It is the day of the Board meeting to decide between ownership or a five-year charter. Charles will present both cases, recommending the latter course of action. The final decision, however, will be made by the Board.

The Board meeting starts at 10:00 and Charles is waiting his turn, scheduled right after a report on the new terminal. At 11:00, he enters the Board room, sits down, and waits while the Board members read his report.

Jason is the first to speak. "Did you read in Sunday's paper about the Greek shipowner who rented an entire hotel in London and stuffed it with people from all over the world to celebrate his divorce from his third wife? The hotel staff made a fortune in tips. The whole party must have cost a bundle. According to the article, the owner was born in poverty—father a ne'er-do-well, mother a scrub woman. Charles, how do you think he became so wealthy?"

"Well, I . . . ."

"I'll tell you how, Charles. By this charter you have in mind. These guys couldn't get a loan for a used car, but by these charters that we give out gratis they can make millions. Whose credit, Charles, do you think is in back of this transaction?"

"Well, the shipowner, Hans . . . ."

"Not so, Charles. It's ours. As I have repeatedly told this Board, I understand our need for spot- and short-term charters—no problem. But as soon as we start issuing seven-year charters, we are better off owning the vessel ourselves regardless of the rates offered us."

"Five years," interrupts Charles. "The sixth and seventh years are optional at our discretion."

"Charles, what does that have to do with the issue? There is only one way for an owner to make it in this world and that is by riding on our backs."

"Amazing analysis, Jake," retorted William. "I've listened to you drone on this subject before and I find it a bit curious. At last month's meeting, we approved a ten-year contract with Wilbank Pipeline to move our products. Why didn't I hear you talk about the fortune Wilbank Pipeline is going to make on our contract?"

"Wilbank Pipeline is a subsidiary of Takeall Oil . . . ."

"Just my point, Jake. We routinely enter into contracts with crude oil suppliers and oil product end users. Not once have I heard you mention buying out the suppliers and end users solely to capture the profits they make in dealing with us. Yet when it comes to ships, you bring out all your cannon fire. The only difference between these companies and this shipping transaction is that the former are public corporations and the latter is an individual. Remember, this steel company was formed largely by the efforts of one man. So if you don't mind, Jake, let's keep this a business discussion. If you can show me that ownership will serve our purposes better than chartering a vessel, then I'll support you."

"Fine, let's get down to brass tacks. Tell me, Charles, why is it that you must charge the company a rate of $7 and this fellow Hans charges us about $5.50?"

"Well, I was thinking about the same . . . ."

"You're very incisive, Charles. Now, I'll tell you why, and Willy here can learn a thing or two. The reason is in 1989. If we charter in, we have nothing at that time because the vessel goes back to the owner. If we own the vessel, we have another 15 years' use out of it. Look at his proposal; a whopping savings in the first year which he whittles away in each succeeding year. He throws us a bone with a two-year option. Who is he trying to kid?

"I don't care how you cut it. We are just giving Hans another ship. All I ask is that you put in your calculations the fact that we have no vested interest in that ship five or seven years down the road, and you'll see that Hans' rates are not lower than yours. We're just kidding ourselves if we think otherwise."

"Jake, it's always a pleasure to sit at the knee of a philosopher-king. The point is that we don't need an 80,000 tonner for 20 years; we need it for five years. It would appear to me that the question of ownership would be more pertinent for the larger vessels we'll need when the new terminal is completed. Charles, tell us about the option."

"Quite simple. If the market rate for vessels of this type is below $6, we don't exercise the option even if we need the vessel; we just charter-in another vessel at a cheaper rate. If the market is above $6, we exercise the option even if we don't need the ship. In this case, we charter the vessel out to someone else at a higher rate and pocket the difference for ourselves. This is a five-year obligation only."

"Tell me, Charles, when our vessel, the *Lemon*, broke down in the middle of nowhere and we were stuck with all those towing charges and that pirate repair yard tried to hold us up, how would the situation be different if it were chartered-in rather than owned?"

"The moment the vessel became inoperative, we would have stopped paying hire, and all the costs and troubles you mentioned would have to be paid for and borne by the owner."

"Then Hans is assuming a business risk in this proposal—he is not just riding on our back."

"Yes. His rate to us is fixed and he's stuck with it no matter what happens."

"Charles, what is your opinion on the value of our 50,000 tonners when the new terminal is completed?"

"Frankly, they're worth less than the 80,000 tonner. We still have some use for them, but most of our oil will be carried in much larger vessels. We may charter them out or sell them at that time."

"Or be laid-up or scrapped, Charles, if there is no market?"

"Yes, of course."

"Fine. Now we are learning for the first time that the new terminal is making our own fleet obsolete. Thank you, Charles. That'll be all. We'll let you know the results."

Charles leaves the Board room but waits in the ready room in case he is called back into the meeting. The talk inside continues.

"Jake, weren't we talking just a while ago that our company cannot earn, nor can we borrow enough, without violating existing debt-to-worth ratios in the loan covenants of our senior debt, nor is it likely we can sell more stock at this time to fund all the capital required by our ten major capital projects? And, Jake, wouldn't you agree that sinking another $30 million in a vessel would further peril the financing of these projects if we choose to do all of them? I'll bet that if we didn't own as many vessels as we do, we wouldn't be so worried about how we are going to raise all the funds we need for our capital expansion program. Do any of you realize how many tens of millions we have wrapped up in our fleet? We are an oil company, not a shipping company, our capital commitment to shipping, including this deal, is preventing us from moving ahead."

After waiting a half-hour, Charles returns to his office. A little later, he receives a call authorizing him to conclude a charter along the lines proposed at the Board meeting. Charles calls the broker, the broker calls the owner, and the owner calls the shipyard manager, who congratulates Hans warmly as he blocks out eighteen months of employment for Building Berth 2, Hull 1010, on a schedule taped to his desk.

The time for celebrating is short. As the news spreads, Hans is already marshalling his forces to ensure that the charter party and the shipyard contract are signed without a hitch. There are many details yet to be negotiated and resolved.

A few months later, Hans' thoughts turn to tying up the financing of the vessel, for he does not wish to put up $10 million in equity nor have to face the cash drain of a seven-year amortization schedule. Although the shipyard credit is fixed at a low rate of 7%, Hans is willing to pay a higher cost of funds to a commercial bank to obtain a more advantageous financing structure. Part of this higher interest will be compensated by the $1 million in savings in the yard price if he does not utilize the credit facilities of the Exim Bank.

Hans calls Ace in to make up a cash flow projection to present to the banks: the three he normally does business with (banks 1, 2, and 3) plus one other (bank 4). He has decided to ask for twelve-year, 90% financing, which he does not expect to receive, but which will be the basis of his initial bargaining position. He also tells Ace to assume a 1983 projected operating cost of $1 million with 6% escalation thereafter and a cost of 7% on the borrowings (Table 14.5).

Hans believes the best way to handle the situation with the banks is to meet each banker, make his presentation, and ask for an informal response after they have had time to think about the matter. Based on these indications of interest, Hans will formulate his next tactical move.

In meeting with his account officer at bank #1, Hans learns that the size of the loan, added to his other loans, will exceed a prescribed limit and the bank cannot consider the loan request.

"I'm surprised to hear this. I didn't know I was approaching a limit in my previous borrowings. Is this something instituted by outside authorities, or is this an internal management decision?"

TABLE 14.5
CASH FLOW PROJECTION FOR BANK PRESENTATIONS

Year	Time charter (T/C) rate ($/dwt/month)	Annual revenue (T/C rate × 80,000 dwt × 11.5 mo/yr)	Operating costs (6% escalation)
1983	$5.00	$4,600,000	$1,000,000
1984	5.20	4,784,000	1,060,000
1985	5.40	4,968,000	1,124,000
1986	5.60	5,152,000	1,191,000
1987	5.80	5,336,000	1,262,000
1988	6.00*	5,520,000	1,338,000
1989	6.00	5,520,000	1,419,000
1990	6.00**	5,520,000	1,504,000
1991	6.00	5,520,000	1,594,000
1992	6.00	5,520,000	1,689,000
1993	6.00	5,520,000	1,791,000
1994	6.00	5,520,000	1,898,000

*Assumes the charterer will exercise the two-year option.
**Assumes that the vessel can be rechartered at the same rate as the option rate.

Surplus earnings to support financing charges (revenue less operating costs)	Amortization of debt	Interest on debt (7%)	Net cash flow
$3,600,000	$2,000,000	$1,610,000	$ −10,000
3,724,000	2,000,000	1,470,000	254,000
3,844,000	2,000,000	1,330,000	514,000
3,961,000	2,000,000	1,190,000	771,000
4,074,000	2,000,000	1,050,000	1,024,000
4,182,000	2,000,000	910,000	1,272,000
4,101,000	2,000,000	770,000	1,331,000
4,016,000	2,000,000	630,000	1,386,000
3,926,000	2,000,000	490,000	1,436,000
3,831,000	2,000,000	350,000	1,481,000
3,729,000	2,000,000	210,000	1,519,000
3,622,000	2,000,000	70,000	1,552,000

"Either way, Hans, it doesn't matter. I cannot book your loan. I could look into syndicating this loan for you. But I must warn you in all fairness that participating banks, unfamiliar with you, may be exceedingly tough; for instance, they may want a bank guarantee. Do you want me to look into this further?"

"No, not yet anyway. Thanks just the same."

Hans tries to contact Frank at bank #2. He is unsuccessful. An account officer by the name of Harold asks Hans to forward the proposal to him. About a week later, Harold calls and sets up an appointment with Hans at the bank.

Hans wonders why Frank doesn't call. Frank has been his account officer for years. He understood and appreciated Hans' shipping activities and expeditiously and competently handled Hans' banking requirements (money transfers, foreign exchange dealings, short-term interest bearing deposits) in addition to lending Hans considerable amounts of money over the years to finance the growth of his fleet. Hans has á great deal of respect for Frank and the two of them transact business in a straightforward manner. Hans has been so satisfied with his relationship with Frank that he has given serious thought of making bank #2 his primary bank rather than more or less dividing his business among three banks.

Hans arrives at the bank and is escorted to a conference room. He is told that Mr. Gladhand will be in to see him shortly. Twenty minutes later, Harold Gladhand arrives at the conference room. While Frank always had at least one deficiency in dress, be it scruffy shoes, a slightly out-of-fashion wrinkled plaid suit, not especially close-shaven, or a loose lock of hair, Harold Gladhand makes his debut in immaculate condition, exceedingly well-groomed in his pinstripe suit. Hans takes an instant dislike to Harold.

"Where's Frank?"

"How do you do. My name is Harold Gladhand."

"That's nice. Where's Frank?"

"As you may be aware, there has been a change in top management in the bank, who have introduced new institutional goals. These goals can only be carried out by people who are sympathetic to the fulfillment of the new overall corporate strategy."

"That's nice. Where's Frank?"

"I am your new account officer. Frank, as you call him, is no longer with us. With regard to your loan request, it comes at a most inopportune time, for all of the accounts are under review by myself and Mr. Archibald, my immediate senior, who is also newly appointed. Our review is not yet complete and we feel that we do not have the time available to thoroughly review a loan with such a large speculative element."

"Speculative?"

"Of course, the length of the charter is considerably less than the requested amortization period; the cash margins are much too thin, which unfortunately seems a common situation with the other loans you have with us. There appears to be an element of risk in your operations which we, as a bank, may not and probably should not be prepared to accept."

"What would you have in my proposal to make this more acceptable to you?"

"As a minimum, the charter period should cover the tenure of the loan. Moreover, the charterer should agree to at least pay the capital element of the charter hire in case the vessel breaks down. Perhaps a keepwell or a comfort letter from the charterer or maybe some sort of insurance might be appropriate so we can divorce ourselves from the consequences of your possible inability to perform."

"What you're talking about is a bareboat charter. If all I did was bareboat charters, then I would be nothing more than a financial institution myself. There would be no purpose for the oil company to deal with me. I am a businesssman in shipping. It is my business to take some degree of risk."

Gladhand mentally notes the idea of calling on the oil company about financing possible vessel acquisitions. Hans mentally notes that this is a hopeless cause.

"Furthermore, we are of the opinion that even with a suitably structured charter, we should not finance over 50% of the market value of the vessel. Moreover, our preliminary investigations show that the covenants on our existing loans to you may not be adequately safeguarding our interests and there is a question on the collateral support on the Zeta loan."

"Look, Gladhand, three points; I am not about to open up previously signed, sealed, and documented deals. They were done openly with legal counsel on both sides, yours and mine, present at all the negotiations. Two, I don't know why you mention the Zeta loan. Three, where's Frank?"

"I don't know. When I arrived to take his place, he didn't tell me nor did I wish to know where he was going. He just took his personal belongings out of his desk and that was the last I saw of him. The problem with Mr. Klaus, as I see it, and which is becoming apparent in our review, is that his lending practices may not have reflected our current banking strategy. For instance, the Zeta loan may be under-collateralized."

"The collateral on that loan is what you agreed to."

"Yes, but in accordance with the covenants of the loan agreement, you promised to maintain asset coverage of 150% of the principal amount outstanding and we have reason to doubt that this is the case."

Hans is taken back by this remark, for he had forgotten this particular loan provision. After thinking a moment, Hans replies, "Do you realize you must have over 300% asset coverage? That loan is more than half paid down."

"It ought to be confirmed, don't you think?"

"At whose expense?"

As Hans leaves bank #2, he is glad that he never carried out his plan to make Frank his only banker. His capacity to borrow funds from this bank ended with a change of account officers.

Hans receives more favorable responses from banks #3 and #4. Both, however, question the $1 million operating cost estimate for 1983 and the 6% inflation rate thereafter. The account officer at bank #3 bases his concern on Hans' unaudited financial statements which Hans submits routinely as required in the loan agreements with the bank. The account officer at bank #4, with no existing relationship with Hans, refers to financial statements of other owners of similar type tonnage registered under flags of convenience. Hans responds individually to both bankers.

"As you know, my three principal costs are crewing, insurance, and repairs. Tankers may be going into layup, and the crews released will tend to hold down wage demands. Besides, as a flag of convenience owner, I can switch my crews if I feel forced to do so. Vessels in layup put pressure on insurance companies to be more competitive because of loss of premium income. I also think repair costs will be held down by shipyards entering the repair business as they run out of work building tankers. Therefore, I feel that inflation will be more moderate in the future than it has been in the past. As you may not realize, my most authoritative source on future inflation rates is the press releases from your own bank economists who say that inflation is now under control."

After some haggling on this issue, both bankers independently agree to a 1983 projected operating cost of $1.2 million with 8% escalation thereafter.

David is the account officer at bank #3. He wants to book another loan with Hans because he has a high regard for the charterer and the owner. In looking over Hans' presentation, David decides that he must disregard the two-year option because he cannot count on it being exercised as a source of repayment on a loan. He decides that the best structure is a five-year loan with a balloon payment. However, he has a problem figuring out the value of the vessel when it comes off the five-year charter. The amount of the balloon payment must not exceed a conservative estimate of the residual value of the vessel at the time. It can certainly exceed the vessel's scrap value of about $2 million. In thinking over this matter, David is influenced more by the attitudes of senior mangement, whose approval he must obtain prior to making a formal response to Hans, than by his own views on the commercial value of the vessel. After due consideration, David concludes that the most he dares to submit to management for their approval is a five-year loan with a $5 million balloon payment.

David's next step is to determine the surplus of cash available to service debt; and from that, the amount of the loan (Table 14.6).

TABLE 14.6

Year	Time charter rate	Annual revenue	Operating costs (8% inflation)	Surplus to service debt
1983	$5.00	$4,600,000	$1,200,000	$3,400,000
1984	5.20	4,784,000	1,296,000	3,488,000
1985	5.40	4,968,000	1,400,000	3,568,000
1986	5.60	5,152,000	1,512,000	3,600,000
1987	5.80	5,336,000	1,633,000	3,703,000

David then arbitrarily selects $15 million as the loan amount to be repaid at $2 million per year, semiannual payments, for five years. The remaining $5 million is due in full at the end of the fifth year (Table 14.7).

TABLE 14.7

	Debt amortization	Interest (assume 10%)	Surplus from operation to service debt	Net cash flow	Cumulative cash position
1983	$2,000,000	$1,400,000	$3,400,000	—	—
1984	2,000,000	1,200,000	3,488,000	$ 288,000	$ 288,000
1985	2,000,000	1,000,000	3,568,000	568,000	856,000
1986	2,000,000	800,000	3,600,000	800,000	1,656,000
1987	2,000,000	600,000	3,703,000	1,103,000	2,759,000

David notes that the cumulative cash position after five years of operation of $2.7 million is more than half the balloon payment. Since

David is willing to have a $5 million net exposure on the vessel at the end of the fifth year, he revises the amount of the loan to $17 million and alters the principal repayment schedule (Table 14.8).

TABLE 14.8

	Debt amortization	Interest (assume 10%)	Surplus from operation to service debt	Net cash flow	Cumulative cash position
1983	$1,700,000	$1,615,000	$3,400,000	$85,000	$85,000
1984	2,100,000	1,425,000	3,488,000	−37,000	48,000
1985	2,400,000	1,200,000	3,568,000	−32,000	16,000
1986	2,600,000	950,000	3,600,000	50,000	66,000
1987	3,000,000	670,000	3,703,000	33,000	99,000

Total debt amortization is $11.8 million, leaving a $5.2 million balloon due in full at the end of the fifth year. If Hans is doing well at the end of the fifth year, the bank will probably refinance the balloon payment. David realizes that the cumulative cash position of only $100,000 after a five-year period affords no coverage at all for Hans if the 10% interest rate assumption on a floating rate loan or if the operating expense and escalation rate assumptions are underestimated. There is no coverage if Hans must face extraordinary items such as a vessel breakdown whose cost includes both repairs and the loss of income until the vessel is back operating. However, David is confident of Hans' ability to fulfill his operating responsibilities and to make up any potential cash shortfalls from other vessels in his fleet. David also feels very comfortable with the creditworthiness of the charterer.

David's main concern is the assessment of the residual value of the vessel that limits the borrowing to $17 million, far below Hans' request of $24 million. The transaction as it stands isn't any better than the Exim Bank financing. David is frustrated; he feels he will have great difficulty in obtaining senior management approval for a larger balloon.

The terms of the loan include a first mortgage on the vessel, an assignment of charter hire (the bank being named loss payee on the hull insurance policy), a requirement of having hull marine insurance in force in excess of 120% of the outstanding debt, the safekeeping of the stock of the one shipholding company in the bank's custody, and the bank having the operating account for the one shipholding company.

The first mortgage will be filed in the nation of registry after verifi-

cation that the vessel is free and clear of all liens, has a proper certification of ownership, and has settled other legal technicalities. A plaque
is customarily mounted on the bridge of the vessel with the name of the
first mortgage holder (mortgagee). The assignment of charter hire to the
bank means that the payment of hire is directed to a special account
under the bank's control. If an owner is in arrears meeting his debt
obligations, the bank may refuse to transfer the hire to the owner's
account, keeping what is due to the bank. This is done gingerly because
an owner may lose his charter if he is starved of operating funds. This
would leave the bank in a worse position than before. The assignment of
charter hire is incorporated in a charter party and requires the approval
of the charterer, which cannot be unreasonably withheld. The naming
of the bank as loss payee is intended for the event of total actual or
constructive loss of the vessel, and not so much for the settlement of
minor claims. In case of a loss of the vessel, the bank receives the proceeds from the settlement of the policy, pays off all existing indebted-
ness, and passes any remaining funds to the owner. There are other
matters dealing with insurance such as the requirement for war risk
insurance and mortgagee's interest where the underwriters promise to
pay off the outstanding debt even if the owner is in breach of warranty
with regard to the circumstances surrounding the loss of the vessel. The
safekeeping of the stock by the bank is a precautionary measure because
the stock of one shipholding company in flag-of-convenience/necessity
countries may be in bearer form, that is, he who possesses the stock
owns the company. Safekeeping the certificates in a bank vault ensures
that the ownership of the company remains with the borrower.

David is aware that the vessel needs construction financing. In most
countries, the ownership of a vessel under construction remains with
the shipyard until delivery to the owner. To handle the financing during construction, David requires the assignment of the stock of the
shipholding company holding the shipyard contract, the assignment of
the shipyard contract, verification of suitable shipyard insurance, and
some sort of performance guarantee.

The assignment of the shipyard contract and the stock of the
contracting company to the bank permits the bank to authorize the
completion of the vessel, if the owner cannot or does not fulfill his
obligations. A three-quarters completed hull has very little value to
anybody if the owner decides to, or is forced to, abandon the vessel. By
completing the vessel as the new owner, the bank may be in a better
position to recoup its investment. The yard insurance is to cover such
perils as flooding, storms, and fire which may damage or destroy a par-

tially completed hull. The proceeds of this insurance would either retire advances made for the construction of the vessel if it were a total loss or pay the expenses of repairing the damage. The performance guarantee removes the risk to the bank that the owner will refuse delivery of the vessel. An owner may refuse delivery of a vessel because shipyard contract specifications with regard to vessel performance, or time of delivery, have not been met. It is possible that the shipyard may become financially insolvent and cannot complete the vessel's construction. The shipyard pays a fee to the insurance company underwriting the performance bonds or to the commercial bank guaranteeing the construction loan. A creditworthy parent corporation, owning the shipyard along with other industrial enterprises, may issue a refund guarantee, which accomplishes much the same purpose as a performance bond or bank guarantee. An underwriter of performance bonds or guarantor of construction loans must be very familiar with the capacity of a yard to fulfill its contractual obligations and with its financial health. The loan agreement on the contruction loan will also contain a material adverse change clause. This permits the bank to cancel a formal commitment to the owner prior to the actual funding of the loan if there is a change in the owner's business interests that imperils the transaction.

All these terms are fairly typical in a vessel financing, and David knows that Hans will find nothing unusual in any of them. He calls Hans to discuss the situation, including pricing of the loan. They agree not to take the transaction to senior management at this time.

Henry is the account officer at bank #4. Hans has already called on Henry and acquainted him with the shipping deal. After making a few preliminary inquiries to his contacts in the shipping industry on Hans' reputation, Henry calls Hans and tells him that he has been favorably impressed with the proposal.

"Our credit people, Hans, are very tough and you'll have to release a great deal, if not all, of your fleet information. We may need your help to develop some credit information on the charterer."

"I am not in the habit of releasing my fleet information. I don't keep credit information on the charterer and I am hardly in a position to ask for it. Certainly you, as a bank, must have access to credit information. One thing I can tell you, Henry: I don't enter into any charter with anyone except a first-class charterer. In fact, I have turned down business because I didn't have confidence in the charterer. In one case, I demanded and received a parent guarantee on the payment of the charter hire that other owners did not have. When the shipping subsidiary of that company tried to renege on their charters, they left me alone."

"You may not believe this, Hans, but we don't keep information on companies which do not have an account with us. Since the charterer is publicly traded, we'll be able to get what we need. If the charterer were a private company, this could be a difficult problem. I do need a name of an individual in the chartering department of the oil company to confirm the existence and terms of the charter."

"Don't you people trust anybody?"

"Oh, yes, but only when it doesn't matter! As far as your fleet information is concerned, my own knowledge of your reputation would be sufficient if I were making a decision on my own. But I don't. The bank has set up a credit evaluation group, and no commitment is made without their approval. They don't approve anything without a detailed analysis of your situation. Frankly, if you want to maintain your privacy, and I appreciate your feelings, there is simply no point in continuing with this discussion. I am powerless to recommend anything without a credit department blessing. Let me say, however, that this is a problem we face with every new client. Once the tortuous exercise is over, all other transactions merely involve a catching up on the current situation. Nevertheless, you can expect the credit department on their first go-round to be very inquisitive."

"I'm not used to credit people prowling around my affairs with a magnifying glass."

"Hans, I want to do business with you. I'm confident we'll make a proposal to you—though I can't guarantee it, of course. The decision is yours, not mine. I can do a lot of things, but not an end run around our credit people. I'm afraid that you must view it as a cost of doing business with us. Naturally, all your data will be held in strictest confidence."

"That's what all the brokers tell me. I can't think of a better way to make a public announcement than to tell a broker to keep an item for his ears only."

"We're not brokers and our dusty files . . ."

"Never mind, I'm just badgering you. I accept the fact that if I choose to do business with you, I must divulge my fleet information. Send a letter to my vice president on what you want. But if I answer it, I expect you to produce and I'm going to hold your feet to the fire."

"Hans, I promise you the world."

"Henry, I expect you to deliver."

Within a week, the vice president receives the following letter, which requests the following information:

For the existing fleet, please provide the following information for each and every vessel:

1. Vessel name, type, main characteristics, year built.

2. Charter (if any), type of charter, name of charterer, charter rate, and period.

3. Debt (if any), amount originally outstanding, and institution holding the debt, current amount outstanding, amortization schedule, interest rate, year debt to be paid off, collateral supporting debt including junior mortgages, guarantees, etc.

4. Current operating costs, including breakdown of costs.

5. Current market value of vessels with and without charters.

For vessels under construction (if any), please provide details of financing and charters already arranged, or state of negotiations if not arranged.

Please provide:

A. A description of vessels and terms of all chartered-in vessels (if any) and their employment, or chartering-out, details.

B. All other employment contracts such as contracts of affreightment not mentioned above with pertinent details.

C. Contact names and phone numbers for your most important lenders, charterers, and suppliers for your vessels.

D. Three-year audited statements of all subsidiaries, and a consolidating and consolidated income and balance sheet statement.

Hans calls Henry. "Henry, I received your credit people's request. Before I do anything, you should realize that I have never had my statements audited and don't intend to start."

"Hans, what can I say. Our bank examiners are coming down pretty hard on us for making shipping loans in the tens of millions of dollars without audited statements. The most I can do for you is to book the loan with the condition that you will from here on out have audited statements. I'm quite certain that we can do away with performing a formal audit over the past three years. But the requirement for future audited statements by an acceptable accounting firm cannot be avoided."

"Another cost of doing business with you people."

"I'm afraid it is. While we're at it, I hope you realize that we are going to charge you a set-up fee, a commitment fee during the construction period on the undrawn balance of the loan, possibly a management fee if you try to squeeze our interest spread too much, and you're going to pay all our legal expenses and other closing costs."

"I realize that, but I know that you are going to use the cheapest lawyers in town because this transaction is as simple as a closing on a house."

"No, the lawyers we use are probably the most expensive in town; three or four hours of their time is worth my weekly salary. There is little incentive on the part of the bank to hold down legal charges because you're paying for them. Closings are nontrivial undertakings as are their costs."

"All the cost of doing business at your bank?"

"This bank and, as you already know, every other bank."

"Yes, I know. Another matter: is it necessary to give a detailed breakdown of operating costs? I consider this a confidential matter. Wouldn't an average total figure for each vessel do the job?"

"Give it a whirl, Hans, and see what happens."

"I presume your credit people are going to do a cash flow on my fleet with all this information."

"That's right."

"Out of curiosity, how long are they going to project my earnings?"

"I'm not exactly sure, Hans. Maybe five years."

"That's interesting, Henry. Tell me, what rates are they going to use for ships coming off charter during this period? How are they going to work all these contracts of affreightment into their calculations? Sometimes I use my own ships, sometimes I charter-in vessels to meet these commitments—whichever is more profitable. I have one other vessel, a small liquid gas carrier, on order without a charter. I am purposely not negotiating a charter because I feel that I'll be much better off by delaying this matter until the vessel is delivered in three years. How are your people going to handle this? Are their judgments better than mine?"

"Off the top of my head, Hans, I can say that that's their problem. But their evaluation is of critical importance to me and to you because I can't offer you a commitment without their blessing. They'll be calling up your vice president for more information and they'll probably ask for an opinion or two. It's here where you or your vice president can influence their thinking. Actually, Hans, neither you nor the credit people can answer those questions. There will be a nice, thick credit file on you with cash flow projections of 14-digit accuracy. At the end of the day, it is going to be a judgment. Given the world as it is today and guessing at what the world will be like tomorrow, will Hans be around as an ongoing concern? Do his inflows and cash reserves come reasonably close to meeting his outflows? If their answer is yes, I'll be making a proposal to you. If you like the terms, maybe we'll have a closing. If their answer is no, it's been nice talking with you and maybe we can do something at another time."

"Can't you influence their thinking?"

"Hans, in your position, you slam your fist on the table and that ends the discussion. The decision is made. I am a salaried employee paid to book loans. The credit people are also salaried employees to prevent me from booking, in their opinion, bad loans. It's a check and balance system."

"Sounds like driving an automobile with the accelerator and the brake pedals fully depressed."

"Hans, I promise you I'll do my best because I want to do business with you. The first transaction is always the worst. One good thing about a thorough credit evaulation is that it gives us an appreciation of your business and confidence in you. The second transaction and all others are much easier than the first."

"We'll see."

Henry is confident that the credit department, after the usual hair-splitting arguments, will give their blessing. The liquid gas carrier may pose a serious obstacle because the credit people routinely assume the worst in charter markets in their projections. Henry has often remarked that if such a depressing scenario is truly in store, why is the bank making loans to anyone. As the credit group is gathering and analyzing the information, Henry thinks about creating a financial package that is both attractive to Hans and secure for the bank. From conversations with Hans, Henry is familiar with the availability of shipyard credit for 70% of a $25 million yard price, and that the seven-year amortization is too much of a strain on charter revenues. Henry's first thought is to lend money to fund the difference between the inflow from the charter and the yard credit outflow. This way Hans can take advantage of the low-cost yard credit with his actual cost of interest depending on the mix of the yard credit and the commercial loan financing the vessel (Table 14.9).

Henry constructs Table 14.10 where the interest expense on the bank's debt is added to the principal outstanding at the end of the year and the cash flow available after servicing the Exim debt is applied to the total amount owed to the bank. In other words, Hans does not have

TABLE 14.9

Shipyard price with Exim financing	$25,000,000
Predelivery interest and expenses	3,000,000
Total capitalized cost	$28,000,000
Owner's equity	$3,000,000
Exim bank financing (70% of shipyard price)	$17,500,000
Interest rate (fixed)	7%
Tenure	7 years
Bank #4 loan	$7,500,000
Interest rate (floating; assume average	
rate of 10%)	10%
Tenure	See schedule

Year	Time charter rate	Annual revenue	Operating costs (10% inflation)	Surplus to service debt	Amortization of Exim debt	Interest on Exim debt
1983	$5.20	$4,600,000	$1,200,000	$3,400,000	$2,500,000	$1,138,000
1984	5.40	4,784,000	1,296,000	3,488,000	2,500,000	963,000
1985	5.60	4,968,000	1,400,000	3,568,000	2,500,000	788,000
1986	5.80	5,152,000	1,512,000	3,600,000	2,500,000	613,000
1987	6.00	5,336,000	1,633,000	3,703,000	2,500,000	438,000
1988	6.00*	5,520,000	1,764,000	3,756,000	2,500,000	263,000
1989	6.00	5,520,000	1,905,000	3,615,000	2,500,000	88,000
1990				3,615,000**		
1991				3,615,000		
1992				3,615,000		
1993				3,615,000		
1994				3,615,000		

*Assumes exercise of option.
**Assumes vessel can be chartered at rates that preserves a surplus to service debt of this amount.

to apply funds from other sources to meet the cash deficits as long as the vessel can generate the anticipated revenue, the operating costs turn out to be within expectations, and the average interest rate on the floating rate loan does not exceed 10%.

Henry realizes that this technique, successfully applied in other shipping transactions, plainly does not work in this instance. In 1983, bank #4's exposure is $7.5 million on a vessel with a five-year charter. At the end of 1987, its exposure has increased to nearly $10.5 million with possibly no employment opportunities if market rates are depressed. In addition, the bank doesn't even have a first mortgage

TABLE 14.10

Year	Cash flow after servicing Exim debt	Beginning of year, bank #4 debt balance	Year-end debt balance after applying cash flow	Interest expense on average amount outstanding (10%)	Year-end debt balance after adding interest expense
1983	$ −238,000	$ 7,500,000	$7,738,000	$ 762,000	$ 8,500,000
1984	25,000	8,500,000	8,475,000	849,000	9,349,000
1985	280,000	9,349,000	9,069,000	921,000	9,990,000
1986	487,000	9,990,000	9,503,000	975,000	10,478,000
1987	765,000	10,478,000	9,713,000	1,010,000	10,723,000
1988	993,000	10,723,000	9,730,000	1,023,000	10,753,000
1989	1,027,000	10,753,000	9,726,000	1,024,000	10,750,000
1990	3,615,000	10,750,000	7,135,000	894,000	8,029,000
1991	3,615,000	8,029,000	4,414,000	622,000	5,036,000
1992	3,615,000	5,036,000	1,421,000	323,000	1,744,000
1993		1,744,000	0	87,000	0

since $5 million of shipyard credit is still outstanding. Although this financing package is not possible to be done as structured, Henry decides to explore another avenue.

Henry goes over the information that the credit evaluation group has received from Hans. His attention is drawn to vessels A, B, and C that are all on profitable charters fully covering the underlying debt and are all coming off charter, debt free, in 1987. Henry conservatively estimates that the vessels, as a group, generate $1.5 million a year above their current operating costs and debt servicing obligations. Knowing that owners prefer to borrow as much as they can, Henry proposes to finance 100% of the acquisition of the tanker in conjunction with the Exim funds, using vessels A, B, and C as substitute for the owner's equity investment. Using the same basic financial structure as before, Henry prepares a new cash flow projection (Table 14.11).

Henry feels that he can justify a loan of $10.5 million on the basis of a four-vessel fleet mortgage to his seniors. The bank's exposure at the end of the fifth year of nearly $6 million is collateralized by a second mortgage on an 80,000-dwt tanker ($5 million is still outstanding on the first mortgage held by the Exim bank) and first mortgages on three other vessels. Although all these vessels may be without charters at that time, Henry feels comfortable with the assets. In his mind, the four vessels

TABLE 14.11

Year	Cash flow after servicing Exim debt	Net cash flow from vessels A, B & C	Total cash flow to be dedicated to servicing bank #4's debt	Beginning debt balance	Year-end debt balance	Interest expense on average amount outstanding (10%)	Year-end debt balance after adding interest expense
1983	$−238,000	$1,500,000	$1,262,000	$10,500,000	$9,238,000	$987,000	$10,225,000
1984	25,000	1,500,000	1,525,000	10,225,000	8,700,000	946,000	9,646,000
1985	280,000	1,500,000	1,780,000	9,646,000	7,866,000	876,000	8,742,000
1986	487,000	1,500,000	1,987,000	8,742,000	6,755,000	775,000	7,530,000
1987	765,000	1,500,000	2,265,000	7,530,000	5,265,000	640,000	5,905,000

will certainly have a market value in excess of the total bank and Exim debt of $11 million.

Henry reports to George, who has recently assumed his present position as Henry's superior. Though George has extensive lending experience, he has had limited exposure to shipping loans.

"Specifically, Henry, what is our collateral position?"

"Initially, we will have a second mortgage on the newbuilding, second mortgages on Vessels A and C, and a third mortgage on Vessel B. Now the present second mortgage on B serves as collateral on a loan made on Vessel E, which will be fully paid off two years after delivery of the newbuilding. This liquidates the second mortgage and we automatically move from third to second mortgagee. When the first mortgagee's loan is paid off in the third year of the charter, our second mortgage becomes a first mortgage. Soon after that, we'll have first mortgages on Vessels A and C as their loans are amortized. Remember, George, all these loans are being liquidated by existing charters."

"Yes, Henry, but at the end of the fifth year, if market conditions are depressed, we may have four unemployed vessels on our hands since the option on the 80,000 tonner will probably not be exercised. There is still a $5 million mortgage outstanding on the Exim credit that must be paid off. Why don't you have Hans put up the $3 million anyway and take the three ships. Our exposure will be a lot less in 1987."

"Because I don't think Hans will stand for it. I think giving him 100% financing will be just the bait. I am trying to structure the loan so that we are in a secure position, yet we stand out enough to separate ourselves from the competition. I think this the way to do it. Remember, you judge my performance by the amount of loans I book."

"And pricing?"

"I think I can convince Hans that our approach to this loan justifies a competitive rate."

"I'll tell you right now, Henry, that there will be no discussion on rates. If Hans doesn't like our going rate, the deal's off. I think we are assuming a risk that justifies our spread. Let's go back to our security position. Take Vessel B. What would be the debt on this vessel, say, on delivery of the newbuilding?"

"Roughly, a first mortgage with about $5 million still outstanding, a second mortgage with $2 million still outstanding, and our third mortgage."

"What will be the amount of our third mortgage?"

"I haven't thought of what amount to assign—say $4 million. I think the vessel must have a market value of $10–12 million."

"Okay. Let's say a first mortgage of $5 million, a second of $2 million, and a third of $4 million. Now Hans goes belly up at that time. Where do we stand?"

"Actually, we're in bad shape all around because a junior mortgage holder cannot enforce his rights without the permission of the first mortgagee."

"Henry, we can't even become a junior mortgage holder without the permission of the first mortgagee, isn't that right?"

"Yes, and it may well be that the Exim bank will not permit us to have a second mortgage on the newbuilding. If this is the case, we can get a negative pledge from the owner not to place any mortgage on the vessel. When the present debt is paid off, we can then obtain a first mortgage to protect our position."

"That's a large step backward, Henry, because if a vessel is auctioned off to liquidate debt and we have a junior mortgage, we may get something. Where do we stand with a negative pledge when a vessel is auctioned off? The vessel goes to the buyer, the proceeds of the auction go to the first mortgage holder and other claimants. Then all we have is a negative pledge on a one-ship holding company with no vessel and no cash. The one thing I don't like about loans to flag-of-convenience vessels is that I don't know where I stand in a liquidation. Take, for instance, the *Bete-Noire* loan. The borrower is a French shipping company and its vessels fly the French flag. Its center of operation is in France. Management and the crews are all French citizens. I have access to the French court system. I know nothing about their system of justice. At least I know that problems can be worked out in an established judicial system whose decisions are enforced by French authorities. What do we have here, Henry? An owner whose legal residence and citizenship has changed over his lifetime. He charters out of London, operates out of Bermuda, crews from all over the world. His vessel may never call on any port of its country of registry, if it even has a port. The vessel's only connection with the country of registry is a notation in some file. Even the stock of the owning company is unregistered—in bearer form to be handed over from party to party without anyone knowing it. If he goes bankrupt, where do we go to press our claim?"

"Nice points to bring up, George, after we have booked hundreds of millions of dollars on this basis. Look, we can seize the vessel, if we had an enforceable claim like a first mortgage, in any port in the western world. Thanks to Britain, most maritime countries have a body of admiralty or maritime law, which is remarkably consistent around the world. The United States picked up its maritime law from Britain when it, like Canada, Australia, New Zealand, and several other countries, was a British colony. And Liberia's maritime law was adopted almost word for word from U.S. maritime law when it was a colony of the United States. Let's look at facts. All vessels in Hans' fleet will call on ports in North America, Europe, Japan, Australia, and other industrialized countries because that is the destination of most commodities and the source of most finished goods. So the vessel is in a port in the United States, say, and we know it. We have a legitimate lien on this vessel and we take it to the proper federal court. The court issues an order and a marshall goes down and arrests the ship. Now it can't leave port. I don't care what flag Hans has the vessel under, where Hans lives, where he votes, where he operates out of or anything. I have his ship. If Hans wants his ship back, he has to show up in court, establish his ownership, and post bond equal to my claim. Then and only then is his vessel free to leave port. Now we fight it out in court. If Hans wins, he gets back his bond. If I win, the settlement is made out of the posted bond. I don't care about anything as long as Hans shows up and posts his bond."

"And if he doesn't?"

"The vessel is auctioned off after notice is widely publicized and the proceeds liquidate claims in the order prescribed by the court."

"That's nice for the ex-British colonies. What about Japan, Germany, and Italy?"

"As I understand the situation, their maritime law is similar in intent. Obviously, our lawyers work through their correspondents in these and other countries to carry out the enforcement of a lien. It's possible that we might choose not to arrest a vessel in a particular country because of the nature of their laws."

"Why would Japan or Italy or anyone else bother enforcing our lien. They have no connection with the vessel—it is not owned or operated by their citizens or registered in their country. The vessel just happens to be in their port. Is there an international convention binding these nations to cooperate in this manner?"

"No. I think it is just a matter that Italy, for example, wants to be able to enforce its liens against a vessel in port, say in Germany or any other nation. When a German supplier of bunkers asks the Italian authorities to arrest a Japanese flag vessel for nonpayment, the Italians cooperate for they want reciprocity in the enforcement of their liens for a vessel in a German port."

"Let's go back, Henry, to the auction of Vessel B. There is a first mortgage of $5 million, a second of $2 million, and our third of $4 million. Right?"

"Yes, but George, remember, as you say, we are powerless to enforce our rights to have an auction without the permission of the first mortgagee. As you mentioned, we can't even get a junior mortgage without his permission. Moreover, the first mortgagee can take legal action to our detriment and we can't do anything to stop him. Our rights are truly subordinate to his. It is the first mortgage holder who takes possession of the vessel when his loan is in default, not our loan."

"I understand. Let's assume we were granted permission to become a junior mortgage holder with a third mortgage of $4 million. If the vessel were auctioned off by the first mortgagee for $11 million, we would have our position liquidated at 100¢ on the dollar."

"Not quite, George. First, go back to when we registered the mortgage of the vessel in the country of registry. We first ensure that there are no other liens registered against the vessel other than the senior mortgage holders. This being the case, the mortgage holders generally rank ahead of all other claimants except unpaid crew wages, salvage claims, court costs, and unpaid taxes. These claims have a higher priority than mortgage holders. Other claims may come before us; it all depends on how the court ranks the priority of liens. Let's say these prior liens total $2 million. Then we only get 50¢ on the dollar: $11 million proceeds less $2 million for prior liens, $5 million to the first mortgagee, $2 million to the second and the remaining $2 million to us. That's only half our mortgage. If prior claims total $4 million, we get nothing, as does every other lien which ranks below us. And the new owner of the vessel has no obligation to prior liens, whether or not filed with the court, when he assumes ownership. All liens are liquidated forever by this process, regardless if the claimant received 100¢ on a dollar, 50¢, or nothing. The vessel starts a whole new life again."

"Sometimes I wonder about our investing in shipping . . ."

"George, the assets float. It's hard to nationalize an asset that is not fixed to the ground. You're thinking too much about these things. Look, this world is an ongoing concern and so is Hans. If things get rough, Hans is in a much better position than many owners. With the exception of the liquid gas carrier, every vessel with a significant amount of debt is covered by a first-class charter. His vessels with little or no debt are on the spot market. That's fine as far as we're concerned. If the market falls away from Hans, he'll lay up these vessels and cut his operating costs to the bone. There is no significant amount of debt on these ships to sink him."

"I'm not disagreeing with you, Henry. All I'm saying is that our collateral in the beginning of the loan, aside from the charter, is unsecured subordinate debt because we effectively have no rights to exercise. When we do have real security in the form of first mortgages, we have no charters to fall back on. If we decide to go ahead on this transaction, we had better have Hans sewed up tight just in case your rosy view of the world in eight years or so doesn't materialize. Once we sign the loan documents, that's it. I'll call the credit group and have them draw up a suggested list of loan covenants."

"Hope their shopping list doesn't kill the deal, George."

In a few days, Henry receives the list from the credit group entitled "Suggested Conditions Precedent." Conditions precedent are all the terms and conditions to be written into a commitment letter from the bank to the borrower. A commitment letter cannot become legally binding on the part of the bank until all the conditions precedent have been satisfied. Once the conditions precedent are satisfied, then the bank is legally bound to meet its obligations.

Besides the mortgages, assignment of charter hire, designation of the bank as loss payee on the marine insurance, minimum marine insurance to be carried on each vessel, suitable yard insurance and performance bonds, a material adverse change clause, and an operating account, there are:

- Restrictions on dividend payments on all shipholding companies for Vessels A, B, and C and the newbuilding.
- Cross default clauses where a default in any of these four companies automatically triggers a default in the other three. In case of default, all debt becomes due and payable.
- A cross guarantee among all four companies, each guaranteeing each other's debt.
- A minimum working capital requirement for the shipholding company owning the 80,000-dwt newbuilding vessel equal to two months of operating and financing costs.
- An escrow account whereby all the surplus cash generated above that needed to meet all operating and financial obligations for the four vessels is deposited in an interest bearing account where withdrawals can be made only with the approval of the bank.
- A guarantee by the parent holding company for all the individual shipholding companies.
- A personal guarantee from Hans.
- No disbursement of funds for the 80,000-dwt newbuilding until the liquid gas carrier on order is fixed, in the opinion of the bank, to an acceptable charterer at a satisfactory rate.

- No further major capital commitments without the prior permission of the bank.
- All future income and balance statements of all the shipping companies to be audited by an acceptable accounting firm.

Henry immediately calls back the head of the credit group.

"Do you really think the first mortgagee on Vessels A, B, and C is going to subordinate his position to ours by permitting us to have cross-default and cross-guarantee clauses and dividends restrictions? When have we ever subordinated our position without some sort of quid pro quo? These items are not even at Hans' discretion to give or withhold. It is going to be rough enough getting him to agree with your shopping list without your asking for something he can't give us whether he wants to or not."

The credit group head tells Henry that he'll look into the matter.

That evening Henry and Hans meet at a restaurant. Before dinner, Henry tells Hans of his plan to structure a package which, in conjunction with the Exim credit and Vessels A, B, and C, will provide 100% financing. Hans responds favorably, already thinking of new investment possibilities for the $3 million in equity that is no longer required for this transaction.

"What are the terms, Henry?"

"You're not going to like them."

"Henry, I assure you that there is nothing you can say or do that would phase me in the least. And don't give me a little piece at a time; I take my medicine in one gulp."

Henry explains the position of the bank: the lack of collateral support in the initial stages of the loan, the lack of charters in five years, and the need to establish a secure position at the onset of a loan to safeguard the bank's interest. This includes building in triggering mechanisms in the loan covenants which provide leverage on the part of the bank to protect its interests at an early point of a potentially degenerating situation. There are also the problems of dealing with a client without an already established banking relationship. Henry mentions his run-in with the credit people on the cross-default and cross-guarantee provisions.

"Henry, I wouldn't bother to meet you if I didn't think there were a chance of doing some business together. I'm an owner. Two things control the size of my fleet: the marketplace, which places a value on the services rendered by my fleet, and the availability of credit. I have always been able to get credit as long as the market is with me and not against me. I'll admit that I have been forced to pay higher rates of interest than I'd like and maybe agree to terms I preferred not to have. As long as I run my business right, I have access to credit. If it isn't you, it's someone else. The only real constraint on me is the marketplace and how I react to it.

"You lend money. I borrow money. I don't enter into a shipping transaction unless I can see myself clear as dictated by the market. I may be wrong, so you have to tie me down to make your own position secure. I understand that. What you may not understand is that all your covenants, guarantees, the carefully placed financial mine fields, like the cross-default clauses which trigger a massive explosion if I ever err, won't do a thing for you if the market falls away from me. No covenant in any loan agreement is going to save your hide if the market says my ships aren't worth the steel they're made of. I have no qualms over the assignments, mortgages, insurance—all that is usual for the business. Minimum working capital requirements, who cares? But the escrow account, and perhaps the dividend restriction clauses, should not be an open checkbook for you people. Surely we can establish some sort of criteria where deposits in the escrow account are no longer necessary once they build up to a level which keeps you happy. For instance, I don't see why I have to make further deposits in an escrow account if its balance exceeds the amount of outstanding debt. Do you?"

"No."

"And maybe at some point, I'd like to be able to pay dividends to free money for other uses."

"I think we can work out an accommodation."

"Let's see, you asked for the guarantees of the shipholding company for the 80,000-dwt bulker, one from the parent holding company for all my vessels and a personal guarantee. The shipholding company can guarantee its own debt as far as I'm concerned. I don't go for cross guarantees among these companies because that infringes on the intent of limited liability of a one-ship holding company. The parent company guarantee is something I have to take under advisement. I know some owners do it, but I never have. You realize that the parent company has nothing but a little cash to handle office expenses and holds the stock for each of the one-ship holding companies. I'm not sure what substance that guarantee has, do you?"

"No, not really."

"On my personal guarantee, I can just tell you that you're not going to get it. I have never given it and am not about to start. I'm not going to give you a statement of personal wealth either, so don't bother to ask."

"Maybe I can persuade the credit . . ."

"And while you're talking to them, you can tell them there is no way that I am going to have to go on my bended knee to them everytime I want to make a new capital commitment. I am not that far in hock to the banks and I don't intend to get there. If, by chance, things go bad for me, then my punishment for being wrong, besides losing money, is to genuflect before the creditors. On fixing the liquid gas carrier, you can tell the credit people that there are no charterers willing to take that vessel at this time. So it's not a matter of my agreeing or not agreeing to this demand to fix the vessel. Their demand is simply out of touch with reality. Besides, I wouldn't agree to it anyway. My personal guarantee, the bank's approval of capital expenditures, and fixing the liquid gas carrier are all non-negotiable rejections. This is the cost of doing business with me."

"Hans, we still have a basis for a deal. Fighting over terms indicates solvency. I always worry about borrowers who blandly accept all our terms. When I go back, I may have to increase the pricing of this loan a bit to compensate for some retrenchment in terms."

"Believe me, Henry, I try not to leverage myself to the point that I am no longer a free agent. If I do get in trouble some day, I know I'll have to take your abuse. As I say, that's part of my punishment."

"I hope this talk doesn't disturb the rest of the evening for us."

"I assure you, Henry, that this has been the highlight of the evening. Maybe you're right: if we can do this one, there'll be others."

"My job prevents me from forgetting that."

The rest of the evening is spent swapping sea stories on people, places and things. During the conservation, Henry mentally plots his timing. In five days, the head of the credit department is taking a three-week vacation and the second-in-charge is easier to influence on matters concerning loan covenants. Hans has also concluded his thoughts. Bright and early the next morning, he is going to call David at bank #3 about a $10 million fleet mortgage loan involving Vessels A, B, and C and the 80,000-dwt newbuilding structured just like Henry's proposal.

Index